JESUS THE MESSIAH

JESUS THE MESSIAH

An Illustrated Life of Christ

Donald Guthrie

ZONDERVAN PUBLISHING HOUSE
OF THE ZONDERVAN CORPORATION
GRAND RAPIDS, MICHIGAN 49506

CONTENTS

PART TWO — TOWARD JERUSALEM

List of Illustrations

Preface

Many deny the possibility of writing a life of Jesus, and it must at once be conceded that no "life" in the biographical sense can be written. It is impossible to produce a psychological study of Jesus. His developing awareness of messianic mission cannot be traced. This book presents an account of Jesus from the perspective of faith. It sees in His deeds and words evidence of the truth of His own claims and of the firm convictions of the early Christians. The many current theories that deny the historical truth of the gospels are discussed in my previous book, *A Shorter Life of Christ*. No further comment on these theories is included in the present volume, for the main aim is to give an impression of the Messiah as He moved toward the climax of His mission. No one who reflects on His life and mission can fail to be affected by it, and in this sense the present study is in the nature of a personal testimony.

It is hoped that the reading of this book will inspire many to more diligent study of the ministry of Jesus. With this in mind, the book is arranged in sections that provide the basis, if desired, for daily studies over a period of six months. The relevant passages are noted together with parallels. The sequence in some parts has been dictated by topical groupings, but mainly the general order in the gospels themselves has been followed.

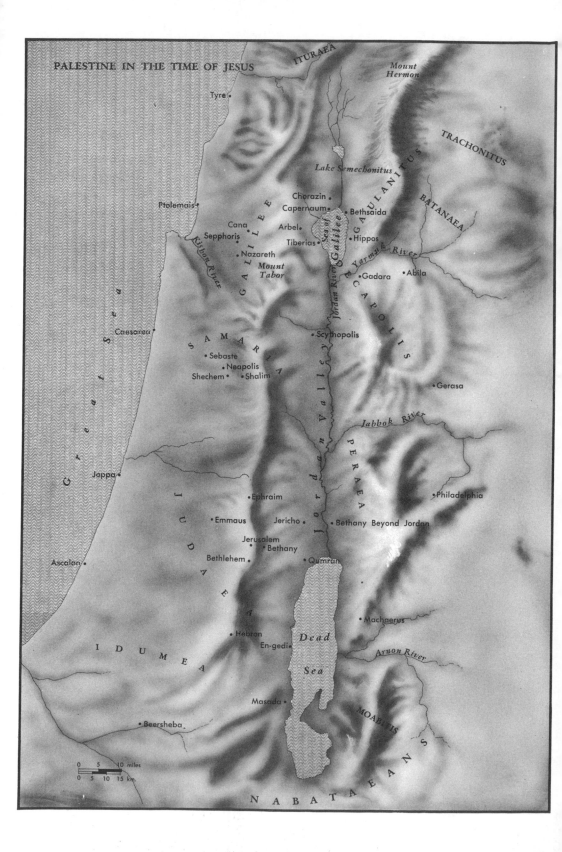

PALESTINE IN THE TIME OF JESUS

Mount Hermon

ITURAEA

Tyre

TRACHONITUS

Lake Semechonitus

BATANAEA

Chorazin

GAULANITIS

Ptolemais

Capernaum
Bethsaida

Cana
Arbel
Sea of Galilee

Hippos

Sepphoris

Tiberias

Yarmuk River

Nazareth

Gadara
Abila

Mount Tabor

GALILEE

Kishon River

DECAPOLIS

Caesarea

Scythopolis

SAMARIA

Sebaste

Neapolis

Gerasa

Shechem
Shalim

Jabbok River

Great Sea

PERAEA

Joppa

Ephraim

Emmaus
Jericho

Philadelphia

Bethany Beyond Jordan

Jerusalem
Bethany

J U D A E A

Bethlehem

Ascalon

Qumran

Jordan Valley

Jordan River

Machaerus

Hebron

Dead Sea

En-gedi

I D U M E A

Arnon River

Masada

M O A B I T I S

Beersheba

N A B A T A E A N S

0   5   10 miles
0   5   10   15 km.

PART ONE — FROM BETHLEHEM TO CAESAREA PHILIPPI

1

Announcements and a Herald's Birth

Introducing the coming one

John 1:1-18

Not everyone in the ancient world was familiar with the idea of a special person who was to come, known by the Jews as the Messiah. The Jews had many ideas about what kind of person He should be and what He should do, but the non-Jewish world would have been largely mystified by the term "Messiah." Especially was this true of those whose thinking was influenced by Greek culture. This widespread culture also affected some of the Jews who lived away from Palestine. The Greek world had other terms to describe the link between deity and man — more abstract terms such as Logos, Light, Life, and Truth. Anyone presenting the Jewish Messiah to the Gentile world of the first century would first have to show His relevance to current Greek thought. This is exactly what John did at the beginning of his gospel.

One of the most learned Jews who lived at the same time as Jesus was Philo of Alexandria. In his writings he attempted to show the close connection between Jewish and Greek culture. His favorite term for describing the means by which God maintained contact with the world was *Logos* (Reason or Word). John took over this term in introducing Jesus Christ to his readers; but he went beyond Philo's use of it, for the Alexandrian never used it of a person. John, however, saw Jesus as the complete fulfillment of what Philo was groping for.

In the introduction to his gospel, John includes the pre-existence and deity of Christ. He affirms that Jesus, whose teachings and acts he was going to describe, is God, the Creator, and Light and Life of the world. One might think such comments should have been left to the end, to be drawn as conclusions from what Jesus actually did and said. Most writers would have arranged it that way. But John made it clear at the beginning that the *person* he was introducing is no ordinary man. He was introducing the perfect link between God and man. When he said that the Word became flesh he was saying what Philo never would have said. Philo would have rejected the idea completely. Most men consider it incredible that God could become man. Why, then, begin a gospel introducing Jesus Christ with ideas most men find incredible? For John the answer was clear. He knew that no real sense could be made of the life of Jesus if He were treated as no more than an ordinary man. He knew that if Jesus were not understood to be God, what He did and said would become increasingly incredible. This fact must be faced at the outset — Jesus the Messiah cannot be understood by ordinary human standards.

John well knew that many would not accept his starting point for the story of Jesus. He himself had no doubt that the Light had shone, but he equally recognized the dense darkness around him. He considered that any light a man has may be traced to Jesus, who for John is the true Light that has come into the world. Nevertheless, neither the world at large nor the Jewish people received Him. John thus gave a preview of the general reaction of people toward the Messiah. He did not want anyone to think that he was about to relate a success story in the popular sense of the term. Rather, he was presenting a Messiah who challenged men to believe in Him. John's purpose was to give people the assurance at the beginning that if they believe that Jesus is the Messiah and Son of God, they themselves will become children of God. The whole purpose of the gospel records is to make clear what this means. It sums up the mission of Jesus.

John's towering concept of Jesus is evident from his experience of having seen His glory, which he further described as being the glory of the only begotten Son of the Father. Moreover, he saw Him as the source of all grace and truth. Again, one might think this a strange way to begin a gospel. What John wrote means little to those who know nothing of Jesus. However, when it is borne in mind that he had come to believe in Jesus in a special way, his language becomes intelligible. He placed his mature reflections about Jesus at the beginning. The other gospel accounts do not begin on so exalted a plane, but their portraits of Jesus the Messiah require such an explanation as John gives. None of the evangelists intended to write a biography of Jesus in the strict historical sense. John made his own purpose perfectly clear — that men may come to believe in Jesus as Messiah and Son of God (John 20:31). The Jesus that John and the other evangelists present is one in whom men could and did come to believe. Anyone attempting to write a life of Jesus from any other perspective will be faced with a dearth of data, since all the records have a missionary slant. A historical account of the acts and words of Jesus is valuable only if it is geared to its theological purpose.

Announcing the birth of a herald

Luke 1:5-14

The Messiah did not come unannounced. A coming king must have at least one attendant. It was customary for oriental monarchs to have a special herald to make way for them, but why should this apply to God's Messiah? Could not the heavens be suddenly opened and a heavenly voice announce to the world His mission? Such a method would have led men to think that His mission was designed to be spectacular. God chose otherwise; a human forerunner was selected. The herald's task was an honored one, and it would surely be expected that some notable person would be selected — yet God's choice fell on one among the lowly. The herald was to be born of humble stock.

The first hint of his coming was given to his father in unusual circumstances. On an October morning, Zechariah, a country priest on his half-yearly turn of duty in the Temple at Jerusalem, and the other priests on duty were gathered to await the casting of lots that would determine which of them would have the honor of offering the incense. This highly coveted privilege was never granted to a priest more than once in his lifetime. Zechariah, now an old man, must have long hoped that the privilege would fall to him. Probably fifty others waited with him, all moved with the same expectancy. That day the lot fell to Zechariah.

No one more deserved the honor. Zechariah and his wife Elizabeth, who also belonged to a priestly family, were well-known for their religious integrity and sincerity. They loved the commandments of God and sought to live in harmony with them. There was, however, one ground for reproach. They had never had a child and Jewish society disdained barrenness. They had for many years longed for a child, but had long since given up hope. They had reconciled themselves to being childless. It is most unlikely that any thoughts of their affliction occupied the mind of Zechariah that day in the Temple, except as desires long suppressed — as dormant prayers as yet unanswered.

As Zechariah stood alone in the Holy Place in front of the altar of incense, he became aware of another presence. It was not a fellow priest, for no one but the chosen representative for that service would dare to enter. Standing at the right of the altar was a heavenly visitor, whom the evangelist later named as the angel of the Lord. His presence overwhelmed Zechariah, as all men are overwhelmed in the face of the mysterious. He had probably never heard any fellow priest report seeing so extraordinary a vision while offering the Temple incense. He was afraid until the angel spoke. Zechariah may have heard of similar heavenly appearances to Simon the Just and to Ishmael, son of Elisha, but why should this visitation be made to him?

What Zechariah heard startled him — his prayer for a son was to be answered, and his son's name was to be John. Both statements surprised him. His wife was surely too old to bear a son, and Jewish custom required that the name of the father should be borne by the son. Why this unexpected announcement? The message was not specific about the part the son of Zechariah was to play in heralding the Messiah, but it revealed some of the characteristics of the coming child. His coming, like the coming of the Messiah, was to be an occasion of great joy, both to his parents and to many others. Births usually bring joy, but what marked out the promised son of Zechariah is that he was to be great before the Lord. There could be no more heart-warming prospect for godly parents-to-be than this. No father could wish for anything nobler for his son. In the life of John some of his greatness would be reflected glory, though the Messiah Himself later stated that John was the greatest born of women. This prenatal announcement of John's coming greatness must have cheered the aging priest, whose prospect of living to see that greatness for himself was remote.

The prospects for John

Luke 1:15-25

The message to Zechariah made clear that the greatness of John would occur in two dimensions — personal and social. He was to be a lifelong Nazarite, living a life of strict self-discipline. It was strange for an unborn child to be committed to such a course, but this was one of the indications that the birth of John was part of a divine plan. The child would be filled with the Spirit, a reminder that his greatness was not to be of his own making. His task would demand more than human resourcefulness. That task was essentially evangelistic. Zechariah realized how many sons of Israel — members of the Jewish nation — were astray from God. The prospect that his coming son would turn many back to God must have gladdened his heart. What could have fired his imagination more than to learn that his boy would be compared with Elijah! Every pious Jew admired the courage of Elijah and would covet the same power. Few, however, came near to it, and none nearer than John the Baptist. To herald the Messiah was no weakling's task, and God's chosen herald was to be given no less than the spirit and power of Elijah. Zechariah would recognize the source of the allusion to a second Elijah, who was to turn the hearts of the fathers to the children. His coming had been predicted some four hundred years earlier by the prophet Malachi. The Jews were familiar with the expectation that Elijah would herald the Messiah. It is probable that Zechariah told his growing boy much about Elijah. None of the other great heroes of Israel's history so fired the imagination of John. He not only came to display the spirit and power of Elijah, but he even copied his very garb. That prophecy of Malachi was likely among John's favorite passages of Scripture. No doubt Zechariah also told him of his future destiny. At an early age John would learn of his role to make ready a people for God. His was to be the humbler task.

However inspired Zechariah was at the thought of being the father of the Messiah's herald, he had one serious misgiving. He was concerned about his and Elizabeth's advanced age. Doubt began blotting out the glorious prospects, as if Zechariah had hit upon a snag that the angel's announcement had not taken into account. Those prospects seemed built on an impossible foundation. He could not reasonably be expected to believe that a son would be born to the aging Elizabeth. Doubt came to him in the hour of his greatest honor. His doubt was couched in a tentative question, "How shall I know?" — as if the angel's words were not enough.

The interview in the Holy Place did not end without a further announcement. The messenger introduced himself as Gabriel, as if Zechariah would at once recognize his significance. Gabriel is mentioned in the book of Daniel as the messenger of good news to Daniel, and Zechariah should have been aware of this. Jewish tradition considered Gabriel as a messenger of justice and Michael as a messenger of mercy, but Gabriel's function here was to announce good news, as to Daniel. Because of his doubt, Zechariah was to remain speechless for some months until after the birth of John. The consequence of his unbelief seems harsh, but the cloud of judgment was lined with mercy, for his affliction gave the old priest more time to contemplate. Perhaps he needed it in preparation for bringing up the herald of the Messiah.

The limiting effects of his dumbness came forcibly to Zechariah the moment he left the Holy Place. He could not explain to the people what had happened. He had been inside the Holy Place longer than was usual for the officiating priest. There was always a certain sense of awe whenever a representative of the people stood alone on the other side of the veil. In this case, the awe was deepened by Zechariah's delay. Presumably the people never knew what happened. Zechariah might have written some explanation for his priestly colleagues, but he may have been too sensitive about the whole matter to give the reason for his inability to speak. Nevertheless, it was obvious that Zechariah could not pronounce the usual benediction. Observers might have imagined that he was stricken with paralysis, although he could make signs with his hands. The whole scene supplied an air of mystery, which preceded and prepared for an event of great significance. Luke, who alone relates this incident, saw its importance as a prelude to his story of the Messiah.

Announcing the birth of the Messiah

Luke 1:26-38

Not without good reason, the evangelist recorded the announcement to Mary before he completed the account of John's birth. The two events are inseparable. The significance of Zechariah's expectation depended on the coming Messiah. John's importance hinged on the fact that he was to be contemporary with the Messiah. The close link between Mary and her kinswoman Elizabeth in the prospective births of their sons is brought out vividly in Luke's narrative. For five months Elizabeth lived in seclusion — a time when she must have often mused on the remarkable fact that the Lord had removed her reproach in her old age. It is not difficult to imagine how she longed for the day of John's arrival, when all would know that the Lord had favored her. As yet even Mary did not know. Although Elizabeth knew that her coming son was destined to herald the Messiah, she knew nothing as yet of the fact that the Messiah Himself was to be a kinsman of hers.

At this time, in Galilee, Gabriel appeared to Mary. In what form he came is not known. In some way she discovered his identity. Presumably he announced his name in the same manner as he had to Zechariah, or else Mary recognized that he was the same angelic visitor when she later compared notes with Elizabeth. Luke simply says that the angel was sent from God, and he must have received this information from Mary herself. The vision came during the time of Mary's betrothal to Joseph, which, according to Jewish custom lasted for one year before the marriage was consummated. Mary belonged to the house of David, a highly important fact for Luke's story. Nothing is known of her home life up to this time. The evangelist's sole concern was the unborn child. His account was designed to show the supernatural character of the Messiah's birth.

Reverent restraint characterizes the dialogue between Mary and Gabriel. The initial greeting is remarkable for its description of Mary as the "favored one." The word means "endued with grace" and thus calls attention, not to any achievement on Mary's part, but to the fact that God had chosen to bestow special favor on her. No wonder she was at once bewildered and fearful. After allaying her fears, Gabriel proceeded to show in what ways she was so highly favored. The announcement about the coming Messiah whom she was to bear is extraordinarily concise. In a few words the angel revealed His name, His coming greatness, His nature as Son of God, His fulfillment of all the hopes surrounding the restoration of the Davidic kingdom, and the eternal character of the Kingdom He was to establish. It can hardly be supposed that Mary's mind at this time grasped all of the significance of this, but she later meditated much upon it. What concerned her was that her marriage was not yet consummated. Her question, "How can this be?" must be distinguished from Zechariah's "How shall I know this?" His was asked in unbelief, hers in bewilderment. Moreover, Gabriel answered hers because her mind was ready to acquiesce. In the concise statement, "The Holy Spirit will come upon you," there is profound theological significance. Its full sense would not dawn on Mary's mind until she would see the Messiah fulfilling His mission. Only then would she realize that He who could die for His people's sins and could vanquish death by His own resurrection must have a supernatural birth.

The idea of the Holy Spirit coming upon people for special tasks was familiar to Jewish minds, but, far more wonderful than that, Luke's narrative delicately suggests — if it does not explicitly state — that Mary's conception was to be attributed to the Holy Spirit. Those looking for a scientific explanation of the Virgin Birth will not find one here. There are no parallels to the Messiah's birth and hence no data on the basis of which any general laws can be deduced to support it. Pagan parallels of divine births contain no resemblance to it. This event was unique. Its unprecedented nature is not surprising. The power of the Highest that was to overshadow Mary may be compared with the brooding of the Spirit over an emerging creation. The miracle of the Incarnation would be performed by the same power that brought the created order into being. Mary had no doubt, even at this stage, that the unborn child was to be no ordinary human being, but rather the breaking forth of God into human life. Unlike any other child, the Messiah was to be holy, the Son of God. In the light of this announcement, which serves as a preface to His birth, the life and teaching of Jesus must be understood.

Gabriel also informed Mary of Elizabeth's child and assured her that with God nothing is impossible. Why was a heavenly message required to inform her of this? Possibly her need to share her revelations with a sympathetic mind had already induced her to think of Elizabeth, and her sympathy would deepen considerably when Mary realized that Elizabeth was pregnant. This question is meaningless to those who deny the Virgin Birth, who do not recognize the divine nature of the Messiah, and who regard Luke's narrative as a product of poetic imagination in which supernatural embellishments were utilized to heighten the narrative. However, if God actually was in Christ when the Word became flesh, it is not illogical that a supernatural activity accompany the event. Mary's comment, "I am the handmaid of the Lord; let it be to me according to your word," shows the humility that possessed her. For so sacred a task as mothering the Messiah, no greater quality than readiness to accept the divine arrangement was necessary.

Private dialogue between Mary and Elizabeth

Luke 1:39-56

Mary's first thought was to visit Elizabeth. The distance from Nazareth to the hill village of Zechariah in Judah was about a hundred miles and it took some time for her to make the hurried journey. When she arrived, she received a remarkable greeting from Elizabeth. Mary's relative had pondered the destiny of her own son; but until Mary came, she had no indication of who the Messiah was to be or when He was to come. She interpreted a sudden and unexpected movement of the fetus within her as a sign that she was face to face with the mother of the Messiah. The intuition was supernatural. Luke states that Elizabeth was filled with the Holy Spirit when Mary greeted her.

"... Mary arose and went ... into the hill country, to a city of Judah, and she entered the house of Zechariah and greeted Elizabeth"
— LUKE 1:39, 40

Ein Kerem, a village in southern Judea, is traditionally claimed to be the birthplace of John the Baptist.

There is no need to suppose that the unborn child supernaturally recognized the mother of his Lord and consequently leaped, although Elizabeth exclaimed that the babe leaped for joy at Mary's greeting. One Jewish tradition relates that unborn babes joined in an "Amen" to the hymns of praise at the Red Sea. However Elizabeth understood the movement of the unborn baby, she rightly interpreted Mary's situation, and she remarkably confirmed what Gabriel had already told Mary. No doubt could remain in Mary's mind of the reality of the angelic message. This was not something that had happened in her own imagination. Although Luke does not say so, she may have heard from Elizabeth an account of Gabriel's revelation to Zechariah. God confirms His acts with many signs, not the least of which are the seemingly incidental coincidences that are later seen to be by design. In the months that followed, Mary must have often praised God for the remarkable reaction of Elizabeth when she met her.

The sheer blessedness of the woman chosen to be the mother of the Lord powerfully impressed Elizabeth. This was the highest honor any Jewish woman could have. Elizabeth showed the spontaneous reaction of a generous-hearted woman who was content with the lesser honor of being mother of the herald. Mary's response to Elizabeth has become a much-loved Christian hymn, the *Magnificat*. Some texts attribute the hymn to Elizabeth and not to Mary, but this is unlikely. The song is steeped in Old Testament allusions; there are reflections from Genesis, 1 Samuel, Psalms, and Micah. The style is that of Hebrew poetry. The whole song is modeled on the Psalms. It was a spontaneous outburst of praise to God from one who had mused much on the Scriptures. Some suppose that Luke composed the song and put it on Mary's lips. Others claim that he found the song in a collection and adapted it. The atmosphere of the song, however, perfectly fits the occasion of the two women in holy and joyous conversation together; any thought of adaptation or invention seems incongruous.

Only one statement in the hymn explicitly marks it out for this occasion, but this statement is all-important — that God had regarded His handmaid's low estate and all future generations would therefore call her blessed. The rest of the Magnificat extols the Lord and might have been sung by any pious Jew. Possibly Mary herself adapted words that she had many times repeated — words so much a part of her that she naturally used them on this occasion of great elation. What is cherished in the mind will spring to life when the opportunity demands. Mary's song has elicited responsive praise in the lives of multitudes ever since.

The song, however, has limitations. Its outlook and form belong to the Old Testament. Understandably, Mary could perceive no more than what was revealed to her; the whole hymn is retrospective. Her song stressed what God had already done rather than what He was to do through the Messiah. Nevertheless, this high view of God was her best prelude for an understanding of the Messiah's work.

Running through Mary's song is the refrain of God's strength. Her Savior-God is not prone to terrify in spite of His ability to scatter the proud and overturn thrones. She knew from experience that He is a gracious God who exalts the humble. She twice returned to a theme that meant much to her — the theme of mercy. She spoke of God's filling the hungry with good things, and she spoke from experience, since she came from poor peasant stock. The divine activity which she described would be reflected in the activity of the Messiah who was to be born through her. He, too, would institute new standards of value differing from those generally accepted. Those who were neglected or despised by contemporary society would be His special concern. Mary did not know that her hymn of praise to God would stimulate countless others to the same outburst of praise.

The conversation of Mary and Elizabeth during the following three months that they spent together may be surmised. Their discussions would concern the coming great events as far as their limited understanding could lead them. The whole story is far removed from what might be expected from current Jewish speculation about the Messiah; it carries with it its own authentication. No Jew, looking for a Messiah who was to be Deliverer of His people Israel, would have imagined His coming to happen in the manner predicted to Mary. The absence of ostentation in this simple announcement to a peasant woman could never have been invented by anyone steeped in Judaism. The simplicity of the narrative is intensely moving — it prepares the way for the paradox of the nativity. There are, however, other considerations to ponder first — the part of Joseph in these events, and the details surrounding the birth of John the Baptist.

The reactions of Joseph

Matthew 1:18-25

Just before the birth of John, Mary returned to Nazareth. Her next meeting with Joseph is passed over by Luke, but it is briefly described by Matthew. It was a delicate situation. Could she expect Joseph to believe that her coming child had been conceived through the Holy Spirit? Even the high respect Joseph had for her could hardly sustain the shock of hearing of Mary's pregnancy. Judging only from human perspective, he took it to be a case of unfaithfulness and immediately decided on divorce. In Jewish custom a divorce could be arranged publicly before a court or privately before two witnesses. Sensitive to Mary's feelings, he chose the latter. He was a man of honor. The mark of his personality left on recorded history was that he was just and kind and responsive to the leading of God. That leading in this situation came in an astonishing way.

To the Jewish mind of the first century, dreams were significant. It was accepted that God could communicate with a man through dreams. Many Old Testament examples supported this expectation. Joseph had no doubts about the reality of the vision that was given to him. The angel of the Lord was unmistakable, the voice was authoritative, and the message was completely unexpected. Joseph was addressed as "son of David."

Nazareth, in lower Galilee, was the hometown of Joseph and Mary. Here Jesus spent most of His childhood and grew to manhood.

". . . an angel of the Lord appeared to him . . . saying, 'Joseph . . . do not fear to take Mary your wife, for that which is conceived in her is of the Holy Spirit . . .'"
—MATTHEW 1:20

His Davidic ancestry was more significant than he realized, for the message he received concerned David's greater Son. The angel confirmed what Mary had told him. The coming child was conceived through the Holy Spirit. Joseph may have wondered whether his dream was influenced by Mary's claim, but it could not be so. The claim was incredible, and his mind was not conditioned to support it. It needed confirmation beyond himself. He could not doubt that the remarkable agreement between the angel's message and Mary's words was more than coincidence. It was a word from God.

What did Joseph understand by the Holy Spirit? As a Jew he had a less clearly defined idea of the Spirit than Christians later had. He would have recognized at once, however, that the coming birth was supernaturally prepared. In many instances in Old Testament times God acted through the Spirit (cf. Job 33:4; 34:14; Ps. 104:30; 139:7). At the time Matthew wrote his account, the fuller significance of the work of the Holy Spirit in the Incarnation was better understood. Joseph, however, had enough light to give up his intention to divorce Mary. He recognized that the angelic message pointed to immediate marriage.

A most astonishing aspect of the message was its disclosure of the name and the mission of the coming child. The name indicated the mission, since the name Jesus means Savior. It was a most fitting name for the Messiah who was to save His people from their sins. The pious in Israel were aware that the sins of the people were a major problem. Many, however, who longed for the coming of the Messiah had an entirely different notion. To them the problem was the yoke of Roman domination. The kind of deliverance they expected was political. Nonetheless, before the Messiah was born, God had made it clear that His mission was to be spiritual. The way by which salvation from sins was to be accomplished, however, was not fully revealed at the beginning. Further revelation came later.

Matthew related these events as links of a chain reaching back to Old Testament times. He was deeply sensitive to events that fulfilled ancient prophecies. The coming of the Messiah was not an isolated event. It was the result of detailed divine planning, and some of the details were revealed to prophetic minds. One detail, revealed through Isaiah, was the virgin birth, predicted in the time of Ahaz some seven centuries before. The translators of the Septuagint understood the Hebrew text to mean "virgin," although the Hebrew word could mean "a young woman." Matthew had no doubt of the special significance of a virgin bearing a son. The child to be born was unique, and a unique mode of birth was altogether appropriate to His coming. Moreover, the prophet predicted the name Emmanuel. Matthew noted that this means "God with us," focusing attention on the astounding fact that in the coming of Jesus, God had come to dwell with men (cf. John 1:14). This narrative, if its validity is admitted, makes any humanistic portrait of Jesus impossible. None of the evangelists intended his readers to think that Jesus was no more than any other man. The gospel story commences in a mystery. Incarnation cannot be explained by logic. That God became man is an insolvable paradox.

After the dream, Joseph immediately followed the divine command. His action is an example in prompt, unquestioning obedience, especially for those who possess more light than he.

The birth of John the Baptist

Luke 1:57-80

Elizabeth had moral support from relatives and neighbors. When John was born they greatly rejoiced at the special mercy of God shown to Elizabeth. To bear a child in old age was remarkable enough, but the removal of her public reproach meant even more to a Jewish woman, although Elizabeth's neighbors would have no awareness of the unique importance of this child.

Zechariah rejoiced silently. Each attempt at vocalizing reminded him poignantly of the unbelief he had expressed many months before. He remained dumb during the first eight days of John's life. His continuing inability to speak probably puzzled him, for had not the angel Gabriel assured him that he would remain dumb only until the promised child arrived? Did he fear that his voice was gone forever? The climax came on the day of circumcision, an important event in every Jewish home with a newly born son.

After the ceremony of circumcision a prayer was offered in which the name was bestowed on the new member of the com-

monwealth of Israel. It was usual for the eldest son to take the
same name as his father, and it was assumed by the relatives
that this custom would be followed for Zechariah's and Elizabeth's child.

Elizabeth, however, remembering what the angel had told
her husband, insisted that the child be called John. When Zechariah confirmed the choice by a written message on a tablet, the
relatives were amazed that both were prepared to break with
tradition. It was all the more remarkable without the prospect
of another son to perpetuate the father's name.

As the name was fully in accord with the angel's announcement, Zechariah's obedience was complete and his speech was
restored. His mind and will shown openly to be in harmony with
the divine purpose, his physical condition returned to normal.
The bystanders saw it as a miracle and therefore as an extraordinary omen regarding the child. They reverently wondered
what kind of child John was. They were certain that the hand
of the Lord was upon him in a special way. It would, however,
be many years before it became evident to the people of Israel
that this John was no ordinary Israelite.

Zechariah's first words spoke praise to God. Much had passed
through his mind since he last uttered his words of doubt. Enforced silence had mellowed him, and events convinced him of
a nobler view of God. Under the guidance of the Spirit he composed a hymn. It seems to have been influenced more by ideas
from Jewish prayers (especially the "Eighteen Benedictions")
than from the Old Testament. Zechariah had frequently meditated on these, since they were repeated at the time of the casting of lots for the privilege of offering incense. He had come to
understand more as a result of the sign he had received, for he
now believed that the Messiah would soon come.

The hymn is in two parts, one centering on the Messiah,
the other on John. The former is described as "a horn of salvation," a figure of speech derived from the horns of a bull as a
symbol of strength. Zechariah's idea of a Savior for Israel envisaged a powerful Leader who would deliver the nation from its
enemies. He did not, however, consider this as an end in itself,
but as a means toward a more adequate service to God. This
latter aspect shows the relevance of Zechariah's hymn for mod-

ern times. He saw the spiritual result of the Messiah's mission when he mentioned that "we might serve him without fear, in holiness and righteousness before him all the days of our life" (Luke 1:73 ff.). The first part of the hymn appealed to the Covenant, which was treasured by every pious Jew, although Zechariah did not mention that the Messiah would establish a New Covenant superior to the Old.

Zechariah, in the second part, addressed his baby son prophetically. He was to be a prophet of the Most High. His task was to prepare and to inform. It was in God's sovereign purpose that a herald should be provided, although the Messiah would not be dependent upon him. John's dominant theme was to be salvation and forgiveness, so intimately linked with the Messiah's own mission. With noble poetic imagery, culled partly from the language of the Old Testament prophets, Zechariah saw the faint light over the horizon, which was a sure prelude to the coming day. The light would dispel the darkness and guide the traveler. No nobler concept of the true character of the Messianic age could be expressed than the image of light dispelling darkness (cf. John 1:5).

Luke gives no details of John's childhood and education, nor does he tell of Zechariah's final years. These things are unimportant. Some scholars think John may have been a member of the Jewish community at Qumran, in the Judean desert. The suggestion is not impossible, but what is next heard of him is far removed from the monastic idealists of Qumran. His mission was confrontation rather than withdrawal, challenge rather than protest.

2

The Messiah's Birth and Its Immediate Consequences

The Messiah is born

Luke 2:1-7

So familiar is the Christmas story that it is difficult to re-capture its original significance. The coming of the Messiah was eagerly awaited by many of the Jews. Moreover, such an expec-tation centered on Bethlehem. Neither the common people nor the religious leaders would be surprised to learn that the Mes-siah had come to Bethlehem, for Micah had predicted it. No one, however, expected His coming to happen as it did.

Luke records that Joseph and Mary came to Bethlehem be-cause of the census ordered by Augustus for the purpose of com-piling adequate records for taxation purposes. Each person had to go to his place of origin; thus Joseph and Mary journeyed from Nazareth to Bethlehem. A pagan census therefore was the major factor in ensuring that the Messiah be born in Bethlehem. So important did Luke consider the historical setting of the Messiah's birth that he specifically mentioned that Quirinius was governor of Syria when the census was carried out. Little did he know the problem his comment would create, for it is known that Quirinius was imperial legate in Syria-Cilicia between A.D. 6-9, whereas the birth of Jesus must have taken place about ten years earlier. Some evidence indicates that Quirinius may have been legate twice, suggesting that he held the position at the time of the birth of Jesus. Another possibility, which is less convincing, is that a census was inaugurated by Herod, but was not officially completed until Quirinius' time ten years later. Whatever the explanation, there is insufficient evidence to dispute that a census was organized at the time of the birth of Jesus.

There was no necessity for Mary to accompany Joseph from any requirement of the census. However, she knew the messianic prophecies, and Bethlehem must have been hallowed in her mind.

That there were accommodation difficulties at that time is not surprising. Since many travelers were returning to their birthplaces, available space would soon be occupied. Whether the stable that Joseph finally found was attached to a hostelry or was part of a cave dwelling, as some traditions suggest, is impossible to say. The precise location is less important than the lowliness of the Messiah's birthplace. One wonders whether Mary considered it an anticlimax after her high hopes. Or did she see in it the deeper symbolism? Whatever her thoughts, she kept them to herself.

The two writers narrate the birth of the Messiah with remarkable restraint. Luke condensed the telling of that wondrous event into one sentence, mentioning only the full inn and the manger cradle. The story of the shepherds and Matthew's account of the Magi heightened the impression of wonder at the Messiah's birth. The absence of outward pomp ran counter to all popular expectancy. The lowliness of His birth was nevertheless fitting, since the Messiah was to identify with the lowliest of men. Subsequent events many times reflected the same lowliness.

Homage from shepherds

Luke 2:8-20

In Israel, shepherds were not highly rated. There is some evidence from the Jewish work *Avodah-Zarah* to show that they tended to be despised. Nevertheless, some had the special task of tending the sheep kept for sacrificial purposes. The shepherds of Bethlehem who came to offer homage to the new-born Messiah may have been among these. During the course of their

usual duties they received the revelation that sent them to seek out the Messiah. Why were shepherds chosen for so special a revelation? Their lowly status focused attention on an important aspect of the Messiah's mission. They represented all ordinary people who would later offer homage to the same Messiah.

Luke's narrative is simple and unadorned. The vision is briefly told: the glory shining around the overawed shepherds, the angel of the Lord in the midst of angelic attendants, the message of good news, the specific directions for finding the Messiah in the city of David, and the concluding anthem ascribing glory to God and announcing peace to men. With a few strokes of the pen Luke painted a vivid word picture of the scene. He heightens the strange incongruity of so heavenly a display of glory being seen by a few humble shepherds. Yet it was not incongruous in God's sight. It was part of His sovereign arrangements for the Incarnation.

Some features of the story are especially noteworthy. The extraordinary joy associated with the good news is one of Luke's favorite themes. The Messiah was not to be received as an object of terror but rather as the delight of His people, not only of Israel but of all people. The shepherds may not have understood the universal note in the announcement. It was difficult for Jews

Terraced slopes below the suburb of Bethlehem, Beit Sahur. Bethlehem was the ancestral home of both Joseph and Mary.

to grasp that the Messiah would be shared by the Gentiles. Another feature of Luke's story is the linking of the Good News with peace. The world at that time was far from being at peace, although Roman imperialism had contributed much to more settled conditions. The kind of peace that the Messiah brought was spiritual rather than political. The shepherds would have caught only a glimpse of this Messianic peace.

The announcement to the shepherds clarified certain aspects of the nature of the Messiah. He was both Savior and Lord, who would bring deliverance and exercise sovereignty. Joseph and Mary had already learned something about the Messiah's saving mission, since this was focused in the name Jesus, although His designation as "Savior" was not a complete description of His status. His Lordship also became an essential part of the early view of Him. It was part of an early Christian confession (cf. Rom. 10:9). The emperor who reigned when the Messiah was born was honored with the title "Lord," but the significance of that title for the emperor was severely limited when compared with the rich meaning implied in the Lordship of Jesus the Messiah.

It is no wonder that the occasion of the Messiah's coming was marked by the glory of the Lord. Israel's earlier history knew something of the *Shekinah,* as the glory was called. This was the assurance of God's special presence with His people. The event of the Incarnation was glorious in its execution even though its outward circumstance was humble. This impression of glory was not due to the shepherds' imagination. The awesome quality of the experience filled them with fear. The one adequate explanation is that it was a supernatural manifestation. It had special symbolic meaning. The Messiah had come to his people, even to the humblest of them.

The vision was followed by immediate action. The shepherds were informed that the babe was to be found in a manger in Bethlehem. Luke says nothing of how they found the right location. They may have inquired at the inn first as the most obvious place. Important to Luke is what happened when they found the Messiah. The scene is uniquely simple — a few shepherds gazing at a babe in a manger. What relevance could it have? Because of the vision, the shepherds believed they were looking at the Messiah. They told what they had seen and heard in the fields. Their hearers marveled at their words, but

*"And the angel said to them,
'Be not afraid; for behold, I bring
you good news of a great joy . . .'"*
—LUKE 2:10

Sheep follow their shepherd
in 'Shepherds' Field'
near Bethlehem.

Mary kept her thoughts to herself. She must have recognized in the shepherds' testimony another confirmation of the angel Gabriel's special message to her. The major importance of the pastoral scene is its witness to a historical event. The homage of the shepherds was no fantasy of the imagination, but a reality. God had broken into history, and because of it the Christian Church also worships.

Rites in the Jewish faith

Luke 2:21-24

The Messiah was Jewish, and it was expected that He would conform to Jewish rites. Circumcision as practiced by Jews was the means of incorporation into the covenant people. To the chosen this was a cherished privilege. The ceremony was normally performed on the child's eighth day, and at the ceremony his name was given, as on the occasion of the circumcision of John. As with Zechariah and Elizabeth, Mary and Joseph had no choice in naming their child, for the name had been divinely announced. The circumcision of Jesus was part of the historical circumstances of the Incarnation, but it was more than that, for it was the circumcised Messiah who opened the way for His people into the New Covenant without the necessity of their being circumcised (cf. Acts 15). Though born into the narrow ritualistic religion of Judaism, Jesus later demonstrated the wider outreach of the Gospel. The outworking of it, however, was to come more directly through His apostolic messengers than through Himself.

Later, circumcision became an issue within the Christian Church. Some Jewish Christians could not see how Gentiles could really belong to the Christian Church without being circumcised. They mistakenly thought that the rite itself possessed special value. This may have seemed to them to be supported by the example of Jesus. If Paul and other Christian leaders had not seen the real danger that would result from insisting on circumcision, the Christian Church would never have broken free from its Jewish anchorage.

The rites of purification of the mother and of presentation of the child are recorded by Luke. Joseph and Mary, in accord with their pious regard for the Law, left nothing unobserved. The law of Moses gave special instructions about firstborn sons (Exod. 13:2, 12, quoted in Luke 2:23). A sacrifice must be offered. For the poor who could not afford a lamb, doves could be substituted. That a poor man's offering could have sufficed for the Messiah shows again the contrast between His lowly circumstances and His exalted mission. It is fruitless to speculate why God arranged the coming in such a way, for His ways are inscrutable. It may, however, be suggested that the Incarnation happened as it did lest any should think that the Messiah's power and mission was in any way supported by earthly advantages. Later for the same reason, the Son of Man had nowhere to lay His head. This was not a making of virtue out of poverty, but a demonstration of the Messiah's mission as independent of favorable circumstances. In fact, the lowly circumstances of Jesus' birth and life were illustrative of the purpose of His coming — to be a servant to men (Matt. 20:28; cf. Phil. 2:5-8).

Recognition in the Temple precincts

Luke 2:25-39

Simeon was no stranger in the Temple. Advanced in years, he was respected for his piety. Everyone knew him to be just and devout, an example of the nobler elements in Judaism. He was also forward-looking. The messianic promises fired his imagination and he longed for the Messiah's coming. But why did Luke bother to narrate Simeon's encounter with the child Messiah? Luke explains that the Spirit of God came upon Simeon. When this happens, a man speaks not only for his own time alone, but for all time. The encounter is relevant for any age. The same Spirit who revealed to Simeon that he would see the Messiah before his death and who inspired his prophetic words interprets the words to each successive age. Simeon's song astonished even Joseph and Mary. Surely by now they were not surprised by confirmations of the mission of Jesus? Or was it the remarkable agreement between the song of Simeon and the supernatural visions they had themselves received that overwhelmed them with a sense of God's presence?

Simeon was satisfied. The event he had long awaited had

happened. He could die knowing that God had kept His word. More astonishing is the insight into the universal mission of Jesus that he expressed. He was no nationalistic Jew looking for a political deliverer, but a noble Israelite who recognized the wider implications of the messianic mission. The Messiah was a light for the Gentiles as well as the glory of Israel. There was to be no distinction. The need of Gentiles in their darkness of moral decline and the need of Israel in her glory-departed heritage equally found solution in Jesus. Simeon saw more of this universal aspect of the Messiah when holding the infant Jesus than many in Israel later saw, even when faced with the *fait accompli* of the resurrection. The first Christians were not quick to note the dawning of a new light in Gentile lands at the Messiah's coming to Israel.

However, Simeon also foresaw future conflicts. Many in Israel would stumble over such a Messiah as this, especially in view of the crucifixion. Later, Jewish comments on Jesus Christ were intensely hostile, as rabbinic references show. God's ancient people refused to see the glory that had come through Israel's most

From the Temple area in Jerusalem looking eastward to the Mount of Olives through the arches of one of the gates.

"*Now there was a man in Jerusalem, whose name was Simeon, and this man was righteous and devout, looking for the consolation of Israel . . .*"
—LUKE 2:25

famous Son. The Messiah was to be an object of hatred, a sign to be resisted. Even Mary's high privilege of nurturing the Messiah would know bitterness, likened to the cutting edge of a sword plunged into her heart. Simeon looked beyond this to the time when all hostile thoughts toward Jesus Christ would be plainly revealed. Nothing could show more vividly that the Messiah, now that He had come, would stir up intense opposition.

Another testimony came from the aged Anna. She too was well-known at the Temple, for she constantly worshiped there. She does not appear to have possessed the same prophetic gift as Simeon, but she recognized in the child Jesus the coming Redeemer. He became the topic of her conversation among those expecting the Messiah. There is symbolic importance in Luke's account of these testimonies. Simeon and Anna, representative of Israel's noblest expectations, recognized the Messiah and praised God for Him, whereas high priests and council members, Pharisees and Sadducees, later failed to do so. Because the Messiah did not come as they expected, they not only rejected Him but crucified Him.

Homage from the orient: the astrologers arrive
Matthew 2:1-6

It is strange that Matthew in a gospel intended mainly for Jews should devote space to the homage of the Magi. He evidently considered the incident to have symbolic importance. It showed unmistakably that the Messiah's mission was larger than the boundaries of Judaism. It was to have no nationalistic barriers. Simeon's song had carried the same emphasis. Gentiles would have immediate access. The significance of the story is clear, nevertheless Matthew's narrative has raised many problems. In considering these, the simplicity of the story must not be lost.

The Magi were most probably astrologers, who believed in a direct relationship between the movements of heavenly constellations and the destinies of men. The cult of astrology was highly regarded in oriental countries, especially in Persia, although there is no way of determining from what area the Magi who offered homage to Jesus came. Their purpose is more important than their origin. Although Matthew makes clear that they did not come to Bethlehem by accident, he leaves many details unexplained. He states that they reported having seen the star of the king of the Jews in the east (or at its rising); but he gives no further explanation of the phenomenon. There are only two possibilities: either the star was a supernatural phenomenon specially created to mark the advent of the Messiah, or else it was an unusual occurrence through natural causes to which special significance had been attached by the Magi. The former cannot be excluded since the advent of the Messiah was a supernatural event; yet this does not seem to be demanded by the evidence. The second alternative would fit in with what is known of astrology at the time.

Substantial evidence shows that both in Jewish and non-Jewish writings, heavenly bodies were connected with human events. Jupiter represented the world ruler and Saturn represented Palestine. When a conjunction of planets occurred it was believed to indicate some particularly important event. In 7 B.C., there is known to have occurred a rare conjunction of the planets Jupiter and Saturn, which would have led those versed in the lore of astrology to expect the rise of a person of considerable eminence, whose destiny would affect Palestinians. It would have been natural for Jews to connect this with their own messianic expectations. It is probable that the Magi were acquainted with Jewish expectations because of Jewish settlements in the East. From Matthew's account it is clear that the Magi's knowledge was severely limited. They had merely deduced the arrival of some important king in Israel.

They traveled to Jerusalem, for where else would they expect information about so important an event? They were obviously unaware of the political situation of Herod's territory. They apparently knew little of the tensions between the Jewish people and Herod, the cruel Idumean whom Jewish patriots considered as a tool of Roman imperial power. Little did the Magi know that their quest to offer homage would instigate or intensify political intrigue.

Stirrings at Herod's court

Matthew 2:7-12

Matthew's account must be set against the background of

the character of Herod. Herod's reaction to the Magi's simple inquiry concerning the newborn King would otherwise be unintelligible. His deep uneasiness arose from his awareness of the
political turbulence that news of the Messiah's coming would stir
up among his Jewish subjects. Significantly, Herod himself, in
Matthew's narrative, identified the "king" in the Magi's statement
with the Messiah of current Jewish speculations. He was acquainted with these, for they potentially threatened his throne.
He immediately summoned the chief priests and scribes to inquire about messianic prophecy. The Jewish leaders had no
doubt about the place of the Messiah's birth. There was scriptural support for Bethlehem as His birthplace (Micah 5:2). Matthew quoted the passage because of his special interest in Old
Testament fulfillment.

Minor differences exist between the Hebrew text of Micah
and Matthew's form of it. This may be explained as a rendering
intended to make the text clearer; hence "land of Judah" takes
the place of "Ephratah," and "rulers" displaces "thousands." The
prediction of a ruler to govern Israel greatly concerned Herod,
although possibly Herod did not actually believe the prediction.
He feared the explosive consequences of the Magi's story, which
had apparently already begun to take effect in Jerusalem. Action was needed, and Herod's plan shows the man to be as cun-
ning as he was cruel.

Herod secretly summoned the Magi. The Jewish leaders
must not know of his plan. It was important for him to know
when the star had first been seen, to enable him to calculate the
age of the recently born Messiah. Matthew gives the question but
not the answer. It can only be inferred from Herod's subsequent
action in ordering the death of all children under two years old
that some considerable period had elapsed. Presumably, Herod's
upper limit allowed a generous margin. It is strange that he suggested that the Magi should search for the Messiah and then report back to him so that he himself could offer homage. Why did
he not send his own servants to inquire? Can it be assumed that
in spite of his fears he did not really believe the Jewish leaders'
statement or else did not believe that there was anything in the
Magi's report? It is more likely that he knew that to any Jew
his pretension to offer homage to the Messiah would sound ut-

terly incongruous. This was another reason why he consulted the Magi secretly.

A strange detail in Matthew's narrative is the reappearance of the star. The star seems to have served a double function. At its rising it provided the impetus for the Magi's search. But since they had discovered the location of the Messiah's birthplace through the scribes, what was the function of the star in its movement over the place where the child was (presumably Bethlehem)? At this time the star had no more than confirmatory importance. To the Magi it was a heavenly phenomenon that marked both the opening and the close of their quest. It confirmed that they had found the right child.

Are the details in Matthew's story intended to be historical or merely symbolical? It is difficult to imagine in modern times anyone being led by astrological intuition to journey at considerable hazard to offer homage to a recently born king of whom he knew little or nothing. Matthew's account, however, is related as a straightforward, unadorned narrative. His description of the reactions of the Magi is true to life. If astrology started their quest, there is no reason why it should not confirm it. Their joyful reactions at the confirmation brought by the reappearing star are certainly understandable.

The scene inside the house where the Magi met with Joseph and Mary is described with remarkable reserve — in just two sentences. Yet it has offered limitless scope to the imagination of artists. Matthew gave no details about the dress of the visitors. It is probable that they were wealthy men and therefore well dressed. If so, the contrast between the lowly state of the Messiah's home and the grandeur of those who came to do homage did not impress the evangelist. He was concerned primarily with the homage and the gifts. He did not even suggest, as many have subsequently done, any symbolism in the choice of the gifts offered — gold, frankincense, and myrrh. It seems best to see them as representative of the natural wealth of the country or countries of the Magi. The giving was more significant than the gifts. Before long, a time would come when the Messiah would demand more gifts than these — nothing short of all that a man has.

Herod's child massacre
Matthew 2:13-23

The Magi had reached their goal, but they did not report their findings to Herod. Matthew tells us they were warned in a dream not to do so, although he gives no clue of the content of the dream nor the method of interpretation. This is bypassed to make the essential feature of his narrative stand out in bold relief. He had already given another example of a divine communication by means of a dream, and there were more to come. He intended his readers to understand that special measures were taken to ensure the protection of the Messiah-child. This is evident in the second dream-message to Joseph, advising him to take Mary and the child to Egypt, away from the territory of Herod. Not only did Matthew mention the dream, but he also saw the fulfillment of prophecy in the action taken by Joseph. He quoted a passage from Hosea (11:1), "Out of Egypt have I called my son." He applied the passage quite differently from Hosea's original meaning. In Hosea it referred to Israel as God's son, but here, to the Messiah. Moreover, Matthew implied that a flight into Egypt was necessary to make possible the fulfillment of prophecy. The stay in Egypt was part of God's plan.

Herod's reaction to the Magi's failure to return unveils a sordid story that raises many problems. The heartless brutality of his decision to massacre all male children in Bethlehem under two years old is hard to parallel. Moreover, in spite of all the human suffering involved, Herod did not attain his purpose. The Messiah escaped him.

Some may consider that the brutality of the incident makes its historicity highly improbable, especially since there is no reference to this incident in secular sources. How could an event of such blatant inhumanity have escaped the notice of contemporary historians? It may be answered that in spite of the human pathos involved, its effects were limited to an insignificant area in Palestine. In a world accustomed to reports and acts of human cruelty, the significance of the incident may not have been appreciated. Moreover, the tyrant Herod was infamous for his inhumanity. He ordered the murder of his own wife, Mariamne, and of three of his sons — Alexander, Aristobulus, and Antipater, and several times in his career he indulged in mass executions, sometimes accompanied by torture. He would not have hesitated to destroy a few young children to achieve his purpose. There were at that time few who could parallel Herod for sheer savagery.

How could such flagrant acts be allowed by the Roman emperor Augustus under whom Herod held his position? Augustus was reluctant to interfere in the Jewish situation since it was known that the Jews were the most difficult of his subject peoples. Moreover, he agreed to the slaughter of Herod's sons and was not himself exempt from the use of murder and massacre earlier in his political career. Matthew's account of the massacre, therefore, is not inconsistent with the character of Herod, and there is no reason to doubt its veracity.

Why did he include the story? His main purpose was to illustrate another instance of prophecy fulfilled. Jeremiah, centuries before, related the lamentation over the departure of the exiles from Ramah (Jer. 31:15), and Matthew saw an extension of this in the wailing at Bethlehem over sons lost through Herod's callous murders. Although the circumstances were different, the result was the same. Both Jeremiah and Matthew highlight the bitter human pathos involved. Perhaps Matthew further intended to show with a few strokes of the pen the stark inhumanity of the world into which the Messiah had come.

After Herod's death, Joseph received two more dream-visions, directing him to return to Israel and to settle in Nazareth again. He was at first inclined to go to Judea, but since Archelaus (Herod's son) had taken his father's place, he feared a continuation of Herodian hostility. Matthew again draws attention to the divine overruling in the affairs of the life of the Messiah. He even finds fulfillment of prophecy in the residence at Nazareth, although the passage he cites has caused difficulties because the precise words cannot be traced in the prophets. Most scholars think that the word for Nazarene in the statement "He shall be called a Nazarene" was connected in Matthew's mind with the Hebrew word for branch, and therefore it may be some allusion to Isaiah's prophecy of the Messiah as the Branch (Isa. 11:1). Whatever the explanation, Matthew had no doubt that the home of Jesus could be nowhere else but Nazareth. Having said this he completely passes by the years that Jesus spent there.

3

At Home and in the Wilderness

The years in Nazareth

Luke 2:40

Of the gospel writers, Luke alone tells something of the years that have come to be known as the silent years. Even Luke is most sparing in his information; yet what he recorded suggests certain aspects of the subsequent mission of Jesus. There is the complete absence of the real or supposed fantastic childhood experiences that later became popular through the writers of the apocryphal gospels. Luke presents a thoroughly credible account that singles out one notable incident of Jesus' childhood. Otherwise he makes only two general statements about those years. One of these records the development of Jesus, both physically and mentally; He was notable for His strength and wisdom. Luke also states that Jesus found favor with God, by which he intended to convey some impression of Jesus' religious life. Moreover, His life was favorably viewed by men. Also important in Luke's account is the statement that Jesus was obedient to his parents.

In any home, the greatest influence on a child in his early years is the mother's love and instruction. It was no less so with Jesus. However, Jesus' mother was often mystified. She heard words and saw actions that she never fully understood. She had no one with whom to share her deepest reactions. She could only store her memories. She knew that her own dreams about

Jesus, imperfectly developed as they were from what she had been told before His birth, would one day be fulfilled. Nonetheless, the years of her patient care over the developing life of Jesus were essential in God's plan for the Messiah.

The evangelist leaves the education of Jesus in obscurity, since this was incidental to His mission. All Jewish boys learned about the religious festivals and other important aspects of Jewish life. They were taught about these at an early age by their mothers and would come to appreciate the value attached to them. When they were sent to school, usually at the local synagogue with one of the synagogue officials as teacher, they learned to recite the text of Scripture, beginning with the book of Leviticus. Later, they were instructed in the interpretation of Scripture. A further step in education for those who showed special aptitude was instruction in the minute details of the oral law, which led for some to graduation from one of the schools of the Law. Presumably, Jesus received the earlier elements of Jewish education but did not proceed to the higher schools. Those who did not receive the "higher" education were frequently despised by those who did and were regarded as ignorant and unlearned. Jesus probably was so regarded as He grew to manhood. In this way, God's Messiah had better rapport with the general public. The mission of Jesus was not marked by academic distinction, but was promoted by submission to a humbler position.

That the gospel writers give no consideration to the psychological processes by which Jesus came to a full awareness of His mission further indicates that they never intended to write biographies. To them the mission as performed and accomplished was primary, apart from any theories about how it came to be formulated in the mind of Jesus. Luke's story, however, suggests that such consciousness formed part of Jesus' natural development. There was mental growth, for Jesus "increased" in wisdom. Here is the mystery of human development in a divine person.

The childhood of Jesus was not isolated from life within a family. Other children were born to Mary — Jesus' brothers and sisters, although some have tried to make them cousins of Jesus in order to preserve the "perpetual virginity" of Mary. The names of four other boys in the family are recorded — Joses, Simon, James, and Jude, but the sisters mentioned are unnamed. Of the first two brothers nothing more is written, but the last two wrote epistles included in the New Testament canon. As post-resurrection believers, they had finally shed their initial unbelief in Jesus. Apart from the comment in the gospels that His brethren did not believe in Him, there is no further description of the family life of Jesus. Presumably, it was a normal family life, but the brothers and sisters must have noted in Jesus a strange consciousness of an overriding purpose that none of them could understand.

In addition, the town of Nazareth had no reputation for producing leaders, for John records a remark of Nathanael's: "Can any good come out of Nazareth?" In such a setting, the Messiah grew up. From a human perspective, Jerusalem with all its historical associations would have been a more appropriate setting. The Messiah, however, did not need the credentials of a special place of upbringing. Nazareth, an object of derision, thus became the background of Jesus for thirty years.

The beauty of His natural surroundings — the Galilean vegetation, the hills, and the shifting moods of calm and fury on the Galilean lake — was not unnoticed by the sensitive mind of Jesus. In the gospel accounts Jesus echoes His love of nature through His incomparable illustrations. Such allusions to nature are nevertheless incidental; the natural world was not unimportant to Jesus, but His mission concerned the world of men.

There is passing reference to the trade of Jesus as a carpenter. All male Jews were expected to learn a trade. Even those whose calling was to expound the Law were expected to have experience in some manual task. The gospels are silent on the experience of Jesus in the carpenter's shop; however, it is worth noting that some of His most telling illustrations refer to instruments made in a carpenter's shop, such as the plow and the yoke.

The Temple visit

Luke 2:41-52

Jesus' visit to the Temple at the age of twelve followed the pattern for every Jewish boy. This visit was official, to mark the initiation of a boy into the observance of Jewish ordinances. Officially the boy was to be the age of thirteen, but frequently the pilgrimage occurred a year or so earlier. That it was an important landmark in the growth of a boy into manhood is sufficient reason for Luke to record this Jerusalem visit of Jesus.

Luke says nothing of the impression on the mind of Jesus of the magnificence of the Temple or the holy city. The deep spiritual impact far exceeded any sensory impression. Jesus had come to His Father's house, which was more than a Temple to Him. A time would come some years later when Jesus would violently expel the moneychangers from the Temple precincts to restore His Father's house as a place of prayer. At this time, however, his youthful approach was reflective. He was conscious of His own special relationship to the Temple.

The twelve-year-old Jesus lingered in the Temple when his parents moved homeward with their companions. The hurried return of the parents to the Temple and their frantic search conveys the impression of agitation. To their astonishment, they found Him consulting with the Temple teachers. All who listened were amazed at the astuteness of Jesus. The subject of the discussion is not given. The theme may have been the Passover and its meaning. Luke's concern, however, is simply to show the astonishing spiritual insight of Jesus.

In reply to the mild rebuke of His parents, Jesus posed the question, "Do you not know that I must be in my Father's house?" The form of the question and Luke's comment that the parents did not understand show the spiritual gulf between the Messiah and His earthly guardians. His mind was set on higher things; theirs on the practical business of getting home. The whole incident may have been written off by them as the reverie of a dreamer, but time would prove that His deep interest in the things of God was essential to His life's mission. The meaning of His mission did not suddenly occur to Him at the age of thirty. It developed, through adolescence to maturity. By the beginning of His public ministry the mind of Jesus was wholly conditioned to fulfill His Father's business. After this incident, Luke passes by the next eighteen years.

A voice from the wilderness
Matthew 3:1-6 (Mark 1:1-6; Luke 3:1-6)

The obscurity of the thirty years was finally broken when the herald suddenly emerged in the wilderness of Judea proclaiming in ringing tones, "Repent, for the kingdom of heaven is at hand."

The thirty silent years of Jesus are matched by the thirty silent years of His cousin John. There is not even one incident in his case which breaks the mystery of those years. He may have dwelt for a time with the men of Qumran in the Judean desert near Jericho. If he did, he was at some point constrained to take an independent line. Welling up within him was an irrepressible urge to take a message to Israel. No doubt he had heard from his father Zechariah about the vision that predicted that he was to become the prophet of the Most High to prepare a people for the Lord.

He must have often mused on his own destiny; as he did, his mind turned to Old Testament models, especially Elijah. As the latter came from the wilds of Gilead, so John was in the arid stretches of Judea. Moreover, John adopted Elijah's rustic garb, unorthodox as it was. The rough camel skin and the leather girdle surprised the Judean peasants. John's appearance marked him as an eccentric. When he spoke, however, his hearers could not fail to recognize the voice of an authentic prophet, just as the hearers of Elijah had done. Both men proclaimed stern messages and both matched the severity of their words with the simplicity of their dress.

People must have reacted differently to the abrupt appearance of this strange prophet in the wilderness. Why did he preach there and not in the heart of Jerusalem? The gospel writers suggest no answer, except to note that John began preaching where the Word of the Lord came to him. No one could accuse him of personal self-seeking. His manner of life was simple. He ate locusts with what small quantities of honey he could find in rocky crevices. His first pronouncement of judgment broke like a thunderclap, though with it he brought a message of mercy. More and more people collected to hear him as his fame spread.

Long before the lone commanding figure of John, the prophet

Isaiah had spoken of a voice from the wilderness that would prepare the way of the Lord. Isaiah's words are quoted by all the evangelists, although in different forms. According to the fourth gospel, John the Baptist identified himself as the voice crying in the wilderness, which shows that he meditated on the passage many times. All the gospel writers were aware that the sudden appearance of John was no unprepared phenomenon. He came preparing the way for the Messiah, but his own way was also prepared. There was an air of inevitability about him. In his narrative Luke quoted more of the passage from Isaiah than the others, with the significant addition that all flesh would see God's salvation. The Messiah's mission was universal.

John's message to the crowds by the Jordan is aptly epitomized in the words, "Repent, for the Kingdom of heaven is at hand." It is necessary to know some of the background to appreciate the relevance of John's theme — the Kingdom of heaven — to his contemporaries. Israel was a subject people, forced to submit to the overlordship of the Roman empire. The Jews nonetheless were a people of sturdy independence. They were convinced that Israel was a theocracy, a people owning only the kingship of God. This led them to resist the occupying forces wherever opportunity presented itself. Moreover they strongly resented their Roman masters, yearning constantly for some deliverer to break the yoke of Rome. This widespread expectancy of a coming national leader predisposed them to listen sympathetically to John's message. The preacher himself may have had little conception of the ultimate importance of his words, apart from the need for repentance. Even so, repentance, which was evidence that sin was admitted, was linked with forgiveness. John's message was not confined to pointing out shortcomings; it positively stressed the mercy of God.

Baptism practiced by John was not original. The Jews performed proselyte baptism on non-Jews who embraced the Jewish faith. The men of Qumran also had some baptismal rites. John's insistence on repentance, however, gave the outward ceremony a moral meaning. That which was outwardly seen was evidence of an inward change, an admission both of past defeat and future possibilities. Nonetheless, John's baptism was no more than a preparation for the mission of the Messiah.

Stern words from the herald

Luke 3:7-18 (Matthew 3:7-12; Mark 1:7, 8)

John's audiences were mixed. Matthew and Mark speak of all Judea and all Jerusalem, but Luke speaks more generally of multitudes. All four gospels clearly agree that John's preaching caused a stir among the common people. Many traveled considerable distances to hear this "voice in the wilderness." Those from Jerusalem and beyond traversed arid wastes, but they came in hundreds. The fame of this stern desert preacher held a strange attraction for them, which compelled them to listen. Among those who came were some Pharisees and Sadducees. For them John reserved his sternest words, according to Matthew, although Luke implies that the multitudes were also included. John must have recognized that the religious leaders had no sincere desire for baptism. Otherwise he would not have addressed them as a "brood of vipers." Moreover, he knew that their lives showed no evidence of repentance. They were trusting more in their religious heritage than in their personal piety. Their pedigree as Abraham's sons was more important than the emulation of Abraham's faith. Later, Jesus pointed out the same inconsistency. Appealing to Abraham was a notable feature of contemporary Jewish religion, and John the Baptist regarded it as a major stumbling block to true repentance. His criticism was biting. The stones which lay scattered around the desolate ground were fitter subjects for God's activity than these people. Their claims to proper descent were not backed by moral actions. The illustration of the stones must have startled them, for what could be more remote from life than insensible stones! Yet the strangeness of the imagery pointed to the infinite power of God, a power more important than any physical descent from Abraham.

The ring of judgment in John's words is unmistakable. The wrath to come was to be feared. Here is no soft theology. God is holy and makes holy demands. John saw Him wielding the axe of judgment to slice down the unproductive trees, which were fit only to be burned. The picture John drew was terrifying; small wonder that men sought the baptism of repentance under such thunderous warnings. Luke relates that multitudes cried out,

"What shall we do?" He then gives samples of some of John's special answers. The well-clad were to share with the poorly clothed; the well-stocked, with the hungry. Tax collectors were ordered to be fair, and soldiers were told to stop using extortion to supplement their wages. This is social ethics at its highest challenge, as relevant now as in first-century Judea. Men must match words with actions, to show by the latter the reality of the former. This teaching of John foreshadowed remarkably the moral and social teaching of the Messiah whose herald he was.

One question inevitably arose in the minds of the people. Was John himself the Messiah? His further vivid imagery at once dispelled such thoughts. It was a slave's task to fasten and unfasten his master's sandals, so that the master had no need to stoop. John had so humble a view of himself and so high a view of Messiah that he could not think of himself as worthy to perform even so menial a task. He had no doubt that the Messiah was mightier than he. He knew there would be a significant difference in the Messiah's baptism. His own was water baptism, the Messiah's would be fire baptism, a baptism that was spiritual.

The fire imagery is vivid and terrifying: fire can both purify and destroy. The former is its function here, but the latter is used by John to describe the fate of the wicked. Yet the Messiah's ministry would concentrate on mercy rather than judgment. He would bestow the gift of the Holy Spirit, which John's baptism never could. John spoke of the threshing floor to illustrate judgment. The thresher's fan had no mercy on the chaff. It drove it from the grain and consigned it to the flames. The distinction between the chaff and the grain could not be more vividly illustrated.

In these ways John prepared the way for the Messiah. He preached good news, but mixed it with warnings. Always he was pointing to another. He was no more than a voice.

A unique baptism

Matthew 3:13-17 (Mark 1:9-11; Luke 3:21, 22)

The Spirit who led John to begin preaching was the same Spirit who led Jesus to attend his baptism. Jesus, standing in the crowd, listened to the voice of the herald. He had come to the baptism of repentance. Matthew alone mentions that John was reluctant to baptize Jesus when He presented Himself for baptism. John's reaction showed his awareness of the superiority of Jesus — "I need to be baptized by you." He wondered how so pure a person as the Messiah could need the baptism of repentance. Jesus indirectly dealt with his problem. He said it was fitting to fulfill all righteousness, and by this He meant to act wholly in a righteous way by fulfilling God's righteous demands. This included John's willingness to baptize Jesus and Jesus' willingness to be baptized. The problem still remained how a sinless one could submit to a rite so closely bound up with repentance. Jesus regarded the baptism as a symbol of submission to God's righteous demands. For all other men this required repentance because they could not meet those demands. But in Jesus' life the demands were met, and the rite of baptism took on a new meaning — as marking His dedication to His ministry and mission.

Because John's hesitation is mentioned only by Matthew, some scholars do not regard it as authentic. They treat it as an invention by Christians to lessen the mystery of Jesus' submission to the rite of baptism. Matthew's record, however, is not out of harmony with what might be expected. John may not at this point have recognized the full implications of the messianic calling of Jesus (cf. John 1:33), but he knew something about the messianic character of His life (John 1:29). This was enough to make him hesitate.

John had baptized many others before he baptized Jesus, but for no one else had the heavens opened or the Spirit descended. What happened to Jesus was unique. Its importance cannot be overstressed. The double testimony was not public. The gospel writers give no indication that any of the multitude saw the opened heavens or the descending Spirit. John at least saw the Spirit, and recognized this as a sign that Jesus was the Messiah (John 1:33). The purpose of the event was mainly for Jesus Himself. It marked God's seal upon His special mission.

The Spirit descended in a dove-like way, a figure which all the gospel writers used. Luke mentions the bodily shape of a dove, but the figure is certainly symbolic. It could illustrate the gentleness of the Spirit or His essential mission of peace. An-

A view upstream of the Jordan
River, in the lower
Jordan Valley.

*"Then Jesus came from
Galilee to the Jordan to John, to be
baptized by him"*
— MATTHEW 3:13

other suggestion is that it represented Israel, in which case the
Spirit's descent would show Jesus as the typical Israelite. Whatever the symbolism, no doubt the Spirit's descent was recogniz-
able both to John and to Jesus, if not to others. There is mystery
about this, but the movements of the Spirit can be located only
by spiritual insight. As Jesus' baptism was unique, so was the
spiritual phenomenon that accompanied it.

The most striking feature of the event was the heavenly
voice. Jewish teachers spoke of a "daughter-voice" (*bath-qol*)
from heaven, but the heavenly voice of which the gospels speak
must be sharply distinguished from this. The Jewish idea came
into prominence only because the voice of the Spirit in prophecy
had ceased. Here, at Jesus' baptism, the Spirit is linked insepara-
bly with the heavenly voice. The statement "You are my beloved Son (or, my Son, the Beloved); with you I am well pleased"
confirmed the call and mission of Jesus. In Matthew's version,
the confirmation is given — as it appeared to John — in the third
person, with "This is" instead of "You are." There is no suggestion that Jesus needed a heavenly voice to reassure Him of His

divine sonship; this is unthinkable. The heavenly voice was expressing pleasure in the inauguration of the mission of the Son. The Messiah was moving into action. It was a momentous event that was marked in a special way by supernatural communication.

The tempting of Jesus

Matthew 4:1, 2 (Mark 1:12, 13; Luke 4:1, 2)

After the baptism of Jesus, John continued his preaching. Multitudes still came to the desert to listen and repent. Jesus, however, had withdrawn to another part of the desert alone, locked in spiritual combat. Why did He not begin His mission by addressing the crowds that John had already gathered? The gospels give the answer. He was impelled to withdraw — the Spirit led Him or, according to Mark, drove Him. This could not have been a detail derived from observation. Jesus must have given His own impressions of the experience to His disciples. He recognized a compulsion to be alone, and this was fully in harmony with the Spirit's purpose. His obedience to the Spirit characterized His whole ministry, and it was fitting that so striking an example of this obedience should be seen at the outset.

With this initial step of His public ministry, the whole plan and strategy of the messianic task must have been uppermost in the mind of Jesus. It is against such a background that the temptations that came to Him in the wilderness must be interpreted. They reflect something of His inner conflict throughout the forty days He spent alone. He did not even allow food to interrupt His meditations. Spiritual realities took precedence over physical needs. Those forty days became an intensive period of challenge. The intensity of the temptations almost certainly grew greater as physical strength declined. For this reason, it is usually interpreted that the three recorded temptations belong to the close of the period; in fact, both Matthew and Luke imply that the hunger resulting from the fast was the setting for the first temptation. Nevertheless, these temptations were representative of the whole period.

Some conclude from the appearance of the tempter in the narrative that there is here a use of myth, since the tempter is not a figure who can be historically substantiated. If the narrative, however, rests on the personal report of Jesus, it is evidence that Jesus believed in a personal agent of evil. Although the use of myth was not alien to the Jews, the narrative cannot rest on Jewish mythology — for nowhere in Jewish thought does the idea occur of the Messiah being confronted by the tempter. The gospel writers related more than a symbolic representation of a psychological conflict. They described the real and intense struggle that lay behind the whole ministry of Jesus.

The extended period of fasting has Old Testament parallels. Both Moses and Elijah fasted forty days, but the spiritual result in their experiences is to be distinguished from that in the experience of Jesus. Jesus directly and decisively confronted the tempter and in that conflict was Himself the mighty conqueror. It is highly improbable that the gospel writers were influenced exclusively by these parallels. To them Jesus was unique, and this presupposed a unique clash with hostile spiritual agencies.

They did, however, regard the temptations of Jesus in some measure as samples of what afflicts every man. To the extent that these came to Jesus in His unique function as the Messiah, they cannot serve as examples for others, yet as they illustrate principles of spiritual conflict, they are invaluable as models.

How could one without sin be tempted? Must the temptation narrative presuppose the ability of Jesus to sin? This problem is unique in reference to Jesus. No other man has faced temptation without the disposition to sin since the first man Adam. Yet the writer to the Hebrews spoke of Jesus as "one who in every respect has been tempted as we are, yet without sinning" (4:15), and this points to a common element in His temptations and those of all men. This is a paradox. The human mind cannot imagine the Son of God capable of sinning, nor can it conceive of a real human being incapable of yielding to temptation. Both facets are essential to a true understanding of Jesus. His conflict with evil cannot be dismissed as unreal. There is no completely adequate explanation, since no human analogy is possible. Beyond all doubt, however, is the majestic triumph of the Messiah over all the temptations that came to Him concerning His own special mission. This triumph all four gospel writers affirm.

The threefold test

Matthew 4:3-11 (Luke 4:3-13)

The first temptation related to food. The hungry Messiah was tempted to use His powers to provide physical sustenance. The stones scattered on the barren soil looked like bread. Why not make them become bread to satisfy His own hunger? Moreover, insufficient food was a social problem then as it is an even greater world problem now, and any leader with a solution to it would at once be welcomed. A Messiah who used His powers to alleviate hunger would gain immediate popularity. Jesus at once perceived the snare. His mission was not to be limited to satisfying man's physical needs, whatever compassion He felt for those who suffered them. When He later fed the multitudes, they sought Him only for the food, and He turned them away. This first temptation must at that time have returned to His mind. Also, there was a further sharp barb in the way the temptation was stated: "If you are the Son of God, command these stones to become bread." The tempter was not doubting the

"Then Jesus was led up by the Spirit into the wilderness to be tempted by the devil"
—MATTHEW 4:1

Desert panorama of the wilderness of Judea, east of Bethlehem. A large and lonely area such as this was the setting for the tempting of Jesus.

sonship of Jesus, but was implying rather that the Son of God should be using His supernatural powers. The implication was that any failure to do so would amount to a denial of His true character.

Such temptation can come to other men only to a limited extent. There is always a tension between the material and the spiritual and the danger of neglecting the spiritual in the pressing task of meeting the demands of the material. One common factor between the experience of Jesus and that of other men is the availability of the same weapon of defense, summed up in the formula "It is written." Jesus quoted Deuteronomy 8:3, which makes clear that man needs more than bread. He needs the living words of God. In short, Jesus backed up a spiritual principle with Scripture, which for Him, as for all Jews, would endow it with indisputable authority. Those who face temptation without adequate knowledge of biblical principles give the advantage to the tempter, for it is like fighting without a sword.

The second and third temptations are in a different order in Matthew and Luke. Matthew's order will be followed here.

The tempter took Jesus to the Holy City, to a pinnacle of the Temple. At one point the height of the Temple enclosure above the Kidron valley is considerable. If from this point Jesus were to cast Himself down in order to be miraculously saved, it would have a spectacular impact on the multitudes. This would be no temptation to anyone not convinced that a supernatural escape would be provided. This temptation shows the devil's awareness of the uniqueness of Jesus. If the Messiah were interested in quick success by public acclaim, what better way to do it than by some spectacular action? The temptation was real. The spearhead of the tempter's bait was the quoting of Scripture to support his proposals, or, more precisely, the misquoting of Scripture. He appealed to Psalm 91:11, 12, which assured special protection for the one trusting in God. But the devil omitted the conditions. Jesus counterattacked with Scripture that expressly forbids the tempting of God (Deut. 6:16). Any resort to supernatural methods as proposed by Satan would run totally contrary to God's plan for the messianic mission; it would amount to a rejection of that plan. This, to Jesus, was unthinkable.

Although the form of this second temptation could never

come to other men, the urge to use illegitimate means for legitimate ends is persistent in most people. Whenever it comes, the same answer is valid — God has His own plan, and any method, however laudable it seems, that contravenes that plan is basically opposed to God Himself.

The third temptation focused on the kingdoms of the world. The mission of the Messiah was wider than just the Temple, or Jerusalem, or Judaism. It embraced the whole world. Jesus knew, as He later pointed out, that the whole world is under the influence of the evil one, and that all men are subject to him. The suggestion was that the devil would give back the kingdoms of the world if Jesus would offer homage to him. That the Messiah would bow to the devil was so inconceivable to Jesus that it received only the most cursory rejection. He quoted again, this time the words "You shall worship the Lord your God and him only shall you serve." The Messiah was God's servant, not the devil's. As with the other temptations, this third incident has no precise reference to other men, although one common principle may be noted. It is characteristic of the devil to delude men into thinking that he possesses more authority than he actually does. He offers what he has no right to give.

Matthew and Mark both say that Jesus was attended by angels when the devil left him. It cannot be denied that the gospel writers saw the ministry of Jesus as a constant conflict. Some tend to deny spiritual forces because they cannot be submitted to historical tests, but spiritual forces belong to a different dimension of reality than do bare historical facts. Unless this is assumed, much of the gospel narratives will be unintelligible. The many exorcisms demonstrate the power of Jesus over the spirit world.

Luke pointedly remarks that the devil left Jesus only until an opportune season, which supports the view that further temptations occurred throughout His ministry.

4

The First Events in Judea and Cana

A testimony from John

John 1:19-34

In the synoptic gospels the scene shifts to Galilee after the temptation of Jesus, but John's gospel relates further events in Judea. Jesus returned to the banks of the Jordan to attend the ministry of John, although He was soon to begin His own ministry. During the six weeks that Jesus spent alone in the wilderness, John the Baptist had had further time to reflect. He had come to a deeper understanding of the superiority of Jesus (cf. John 1:15) and had meditated further on his task of making a path for the Messiah.

The religious authorities in Jerusalem, mystified by John's strange behavior and message, sent a deputation to him. The deputation consisted of priests and Levites, who were specially associated with the Temple cultus. They were sent by Pharisees, who placed more importance on religious observance than did the Sadducees. They challenged John to identify himself. He at once denied that he was the Messiah. Then, because of his appearance, they queried whether he was Elijah, whom many believed would return. This also John denied. The third suggestion — that John was "the prophet," a reference to the one mentioned in Deuteronomy 18:15, 18, who was to be like Moses — John also denied. To be considered any one of these — Moses, Elijah, the prophet — would have given John a position of great honor. This demonstrates the true greatness of John the Baptist,

47

that he never for a moment yielded to the temptation to claim to be what he was not. Yet, denials were not enough. The deputation wanted some positive answer to their question. John described himself as "a voice in the wilderness." His mind was not on himself, but on the Messiah whose herald he was, on whom he had seen the Spirit descend some weeks before.

John was then questioned about his baptism. The deputation was puzzled by his description of himself as a "voice." Why should a "voice" institute a rite of baptism independent of anything authorized by the religious schools? Such innovation demanded an explanation. John's answer was not what they expected. He talked about the "coming one." His own baptism, like his office, was only preparatory. The deputation could not have understood, since the "coming one" had not as yet been publicly identified. John was using the title to describe the Messiah, but the messianic ideas of those days were so varied that it is difficult to determine what impression the deputation would have gained. If they had attended the preaching of John the next day, they would have discovered the identity of that "coming one."

The fourth gospel specifically narrates events of the first week of the ministry of Jesus just as it does the events of the concluding week. The events of both weeks are linked by John's striking announcement about Jesus. What John said in the first week had its fulfillment in the last week. His many hearers must have been startled when they heard him declare Jesus to be "the Lamb of God, who takes away the sin of the world." What meaning was conveyed to them by this declaration? As Jews they were familiar with the offering of lambs as sacrifices for sins, but no one ever conceived of a "super lamb" that could atone for the whole world's sins. John may have been thinking of the remarkable passage in Isaiah (chapter 53), which describes Israel as a servant but also contains an allusion to the coming Messiah. It is too much to expect that the hearers generally understood the meaning of John's words. It is more important to consider what they meant to Jesus Himself. Coming immediately after the temptation, the words would have reminded Him of the true character of His mission. He was to become like a lamb suited for sacrifice. This placed Him at variance with current messianic hopes, for no Jew ever conceived of a Messiah who would come to suffer. Moreover, they never connected the Messiah's main task with the necessity of dealing with sin. Jesus began His mission with no illusions about its outcome. The way of victory was for Him a path of suffering.

John had already spoken of the "coming one's" superiority to himself. After he introduced Him in the person of Jesus, he reiterated His superiority. He then made another statement that must have further astonished his hearers — "this is the Son of God." John was speaking of sonship in a unique sense. The ministry of the Messiah would be the work of one who knew and delighted in the mind of God. The herald had done his task magnificently. No one could doubt the exalted opinion he held of the one he announced.

The first disciples

John 1:35-51

Two men who attended the preaching of John the Baptist and had become his disciples were especially moved by his remarkable announcements about Jesus. They may have consulted their leader further about the "Lamb of God." The evangelist does not say, but he records that on the following day John repeated the same title as Jesus came toward him. At that the two disciples left John to follow Jesus. They were in need of much further light before they could understand the significance of their action. They were eventually to behold the Lamb of God being sacrificed. Not until after that sacrifice would their understanding become more fully enlightened.

The dialogue between Jesus and the two disciples of John seems deceptively simple. He said, "What do you seek?" They said, "Where do you live?" He said, "Come and see." They stayed with him that day. Why does the gospel writer narrate such a conversation? There must have been good reason for his doing so. It has the ring of a personal reminiscence. John always remembered that day when he met Jesus. The first words he heard were unforgettable. The informality and friendliness of it all lived on in his mind. It is strange, however, that John said nothing about the conversation between the three of them that day. He recorded only the conclusion reached by himself and

his companion — "We have found the Messiah." The messiahship of Jesus was recognized in the course of the conversation.
How different this was from the spectacular demonstration offered in the pinnacle temptation. The disciples' first glimpse of
messiahship probably was confused — certainly less clear than
Jesus' own conception of His mission — although it was a beginning.

One of the men, Andrew, decided that his discovery was
too good to keep to himself. His brother Simon must know about
it. When Jesus met Simon, He at once announced that he should
be called Cephas, which is the Aramaic equivalent of the Greek
"Peter" which means a "rock." Simon was to spend considerable
time with Jesus before he discovered the deeper significance of
that name. This first encounter illustrates Jesus' insight into human potential.

The following day, Jesus decided to leave Judea for Galilee.
Not only was His own home there, but His first three disciples
were Galileans. In Galilee, Jesus called a man of Bethsaida, a
fishing town on the northern shore of the lake. Philip not only
responded but also introduced Nathanael to Jesus. Nathanael's
first reaction was skeptical because Jesus came from Nazareth,
from which it was said proverbially that no good could come.
Philip, however, knew that a personal encounter with Jesus would
dispel the skepticism. Nathanael's interview with Jesus is more
fully recorded than are any of the other first encounters. At
the outset Jesus paid Nathanael a high compliment. He called
him a guileless Israelite. Nathanael was amazed that Jesus knew
him and even more amazed when Jesus told him He had seen
him under the fig tree. His amazement led to an astonishing
confession — "Rabbi, you are the Son of God! You are the King
of Israel!" Why did Jesus' foresight into Nathanael's character
draw forth such a confession? An Israelite under a fig tree was
no unusual sight, but Jesus had seen more than that. He had
seen the noble aspirations beneath the outward form. He contrasted this man with the scheming Jacob of patriarchal days,
who was nevertheless transformed into Israel, a prince with
God. He saw great possibilities in Nathanael, who would afterward see greater things. Like Jacob, he and the others would see
an opened heaven, with ascending and descending angels; unlike

Jacob's vision, however, this vision would be centered on the Son of Man. This prediction of Jesus was to correct any misunderstanding over Nathanael's addressing Him as King of Israel. His mission must not be interpreted in a political sense. Its major purpose was to deal with man's contact with God, and for this there was only one divinely appointed connecting link — the Son of Man. These men would need more teaching before they could grasp this truth, but Jesus began His ministry with the confident assertion that this understanding would come.

A domestic scene in Cana

John 2:1-11

At the end of the same week, during which the five men began following Jesus, they were all invited to a wedding feast in Cana, a town in Galilee. What happened there is recorded by John, who narrates the story without the least suggestion that the Messiah had no place at a village wedding. Yet His attendance at the wedding may have seemed strange to the disciples. Was following Jesus to consist of a round of social visits? Why did John narrate an incident of this kind? He himself gives the answer. This was the first occasion on which Jesus performed a sign and showed His glory. Moreover, the incident deepened the disciples' faith in Jesus. They had begun to follow Him, but at Cana they really believed in him — John included. No wonder he recorded the incident.

The narrative is simple. The feast ran short of wine. The mother of Jesus suggested that He should be informed. Jesus resisted her approach, pointing out that His hour had not yet come; this statement suggests that she thought that it had. Nevertheless, He commanded that six large jars that were standing nearby be filled with water. When the servants drew from this water, it had become wine. The better quality of this wine caused the steward of the feast to remark that most men keep the inferior wine until last.

Certain problems arising from this account cannot be ignored. Why did Jesus speak to His mother so abruptly? Why did He create so much wine? Is the nature of the narrative historical, or is it symbolic?

"This, the first of his signs, Jesus did at Cana in Galilee, and manifested his glory; and his disciples believed in him"
—JOHN 2:11

Cana of Galilee still retains the appearance of Palestinian villages as they looked in New Testament times.

The remark to His mother ("O woman, what have you to do with me?") must be considered against the background of the divine insight already mentioned. She must learn at the commencement of His ministry that her son was governed by His "hour." John's gospel makes much of this, showing the gradual development until He could say, "My hour has come" (John 12: 23, 27). She must not interfere with this. He alone could decide what action was appropriate.

Why did Jesus make so large an amount of wine? If the water in all six jars of water were turned into wine, the quantity would be approximately one hundred gallons, which seems excessive. The narrative, however, gives the impression that only what was drawn out was turned into wine. This avoids one difficulty but creates another, for it is not clear why all six jars had to be filled if not all were used. Whether the quantity of wine was small or great, the action was nonetheless miraculous.

The question of the nature of the narrative is of great importance. Some see it only as symbolism. According to this view, it symbolizes what Jesus came to do with the water jars of Judaism,

to replace the weak contents of Judaism with the strong new
wine of the Gospel. It is difficult, however, to believe John intended his narrative to be understood in this way. Since the sign
led to faith in Jesus, it has historical validity. Those who reject
miracles are, of course, forced to advocate symbolic interpretation. Since it is not out of keeping with the nature of Jesus
to possess the power to perform miracles, a literal interpretation
is to be preferred. This is not to exclude a spiritual meaning from
the incident. It has already been noted in the first temptation of
Jesus that He did not come merely to meet man's physical needs.
His own mind at the time of the miracle was focused on His
"hour" — the climax of His whole mission. There may be therefore some association between the wine of Cana and the cup of
wine that was later to signify His poured-out blood. Moreover
the jars are described as no ordinary jars, but as purificatory vessels used for Jewish ritual. The Pharisees saw no hope of salvation apart from the observance of many burdensome rites. It is
possible therefore that the passage suggests the power of Jesus
to transform the weakness of Pharisaism, although it is obvious
that He did not Himself bring out this significance, nor did the
evangelist do so in relating the story.

John calls this miracle a "sign," a characteristic word in his
gospel for the miracles of Jesus. The other evangelists do not use
the term in this way, but John was concerned about the value
of miracles as a testimony to the nature of Jesus. He stated this
clearly at the conclusion of his gospel (20:30, 31). In what sense,
then, was this incident a "sign"? John points not only to the
power of Jesus, but also to His glory. The disciples had witnessed
the Messiah involving Himself with a domestic crisis, and against
this background His glory was seen.

The cleansing of the Temple

John 2:12-22

Before setting off for Jerusalem, Jesus went with his mother
and brothers to Capernaum, by the Sea of Galilee. Why did John
mention this in his gospel, since he records no incident on this
occasion? It may be that after the Cana incident it was clearer to
Mary that she must no longer attach herself to Jesus. Perhaps He

was helping to get her settled at Capernaum before moving off on His mission. His mother and brothers apparently did not accompany Him to Jerusalem.

In the Passover season pilgrims from all parts of Israel converged on Jerusalem. Since it was a major festival, Jesus' decision to attend is not surprising. He knew He was approaching the Temple, His Father's house. Although He traveled with many others, His thoughts differed from theirs. They went as pilgrims; He went as the Messiah, although recognized as such only in His own consciousness. On entering the Temple precincts He saw and heard men trading in animals and in Temple currency. There was a prevalence of the extortionate practices He abhorred. Sincere people, who had come to worship God, were cheated. Others may have been shocked by this, but Jesus alone saw its utter incongruity. He saw how alien such practices were in His Father's house. Silently He made a whip of cords, the weapon of His moral indignation. He then moved in and demonstrated His wrath. The traders offered no resistance, hastily fleeing the Temple precincts. The greedy accountants passively witnessed the overturning of their tables. It was a daring act, and yet a moral glory covered it. The voice of Jesus was heard above the chaos — "You shall not make my Father's house a house of trade."

The incident raises problems. Some think that Jesus would never have commenced His ministry with so startling a challenge to the Temple authorities. For this reason they conclude that John's chronology is in error, especially as the other gospels record a Temple cleansing at the climax of His ministry. Thus they regard John's narrative as symbolic rather than historical. A comparison of the accounts, however, shows marked differences between the narrative of John's gospel and that of the synoptics, which suggests that the Temple may have been twice cleansed, although most scholars consider this to be unlikely. A cleansing where John places it illustrates at the outset the relationship between the Messiah and the center of Jewish worship. It shows the profound religious piety that was the basis of His mission. For Him, true religion must never be a means for material gain. That none of the men resisted suggests that they ex-

"And he told those who sold the pigeons, 'Take these things away; you shall not make my Father's house a house of trade'"
— JOHN 2:16

Steps at the eastern side of the Temple area, in Jerusalem.

perienced some twinge of conscience over the legitimacy of their enterprise.

Significantly, Jesus condemned neither the use of the animals nor the use of money in the Temple precincts. The animals were essential for Temple sacrifices, and the money was needed for the Temple tax, which was designed to be used for the support of the cultus. This money had to be paid either in special Temple half-shekels or in ordinary Galilean shekels. Worshipers possessing other coinage had to exchange their money for the authorized coinage. This transaction, however, enabled the money changers to charge excessively heavy fees. Jesus protested against social injustice in the name of religion, a protest that He made on other occasions. Later, the disciples realized that this zeal of Jesus for pure Temple worship had been predicted in the Scriptures (Ps. 69:9).

In spite of the lack of resistance, there were subsequent questions. "What sign have you . . . for doing this?" In other words, "What is your authority?" Perhaps His questioners wanted some supernatural demonstration that would be indisputable evidence of His Messiahship. The answer Jesus gave was even more surprising than the question. "Destroy this temple, and in three days I will raise it up." It is not difficult to imagine the hearers' amazement as they gazed at the magnificent buildings that Herod had planned, which even then were not completed. They must have thought Jesus mad to talk of demolishing it. The Temple was the pride of the Jewish nation. It was inconceivable that anyone could rebuild it in three days, since it had already taken forty-six years to build. The literalists may have accused Jesus of reducing their serious request for a sign to an absurdity. Even the disciples were baffled. They did not recognize that Jesus was speaking of another kind of Temple — His own body. The resurrection finally furnished the key. Those who by their literalism missed the meaning had to do without a sign.

The whole incident is important because it shows that already at the opening of His public ministry, Jesus was thinking about His death. He knew there could be no mission without it. The Messiah would not die by accident, for He was fully aware of the necessity of giving His life.

Dialogue with Nicodemus

John 2:23–3:7

At this point many believed on Jesus. They believed mainly because of the signs that He did. Anything unusual excites interest and enthusiasm. Jesus knew that much of their belief went no further than that. He had an unfailing power to discern between the true and the false, the sincere and the insincere. John comments that He knew what was in man. John had observed Jesus' soul-searching mental penetration. Moreover, he had lived close enough to Jesus to sense the supernatural quality of His insight. He wrote his gospel to show that Jesus is the Son of God.

Against the background of Jesus' penetrating insight, John relates an encounter between Jesus and a Jewish leader. Throughout the dialogue, the Messiah's understanding of the Jewish rabbi's mind is vividly apparent. Nicodemus was an earnest and serious man, an example of the finest in Pharisaism. Jesus did not criticize him as He did some of Nicodemus' contemporaries. Moreover, this Pharisee, unlike most, sought out Jesus because he wanted to know about His teaching. He did so in secret for fear of what his colleagues might think. It was safer in darkness, for although Jesus had not as yet gained a reputation for unorthodox teaching, it was hardly respectable for a leading Jewish teacher to consult with one who had not been taught in the official Jewish schools of theology. Moreover, Pharisees generally were contemptuous of the "common people," and would have numbered Jesus among these. Nicodemus may have been fired with admiration for the courageous action of Jesus in the Temple and wanted to interview Him without his colleagues knowing what he was doing. Or he may have been among those who had acquired some kind of faith as a result of seeing the signs of Jesus.

Nicodemus' introduction seems self-conscious and apologetic. He had obviously prepared his opening gambit carefully. "Rabbi, we know that you are a teacher come from God; for no one can do these signs that you do, unless God is with him." He gave Jesus a title of respect, although Jesus was not a Pharisee. For whom was Nicodemus speaking when he said, "We know"?

This statement implies that he had discussed the matter of Jesus with others. Jesus had become a talking point in Jerusalem. Probably Nicodemus and several others had concluded that the signs pointed to a divine origin.

Whether Nicodemus had prepared anything further for his opening remarks is not recorded; if so he had no opportunity to deliver them, for Jesus interrupted him. With an abruptness which may have unsettled the Jewish leader, Jesus pointed out the need for a man to be born anew before entering the Kingdom of God. John does not state why Nicodemus came, but it is a fair inference that he wanted to talk about the Kingdom.

Jesus took the initiative. Nothing was more important to Him than the Kingdom and men's relation to it. This was the purpose for which He came. The birth analogy confused His learned pupil, who could think only of a literal second birth. As a leader in Israel he was probably mature in years and could see no possible relevance of the words of Jesus to himself. He did not perceive that "earthly things" were being used to convey spiritual truths. The birth illustration, nonetheless, was more appropriate than he knew. It spoke of a new beginning and a new life with new possibilities. The Kingdom that Jesus came to inaugurate was to be achieved, not by a patching up of the existing order, but by a radically new experience.

To unravel the muddle in Nicodemus' mind, Jesus repeated the statement in a more specific form — a man must be born of water and of the Spirit to enter the Kingdom. Much debate has surrounded the meaning of these words. What did Jesus mean by "water" — natural birth, or baptism? If He meant natural birth, there are no scriptural parallels to this use of "water." If, on the other hand, He meant baptism, it must have been interpreted by Nicodemus in terms of John the Baptist's baptism of repentance. That Jesus immediately went on to distinguish between physical and spiritual birth would seem to support the former interpretation. But since this discussion between Jesus and Nicodemus centers in the Spirit, the primary emphasis falls on the need for spiritual birth. If Nicodemus had been baptized by John, it was not enough; or if he had merely been once born, that also was not enough. He must be born of the Spirit. Jesus clearly spoke this as a personal challenge to Nicodemus.

More dialogue and a monologue

John 3:8-21

Outside the guest chamber where Nicodemus and Jesus were talking, the wind possibly was blowing up the narrow streets in fitful gusts. Jesus saw in it a useful analogy to illustrate His point. If Nicodemus was mystified about the activity of the Spirit, he should consider the wind. It whistles up passages and rustles the trees, but it cannot be seen or traced. So is the Spirit's activity. Meteorologists might object and assert that the path of the wind can be traced and its movements predicted with a fair degree of accuracy; but it still remains true that man cannot direct the wind. It is a vivid illustration of the Spirit's sovereignty. Moreover the analogy is natural since both in Hebrew and in Greek the same word is used for both Spirit and wind.

Nicodemus was nonplused. He blurted out his perplexity: "How can this be?" Such perplexity from this noted Jewish leader drew from Jesus the rebuke, "Are you a teacher of Israel, and yet you do not understand this?" Nicodemus was given illustrations from "earthly things," from the process of birth and the blowing of the wind; if he was still baffled, what hope was there for him to understand "heavenly things"? Nevertheless, Jesus proceeded to speak of heavenly things, but it is noticeable that from this point on the dialogue becomes a monologue. That Nicodemus had no more to say suggests perhaps that he did not understand, or that he was deep in thought, — the beginning of the process that led him to believe in Jesus (cf. John 7:50; 19:39).

We will assume that what follows (John 3:13 ff.) was spoken by Jesus, although some think that John recorded his own comments. The latter suggestion is possible, but there is nothing in these statements that could not have been said by Jesus on this occasion.

The teaching of Jesus in the monologue revolved around His mission. He referred to Himself as the Son of Man to draw attention to His earthly status. As a man He would be "lifted up" — a clear reference to His crucifixion. He had been musing on the story of Moses and the brazen serpent (Num. 21:9), a story that illustrated the need for faith: only the people who looked at the bronze serpent found relief from the serpents' bites. By way of contrast, Jesus' messianic mission had much more to offer — nothing less than eternal life.

Thinking of His destiny, Jesus described God's love in sending Him. No wonder this statement (John 3:16) has drawn multitudes to God. The God of Jesus and the God of all men is motivated by love. The depth of that love is evident in its sacrificial character. A love that does not act is not authentic love. When Jesus faced the climax of His mission in the crucifixion, He knew that behind it all was a God of love. This was the mainspring of His mission.

Also, He knew and taught that love cannot be divorced from judgment. The unavoidable condemnation of those who refused to believe in God's mercy must have saddened the Messiah. An analogy was drawn from light and darkness. Jesus knew Himself to be the Light of the world (cf. John 8:12), but not everyone prefers light. As sunlight reveals unsuspected dirt and dust, so those who love evil will resent the exposure of light. Jesus had no illusions that everyone would welcome Him even at this early stage of His mission. He had come into an evil world; many would hate the light of the truth that His mission was to bring.

Jesus and John the Baptist

John 3:22-36

The early ministry of Jesus apparently overlapped the ministry of John the Baptist, although John's ministry was of short duration since by the opening of Jesus' Galilean ministry John had been put in prison (cf. Matt. 4:12; Mark 1:14). Both John and the disciples of Jesus were baptizing in the river Jordan at Aenon, near Salim. This led to a dispute, which gave John the Baptist another opportunity to state his opinions about Jesus.

It was inevitable that increasing baptismal activity in the Jordan would raise questions. What was the relationship between the baptism of Jesus and that of John? John's disciples were the most disturbed because more were flocking to the baptism of Jesus than to their master's. They had failed to appreciate John's emphatic statements about the superiority of Jesus, which accounts for the falling away of John's supporters. No disciple likes seeing his own master eclipsed. Yet, the time had come when John's disciples would do better to follow Jesus, for their master's work of heralding the Messiah was finished.

Graciously John the Baptist accepted the situation. Moreover, he recognized the difficulty facing his disciples. Perhaps they still hoped that their master would after all prove to be the Messiah. If so, John was mildly rebuking them when he said, "I told you I am not the Messiah." He described himself as the bridegroom's friend, not the bridegroom himself. The best man should not steal the limelight at his friend's wedding. His joy is to see the bridegroom's happiness. By this illustration, John put himself in second place. Then he said, "He must increase, but I must decrease." This declaration eloquently summarizes the great life and ministry of John the Baptist.

With his narration of the ministry of Jesus just started, the evangelist John inserted a summary of what happened when God sent His Son. John repeatedly analyzed in his gospel the phenomenon of Jesus Christ. This passage (John 3:31 ff.) dwells on the differences between the earthly approach and the heavenly. The Messiah had not come to speak of earthly things. The words echo what Jesus told Nicodemus — that there are only two possible attitudes toward the teaching of the Messiah; either men reject or else they accept His testimony. There is no middle way. The alternatives are presented in terms of black and white, with no shades of gray. Furthermore, rejecting the testimony of Jesus is to say that God is not true. The challenge is clear and decisive, so identified is the mission of Jesus with what God is and thinks and does. God, however, through the gift of the Spirit, enables men to grasp the truth, and as He gives, He gives unstintingly.

The deep conviction that wrath rests on those who do not obey the Son of God (v. 36) accounts for the strong antitheses in John's portrait of Jesus, and for the unmistakable clarity with which he declares that the most important decision a man must face is the acceptance or rejection of Jesus Christ.

5

Settling in Capernaum

Passing through Samaria

John 4:1-19

As the baptism performed by Jesus' disciples came to be more popular than that of John, the Pharisees became aware of it, possibly through the Jew who had disputed with John's disciples (John 3:25). Jesus, knowing that the Pharisees would look with disfavor on His mission in Judea, returned to northern Palestine (Galilee). He may have left to avoid any further embarrassment to John the Baptist.

The gospel writer saw a divine overruling in this move and even in the route chosen. Because of their great contempt for the Samaritans, Jews normally avoided passing through their area by taking a detour along the Jordan valley. Jesus, however, ignored the prejudice and took the Samaritan route.

Near the ancient city of Samaria was the village of Sychar, on the site of the more ancient Shechem. It stood on the slopes of Mount Gerizim. It had hallowed associations for Samaritans and Jews alike, for Jacob's well was there. It was a refreshing, restful spot for weary travelers. Jesus sent all His disciples to the village to buy provisions and waited alone by the well. His weariness is evidence of His true humanity. Moreover the midday heat was intense and He was thirsty. As any man would, He desired cool, soothing water to moisten His parched lips and to quench His thirst.

Jesus sat on the well without attempting to draw water because traditionally it was the task of women to do so.

For this reason He asked a Samaritan woman, who had just arrived at the well, to give Him a drink. She was surprised that a Jew should ask a favor of her. Her reaction of amazement stemmed from the resentment that the Jews had built up against the Samaritans. Many rabbinical sayings reflect this feeling of animosity. That simple request made her aware that this Jew was different, but she did not as yet know why.

This conversation reveals Jesus' masterly technique in dealing with human problems. He established rapport with her through verbal points of contact, using each as a step to the next, and so He led her by various stages to acknowledge His messiahship.

He first asked the woman for ordinary well water. He then described His power to give the gift of "living water," although she thought He was still talking about the well. She, like Nicodemus, took earthly analogies too literally. The woman explained about the depth of the well and pointed out that Jesus had no bucket, and that even the venerated Jacob could not have done

Recalling the New Testament era, ruins of a Roman aqueduct still stand in a valley in Samaria near Shechem.

"He had to pass through Samaria"
—JOHN 4:4

the impossible. Jesus explained that He was talking about a different kind of water. Its remarkable powers would cause those drinking it never to thirst again. As a spring within, its source would never end.

As the woman understood these words on a physical level, it is no wonder she wanted some of this extraordinary water, if for no other reason than that she would never again have to draw water from the well.

Jesus at this point changed the subject. By His deep perception into human nature He was aware of the chink in her moral armor. Her marital affairs had been a complete failure. He asked about her husband. She denied having one, at which Jesus pulled aside the veil to her past. He mentioned her former five husbands and her present immoral association with another man. Giving no details of what happened to the five, He merely pointed to the woman's moral need. She wondered how Jesus knew all about her and she concluded that He possessed unusual insight. No doubt He was a prophet. This was no small admission for the woman, since the Samaritans acknowledged only the books of Moses, not the Jewish prophetical books. Her opinion of Jesus was developing in a remarkable way. She found it disturbing to be faced with a person whose penetrating insight could unravel both her past and present circumstances. She would rather have hidden her private life, although her neighbors must have known about it. In all probability, others shunned her to such an extent that she could not draw water at the cool of the evening, but was obliged to go at midday alone. She felt the conversation was getting too pointed; she changed the subject, and Jesus graciously responded.

A growing awareness of the Messiah

John 4:20-42

The woman turned the subject to a primary source of contention between Jews and Samaritans — the place of worship. Traditionally, the Samaritans worshiped on Mount Gerizim, whereas the Jews allowed no rival to the Temple in Jerusalem. She clutched at the controversy over the place of worship to sidetrack the moral issue, but Jesus skillfully turned her new theme into a moral and spiritual issue. Worship, He stated, was a matter of spirit, not of place. Since God is a Spirit He cannot be localized. Her view of God was parochial. Her mind was too much tied to Mount Gerizim for the universal teaching of Jesus to have relevance. Once again she changed the subject — this time to the expected Messiah.

Her specific concept of the Messiah cannot be determined. It was probably more vague than the Jewish concept. The Samaritans expected one whom they called "the Restorer." In the woman's mind, the Messiah would come to resolve all religious problems. The implication is that this was still future, and therefore her own problem could wait. When Jesus told her that He was the Messiah, the matter could no longer be procrastinated. This revelation was almost too much for her. She did not know whether to believe it. She left to seek the advice of others, leaving her water jar by the well. She exclaimed to all who would listen. "Come, see. . . . Can this be the Messiah?" So compelling was the woman's announcement that people immediately followed her back to the well.

The disciples had finished their shopping, but were unaware of what had happened at the well. They arrived back just before the woman left. The disciples were surprised that their Master was conversing with a Samaritan woman. The Jews did not hold their own womenfolk in much respect, let alone Samaritan women. Had they expressed their thoughts they would have asked questions, but John says that they remained silent. John probably remembered his own reactions as he wrote the narrative. After the woman left they urged Jesus to eat, but His mind was on spiritual food. His comment concerning this baffled the disciples. He told them that His spiritual food was to perform the Father's will and to finish His Father's work. With little experience of the teaching of Jesus and as yet uncommissioned as apostles, they found it difficult to grasp the true nature of the Messiah's mission. What did He mean by finishing the work? It had just begun. Their perplexity was real, and Jesus helped them toward some understanding of His mission by an illustration from nature. In the fields stretching out in front of them, green shoots were showing, but some time would elapse before harvest. The farming community knew how long the interval would be — four months. These fields illustrated human fields, whose harvest time had already arrived. As the disciples looked where Jesus was pointing, they saw the group of people coming toward them, led by the woman. Many of these people that day came to believe in Jesus as the Messiah. They believed "because of the woman's testimony" (John 4:39). In a natural harvest, the sowers are as much involved as the reapers, and both share in the rewards (v. 36). By such an analogy Jesus laid down a spiritual principle for His Kingdom. The disciples, however, did not learn that in the Messiah's service none could claim precedence over others. Even at the end of Jesus' ministry, they still disputed over who was to be the greatest among them.

The Samaritans of Sychar responded warmly to Jesus. They invited Him to stay longer in their village. He stayed with them for two days. As they listened to His teaching they recognized His true mission as "Savior of the world." No longer based simply on the woman's testimony, their faith became a matter of their own experience. What they meant by "Savior of the world" was limited, but they grasped that if Samaritans were invited to share in Christ, the messianic Kingdom must be wider than the confines of Judaism. They probably reasoned rightly that since they were included in the Kingdom, there was no ground for excluding any people. Jesus did not reject the title, for He knew better than they how prophetic it was. His very name meant "Savior," and this summed up His mission.

Again in Cana

John 4:43-54

Leaving Samaria, Jesus went straight to Galilee, to commence His ministry there. John relates that Jesus quoted the proverb about a prophet having no honor in his own country, to illustrate the move from Judea to Galilee. It is somewhat puzzling that both Matthew and Mark quote the same saying of Jesus as a commentary on His rejection by the people of Nazareth. "His own country" is more easily understood of Nazareth than of Jerusalem in the sense in which it occurs in John. All the gospels show a warm reception of Jesus on the part of the Galileans, and John, who wrote so little about the ministry of Jesus among them, nevertheless specifically mentioned the welcome they gave Him. Jesus' fame preceded Him because of what He had done in Jerusalem. Perhaps some Galileans were among those who believed when they saw the signs that He did. Some of the Galilean pilgrims who had returned from the feast possibly spread the news of the Temple cleansing. The Galileans would welcome a firm stand against a Judean corruption, which sometimes adversely affected them. In Cana it would be widely known what Jesus had done earlier at the wedding feast. That first "sign" was followed by another in the same town. Both signs were a prelude to Jesus' extensive preaching ministry throughout the whole district.

Reports of the healing powers of Jesus had come to an official in Capernaum whose son was dying. He went to see Jesus, but was met with an initial rebuff, although Jesus addressed His rebuke generally to make it less pointed. "Unless you [people] see signs and wonders you will not believe." Why did Jesus state such a rebuke? He knew that for most men faith needed the support of sight. Was it true of this official? Jesus was putting him to the test.

In answer to his request that Jesus should go and see his son, the man was told to return, for his son would survive. Was the man's faith strong enough to be independent of sight? Was he prepared to believe on the basis of Jesus' words without first seeing the result? He did not hesitate. Evidently, the authoritative tone of the voice of Jesus entirely convinced him. As he was returning, he was met by his servants with the news that his son had revived. His faith in Jesus was vindicated. It was deepened when he discovered that the crisis passed at the very hour when Jesus uttered His word of authority. In recording the incident, John mentioned that the official's whole household also believed. It should be noted that there is no interest in the miracle for its own sake, but only for its outcome. For this reason it is again called a "sign." It is evidence to all who hear the Gospel, both then and now, that an absolute faith in the word of Jesus is more important than His physical presence.

Although the miracle of the healing of the town official's son is recorded only by John, a similar miracle, which happened at Capernaum, is told by Matthew (8:5-10) and Luke (7:2-10). The two incidents are sometimes confused as different versions of the same incident. There are, however, reasons against identifying the incidents. In John's account, the official was Jewish; in Matthew and Luke, he was Gentile. This latter feature is seen from Luke's mention of the support given to the centurion by a delegation of Jewish elders because he had been instrumental in helping in the construction of their synagogue. In John's story the person healed was a son; in the other he was a servant. In John's narrative, faith is hesitant and at first inadequate; in the other, faith was so notable that Jesus drew attention to it. In John, the official requested Jesus to come but had to be content with His word; in the other the centurion himself suggested that it was necessary for Jesus only to speak. In the fourth gospel, Jesus made no comment on the incident; but according to Matthew, He remarked about many who would come to sit with the patriarchs, whereas many sons of Israel would be cast into outer darkness. The differences are too many and too varied for the incidents to be treated as variants of one event. It is more reasonable to believe that two healings took place on different occasions.

In the synagogue at Nazareth

Luke 4:14-30

Whereas the synoptic gospels mention the visit of Jesus to Nazareth and the hostility He encountered, Luke alone refers to the synagogue service in which Jesus took part. He placed it at the beginning of Jesus' ministry. Luke may have attached some symbolic importance to what happened. After the temptation narrative, he mentions that Jesus possessed the power of the Spirit to such an extent that His fame spread throughout the surrounding countryside. Jesus taught so effectively in a number of synagogues that the audiences glorified God. It was altogether different at Nazareth, where the whole assembly in the synagogue was filled with wrath. This illustrated what John wrote: "He came to his own home and his own people received him not" (John 1:11).

The synagogue service began with the reading of prayers, sometimes conducted by the person who read one of the prescribed Scripture portions or sometimes by another from the congregation who was appointed by the synagogue chief. It was customary for several people to take part in the sequence of readings, but just one person delivered the sermon. Frequently a visitor was invited to deliver the sermon, particularly if he were some well-known rabbi visiting the district. Probably the invitation on this occasion was extended to Jesus because of the sudden fame that had come to Him as a result of the signs in Jerusalem and Cana.

The preacher was usually handed a scroll, unrolled to the passage he had chosen to expound. Jesus chose His text from Isaiah (61:1, 2):

The Spirit of the Lord is upon me,
because he has anointed me to preach good news to the
   poor.
He has sent me to proclaim release to the captives
and recovering of sight to the blind,
to set at liberty those who are oppressed,
to proclaim the acceptable year of the Lord.

The passage quoted was the basis of the sermon, which may have been on the theme of the dawning of the messianic year. Jesus handed back the scroll to the synagogue attendant and sat down. Everyone was looking at Him. They knew Him as the carpenter and they marveled at His words. Jesus continued, "Today this scripture has been fulfilled in your hearing." This was tantamount to saying that the messianic age had begun, although the people of Nazareth could not believe that their former carpenter was the Messiah.

At first, their reception of Jesus was favorable; the congregation thought well of their preacher. Seeds of opposition, however, were present. Many were struck by His gracious words, but confused by the fact that He was known to them all as Joseph's son. They were too familiar with Jesus. He knew their thoughts; they were wondering how Joseph's son could perform miracles. They had heard what had happened at Cana and were probably expecting some sign in Nazareth. He knew that they were not prepared to believe in His power to perform miracles, as if in their hearts they were expressing the proverb, "Physician, heal yourself." The meaning of the proverb apparently is that one who claims to be a physician must first be able to deal with himself and with his own household. It was one thing to perform miracles in the surrounding districts where His background was unknown, but could He minister to His own people? He knew that their attitude was one of unbelief. This, however, came as no surprise to Jesus. He quoted another proverb: "No prophet is acceptable in his own country." To clarify His point He referred to two Old Testament incidents where non-Israelites were blessed by Israelite prophets. Luke's summary is condensed, but His hearers at once recognized that Jesus was criticizing their extreme exclusivism. Luke says, "All in the synagogue were filled with wrath." Although it was normal for conversation or questionings to follow the sermon, a violent situation developed. They did not reason with Jesus. They manhandled Him out of the synagogue and out of the town to the edge of the escarpment on which Nazareth stands. They were about to cast Him over, but His hour had not yet come. Their murderous intentions were thwarted. His look of moral supremacy may have overawed them. He passed unharmed through the crowd away from Nazareth.

Luke shows the Messiah in the midst of hostility at the beginning of His ministry. The synagogue, like the Temple, was unprepared for Him. Men rejected Him. What happened at Nazareth indicated what was to come from the Jewish nation as a whole.

Jesus, rejected by His own town, returned to Capernaum, which became His main mission center during the period of His Galilean ministry. Those who had been with Him had by now resumed their normal activities, but not long after this they received a more specific call to follow Him.

Calling men at Capernaum

Luke 5:1-11 (Matthew 4:12-22; Mark 1:14-20)

Capernaum lay on the northern shore of the Sea of Galilee. Although in the time of Jesus it was a prosperous town, nothing remains of it now except the site of its synagogue and the ruins of a nearby house. It was here that Jesus made His headquarters during His Galilean ministry. Matthew saw in this the fulfillment of an ancient prophecy (Isa. 9:1, 2). The prophet had envisaged the district of Zebulun and Naphtali as the place where people in darkness would see a great light, and Matthew equates the dawning of this light with the commencement of the Messiah's ministry in Capernaum. Jesus often stood by its shore and watched fishermen at work. He knew where the sons of Zebedee kept their boats and mended their fishing nets. One day He confronted them, challenging them to become His disciples on a more permanent basis. He did not decide to do this on the spur of the moment. It was part of His plan, that they should assist in His mission. John had already been in the company of Jesus, and so had his friends Simon and Andrew. James probably was well briefed by John. The four of them therefore were in some ways prepared for the challenge.

Luke describes how it happened. Jesus was not alone. Crowds of people, having recognized Him, pressed toward Him to hear His teaching. This was His mission, and so important did He consider it that His calling of the fishermen was postponed until after He addressed the crowd. He taught from a boat off shore, so that He would be able to face the audience, and the sea would amplify His voice. Simon's boat was used for the pur-

Fishermen of Galilee with their nets.

"And when they had brought their boats to land, they left everything and followed him"
—LUKE 5:11

pose. Luke does not say what Jesus taught, but both Matthew and Mark record that the theme of His early preaching was the nearness of the Kingdom and the need for men to repent and believe. It was a continuation of what John the Baptist had preached, but with one important difference. The Messiah Himself was announcing it. Repentance was not merely a preparatory measure for the Kingdom; it was fundamental to it. The Kingdom was a moral concept, not a material goal.

Luke says more about the content of Jesus' preaching later, but his main interest at this stage was to record the miracle that had some bearing on the calling of the first disciples. As soon as His address to the crowds was over, Jesus urged Simon to move farther out into the lake to fish. Jesus knew they had fished all night without results. He knew what frustrations this had brought, and He knew that this request to Simon would be no small test of his character. After all, Jesus was no fisherman. Nonetheless at His command, Simon not only launched into deeper water but also let the nets down. The Zebedee boat followed nearby. The catch was as large as it was unexpected. All four men whom Jesus was seeking to enlist as His followers helped to haul it in. They all witnessed what must have appeared to them to be a miracle.

Luke records the reaction of Simon. Because of the unexpected character of the haul, Simon at once recognized the extraordinary insight of Jesus. It occurred to him that if Jesus could penetrate the depths of the sea to locate fish, He had power to see into men. He suddenly became aware of his own sinfulness. He cried out, "Depart from me for I am a sinful man, O Lord." What Simon said the others also thought, for Luke states that they were all amazed. That they were afraid is shown in Jesus' telling them not to be afraid. According to Luke, He then said to them, "Henceforth you will be catching men," but according to Matthew and Mark, He said, "Follow me, and I will make you fishers of men." Some day, after much training and experience, Simon Peter would cast out his "net" on the day of Pentecost and draw three thousand people into the Kingdom of God. How much did he understand at that moment? The mission of Jesus was something beyond the mere working of wonders. Moral issues were involved. The Messiah's work was to make men conscious of their spiritual need. The evangelists all note that these fishermen followed Jesus at once. They were embarking on a period of training to prepare them for future work in the Christian Church. Their number would increase to twelve, and not until then would they be appointed as apostles.

Healings at Capernaum

Mark 1:21-34 (Luke 4:31-41; Matthew 8:14-17)

Mark records experiences at Capernaum that happened on a Sabbath. Matthew and Mark relate the same incidents but in a different order. The precise sequence is unimportant, but Mark's order will be followed. This Sabbath may have been the first since Jesus called the four fishermen to follow Him. The events of that day would stand out vividly in their minds, particulary the miracle performed in Simon's home. There are three different scenes: in a synagogue, in a home, and in the street. Two factors bind the three scenes together — they illustrate Jesus' healing ministry and they happened on the Sabbath.

In contrast to the rejection of Jesus at the Nazareth synagogue, the Capernaum synagogue was more tolerant. It was the custom of Jesus to go there on the Sabbath and teach. The records especially note the astonishment of the hearers at the authority with which He taught. It marked Him as different from the scribes. Not all who recognized His authority fully responded to His message. Authority is impressive and compels men to listen. The authority of Jesus, however, was not merely human. The gospel writers make no secret of the fact that it was also divine. Scribes appealed only to the interpretations of the great teachers of the law, but the teaching of Jesus was direct and challenging.

In the synagogue of Capernaum, it was not only the sermon that witnessed to the remarkable authority of Jesus; the power of His words was vividly reinforced by action. A man in the congregation, possessed with an unclean spirit, suddenly called out, to the astonishment of the rest: "What have you to do with us, Jesus of Nazareth? Have you come to destroy us? I know who you are, the Holy One of God." Why was there such a reaction to the presence of Jesus in the synagogue? Before an answer can be

given, the basic question of the reality of unclean spirits resid-
ing in men must be faced.

It is common to explain these instances recorded in the gospels in terms of psychology, or more precisely, psychiatry. Many
of the symptoms can be explained in this way, but this does not
mean that the notion of demon possession can be regarded as
obsolete. To describe conditions in different terms does not
change their essential character. The significance of demon possession depends on whether it is still meaningful to speak of demons. If demons are not real, Jesus either was deluded, or else He
accommodated Himself to the ideas of His time. The former alternative reflects on His understanding; the latter, on His integrity.
It may be questioned whether demonic influence can be dismissed solely on the grounds that modern medical science does
not recognize it as a scientific category. Facets of the human mind
still baffle scientists and remain beyond the reach of inquiry. The
instances of demonic possession in the gospels may well have
been the result of an intensifying of evil activity because of the
physical presence of Jesus. The most reasonable position is that
the evangelists, and Jesus Himself, viewed demon possession in
this light.

The man's cry in the synagogue revealed that the demon
world was already admitting defeat, acknowledging its imminent
destruction. The demons' fear of the power of Jesus was undis-
guised. There are no recorded instances where evil spirits showed
no fear of Jesus or refused to submit to Him. Their description of
Jesus as the Holy One of God is a remarkable assertion of His
purity of character. It was of high value for such testimony to
be heard, at a time when men were generally failing to grasp the
true character of Jesus. He at once rebuked the unclean spirit,
as He did on other occasions. It is evident that Jesus was not disposed to accept testimony from such a source. He earlier rejected the devil's offer at the temptation, and He would not at
this time accept any "favor" from one of the devil's agents.

As usual in exorcism, a severe paroxysm marked the end of
the evil spirit's domination. Mental disturbance then gave way
to peace. Unlike contemporary Jewish exorcists, Jesus used no
magical means or incantations. He merely uttered an authoritative word. The audience was amazed, and reports of His fame

spread through the countryside. The people were inclined to wonder rather than to believe. The Messiah had, however, not come as a wonder-worker.

After the synagogue incident, Jesus with James and John went to the home of Simon and Andrew. He was told of the illness of Simon's mother-in-law, who was in a feverish condition. Matthew tells how Jesus went and touched her hand, and Mark reports how He raised her up. Luke's statement that He stood over her and rebuked the fever is surprising in view of Luke's medical knowledge. In fact Luke used the same word here as he did when he wrote of Jesus rebuking the unclean spirit. The fever should not be regarded, however, as personal or as connected with evil spirits. Luke's concern was to give another instance of the power of the word of Jesus. He alone notes how quickly her strength returned, and all the evangelists mention that she resumed her normal household duties. This miracle of healing was less public than the synagogue exorcism, but it gave the closest followers of Jesus a further proof of His authority.

On the same Sabbath, in the evening, the calm and quiet of the streets near Simon's house was broken by the clamor of voices. Seemingly the whole of Capernaum clustered at the doorway as many more sick and demon-possessed people had been brought into the streets. Jesus moved among them, placing His hands on the sick, and they were at once healed. The demons who forced men to cry out, "You are the Son of God," were exorcised and silenced. As Matthew wrote about that memorable evening, he noted that the prophecy of Isaiah (53:4) was being fulfilled. Many homes in Capernaum that night rejoiced over bodies mended and mental faculties restored. All marveled at the healing power of Jesus.

Going about in Galilee

Matthew 4:23-25 (Matthew 8:1-4; Mark 1:35-45; Luke 4:42-44; 5:12-16)

The next day after that Sabbath in Capernaum, early in the morning, Jesus prayed alone in an isolated place. Some of the disciples, however, with Simon in the lead, approached Him. They half-chided Him, "Everyone is searching for you." How little they understood the strain of the Lord's mission. A day like the preceding Sabbath made great demands upon the Messiah.

Were they expecting a repetition of His performance on this day? They had not yet grasped that even the Messiah must regain strength through private retreat. They wanted to be on the move. The gospels, however, especially Luke, record many instances when Jesus withdrew from the crowds to pray. He found spiritual freshness in the cool of the morning hours. This prepared Him for further intense activity. He assured the disciples that He must move on to preach in other towns, for this was the purpose of His coming.

Wherever He went He visited the synagogues to preach the good news of the Kingdom. Wherever He was faced with human affliction — whether common diseases, demon possession, epilepsy, or paralysis — His compassion moved Him to alleviate the distress. Fame of Him spread as far as Syria. Crowds came to Him from as far away as the Decapolis, Jerusalem, Judea, and Trans-Jordan. Outwardly, the ministry was successful. Why was such importance given to the healing of people's bodies? The answer is found in the deep compassion of Jesus. His concern for people would not allow Him to pass by their sorrows. Disease and demon possession could not be condoned by the perfect Messiah. It was not His mission, however, to establish a miraculous health service. Moreover, He never gave signs merely for the asking. The healing ministry was not an end in itself. It was an essential part of the teaching ministry. It made men more disposed to listen.

The synoptic writers record a particular case of healing that occurred at this time. Evidently, it was regarded as particularly notable. A leper, flinging himself at the feet of Jesus, pleaded, "Lord, if you will, you can make me clean." Leprosy in those days, as still in many lands today, made a man a social outcast. He was obliged to be segregated from others. That a leper should take the initiative in approaching Jesus was sheer audacity. It moved Jesus to pity, and He touched him and made him clean. The bystanders were horrified at the touching, since this was considered a sure means of contamination — but nothing, not even the hideous disease of leprosy, could in any way defile Jesus. Modern medical science, which has at last discovered a cure for leprosy, has received much of its inspiration from Him who touched a leper in Galilee. When a man in those times claimed to be healed of leprosy, he was required to be certified as clean by a priest. Jesus urged the man before Him to comply with this requirement of the Mosaic Law (Lev. 13:49; 14:2-32). In giving directions to the man, Jesus commanded him to say nothing. Mark says that Jesus charged him sternly. The man disobeyed and the question arises as to why Jesus should have commanded silence. Was it possible for a man cleansed from leprosy to say nothing of what happened? Would he not have been full of praise for Jesus? The sequel shows the reason. People came from every quarter, and the man must know that Jesus had not healed him to court popularity. The healing ministry had limited value in the whole plan of the Messiah's work. One feature of this healing miracle reveals an important characteristic of the messianic mission. In His approach to leprosy, Jesus showed a marked contrast to the Jewish authorities. Whereas they could only isolate the unfortunate sufferers, Jesus was unafraid to touch them. The Messiah was deeply involved with people.

6

Teaching and Touring

By a pool in Jerusalem

John 5:1-14

Some time after returning to Galilee Jesus again visited Jerusalem to attend one of the feasts. John alone recorded the occasion, but he does not say which feast it was. Some scholars have reversed the order in John's narrative, placing chapter 6 before chapter 5. In this way the feast in 5:1 is identified with the feast in 6:4. It is better to keep to the existing order and treat the feast of chapter 5 as unknown. John, more than the other evangelists, linked his narratives to Jewish feasts. This naturally led him to concentrate on the ministry in Jerusalem rather than on the ministry in Galilee. The incident at the pool Beth-zatha led to a further self-revelation of Jesus, especially of His close relationship to God the Father. The occasion also provoked a crisis, for it led to an open clash with the Jewish authorities.

It was on a Sabbath day that Jesus walked by the pool, situated by the sheep gate. It was a well-known spot with a pathetic scene. It was popularly believed that the waters had medicinal properties, and this belief caused the place to resemble an outpatients' waiting room of a hospital. People crowded to the spot with a variety of ailments. Many, sightless or lame, needed assistance from others. This scene would stir the compassion of any sensitive person, and it especially stirred the compassionate heart of Jesus. Around five porticoes near the pool the people clustered, waiting for the opportunity to dip into the water when

78

it was stirred by medicinal springs. Considerable superstition surrounded the healing properties of the water. Some later manuscripts of John's narrative attribute the disturbance in the waters to the action of an angel, but there is no evidence that this was believed in the time of Jesus.

Jesus' attention was drawn to one man among the crowd of needy people. The man's features displayed utter despair. He had been visiting the spot for a long time. Apparently he had had some form of paralysis for thirty-eight years. What earlier

The depth of excavation of the pool Beth-zatha reaches back to the time of Jesus' ministry.

"And at once the man was healed, and he took up his pallet and walked"
— JOHN 5:9

hope he may have had of a cure was virtually extinguished. Yet in spite of the endless frustration of having others forestall him in entering the pool, he still came. Something of that frustration was evident in his response to the inquiry of Jesus whether he wanted to be healed. He complained that no one helped him into the pool. Jesus did not ask him whether he believed, as he asked others on some occasions before healing them. The man, nonetheless, had to exercise faith before healing came, for he was commanded to take up his pallet mattress and walk. As he felt strength coming into his limbs, his faith also developed. Those who witnessed the healing saw that a notable miracle had occurred. A chronic disability had been overcome.

A healthy man whose needs had been met attracted more attention than a chronic paralytic who had been afflicted as long as most people could remember. The legalists promptly noted a technical breach of the law. The man was doing work on the Sabbath by carrying his pallet. Legalistic observance of the laws was more important to them than the banishment of long-standing suffering. It is a sad commentary on human nature when religious observance becomes immune to human feelings. These legalists wanted to know who had commanded the man to carry his pallet and thus to break the Sabbath law. Strangely, the man failed to identify Jesus. Jesus came up to him later in the Temple and told him to sin no more lest something worse should befall him. He was probably taken aback by such a command, but Jesus was reminding him of the need to face spiritual as well as physical issues. Restoration from physical paralysis did not necessarily carry with it restoration from moral paralysis. With penetrating discernment Jesus knew the man's spiritual needs. This is no suggestion that the former physical condition was caused by sin. Jesus, however, was concerned for the whole man.

A clash with religious authority

John 5:15-47

The man healed of his paralysis immediately informed the Jews who had quibbled about Sabbath observance that it was Jesus who had healed him. Why did he implicate Jesus? He was probably too naïve to recognize their real intention, or else he was anxious to clear himself. If he could transfer the blame of the Sabbath breaking to Jesus he could absolve himself of the responsibility. Apparently it did not worry him that he was implicating Jesus. He probably was unaware of the mounting tension between the Messiah and the religious authorities; unaware that the Messiah had come into a hostile environment.

When Jesus claimed that He was working in conjunction with the Father, the hostility was intensified, for they had rightly charged that Jesus was making no less a claim than equality with the Father. Had His opponents recognized that the claim was true, they would have seen the futility of opposing Him — but they regarded Him as an impostor. Their concept of God was so bound up with their narrow interpretation of Sabbath regulations that they could not see how anyone who broke the Sabbath could even be sincere in claiming equality with God. Their hostility mainly arose, however, from the fundamental Jewish conception of the unity of God, which meant that no one could be equal with Him.

Their theological quibbles prompted Jesus to expound briefly the nature of the Father-Son relationship. The idea of God's Fatherhood was not alien to the Jewish people. They were familiar with the concept of God as Father to His people Israel. The teaching of Jesus that God was Father in a personal sense, however, went beyond anything they had known. What Jesus said on this occasion revealed His own approach to God. As the Son, He came to do the Father's will. He had voiced this sentiment in the Temple at the age of twelve. Now it became the dominant factor in His mission. As the Son, moreover, He shared the Father's resources — even to the extent of having power to raise the dead. The Father gave to the Son the execution of judgment, but Jesus desired that men escape the judgment by hearing and believing. On the future day of resurrection, the distinction will be made between those who have done good and those who have done evil.

His opponents, listening to these extraordinary statements, could not understand how Jesus dared to make them. None but the heaven-sent Messiah had the right to do so, but they could not believe that Jesus was the Messiah. Knowing their thoughts,

Jesus pointed out that His claims were not based solely on His own testimony. If they had been, they would have seemed self-centered. His hearers had already heard the testimony of John the Baptist, whom Jesus described as a burning and a shining light. Testimony from such a man must be true, although this would be no more than human testimony. A more important witness was the Father Himself. His testimony to the Son is found in Scripture, which they all possessed. Yet they failed to recognize that the Messiah foretold in Scripture was the one speaking to them. Jesus concluded that they were condemned by their greatest authority — Moses. This challenge was an insufferable insult to them since they regarded themselves as Moses' men. Zeal for the Mosaic Law was a mark of the Pharisees. Yet Moses wrote of the Messiah, and these "men of Moses" not only failed to recognize Him, but they also opposed Him. John recorded no more of the discussion after this point, and his readers can only imagine how these critics of Jesus reacted. The narrative shows both the clarity with which Jesus understood the precise nature of His mission and His dignified disregard of any hostile intention to thwart the purpose for which He came. It shows also that at an early stage could be heard the first rumblings of the storm that drove Him to Calvary.

A sample sermon

Matthew 5:1-12 (cf. Luke 6:17-49)

The scene shifts to Galilee and is focused on the teaching ministry of Jesus. The gospels record many sayings of Jesus along with several of His discourses. The most famous discourse is the Sermon on the Mount. As a complete sermon it occurs only in Matthew, but Luke has a shorter sermon reported to have been delivered on a plain; it contains similar material. Some of the sayings in Matthew's sermon also appear in isolated statements in Luke. Two explanations are possible. Either the "sermon" form is Matthew's own work, or else much of the teaching of Jesus was repeated in different forms and on different occasions. Good teaching is worth repeating, and none was more worthy of repetition than that of Jesus. There is no adequate reason to insist that the content of the Sermon on the Mount was delivered on just one occasion.

The sermon begins with the Beatitudes, a sequence of sayings so called because they are all introduced with the word "blessed." They are clearly intended to be treated as a literary unit. They enshrine profound truth in brief form. Easily remembered, they challenge the mind to serious thought.

The first Beatitude leads not only into the remaining Beatitudes, but also into the whole sermon. The lofty moral teaching that the sermon contains was not addressed to all indiscriminately, but to the "poor in spirit." Many would soon conclude that these demands were impossibly high. Only the "poor in spirit" have right of entry into the Kingdom. Who are they? Was Jesus putting a premium on poverty? Did He so disregard this world's possessions that poverty was a necessary requirement for the Kingdom? Some have supposed it to be so, but this arises from a misunderstanding of the kind of poverty Jesus intended. Matthew's record clarifies that it is spiritual, not material, poverty that Jesus had in mind. It is the quality of those who are humble enough to recognize their spiritual barrenness. Such a quality is not found naturally in man, although the requirement has within it a universal application. Whether a man has much or little, is wise or dull, has won success or known failure, he is capable of possessing poverty of spirit. By this opening statement Jesus was virtually saying that those who do not fall into this category will not benefit from listening any further.

As the first Beatitude is spiritual, so are the rest. The "mourner" is one who laments his spiritual condition, who perceives his need and his inability to meet it. Special comfort is in store for those whose spiritual experience leads through the valley of weeping.

The "meek," as a class, have never been the most honored of men. The Greeks in the time of Jesus regarded meekness as a craven weakness. Jesus set high value on meekness, by which He meant that His followers were to be those who know they have no grounds for boasting. A man who knows this cannot easily feel insecure. The adversities of life leave him unmoved in his dependence upon God, wherever he is. In this sense man can inherit the earth. This teaching of Jesus is still relevant today — in an age of big business, of massive technological advances, of clashing ideologies. With all his achievements man still has not begun in any real sense to "inherit" the earth. Rather, man's "advancements" threaten to destroy the earth, but the followers of Jesus know that His way is the only way.

There is blessing for the hungry and the thirsty in the realm of righteousness, but not in the realm of possessions. And there is blessing for those who are merciful and pure, both qualities existing preeminently in God. The men of the Kingdom are to be like Him. No one can listen to these statements of Jesus without seeing his own faults. The master Teacher knew that man's true state is best seen against a background of the noblest ideal, as black becomes the most sharply black against glistening white.

The last three Beatitudes affect human relationships. In a world of strife, peacemakers are at a premium. It is easier to begin a quarrel than to stop one. Jesus knew that peacemakers would be acting as true sons of the heavenly Father, who is the Peacemaker *par excellence*. The men of the Kingdom, however, will be persecuted rather than welcomed. Righteousness is not a quality for which men clamor. All too often it is an object of scorn. The men of the Kingdom possess a spiritual dynamite, and this quality rouses the basest opposition of men. They are nonetheless blessed to suffer for the sake of their king. They know this is no new phenomenon. Prophets suffered before them and many men of the Kingdom have since suffered for the same cause. The Messiah set before His prospective followers a vivid, realistic picture of what they might expect. The challenge was tough, but it carried with it the abundant rewards of spiritual blessedness.

Thoughts about the Law

Matthew 5:13-48

A good sermon is perfectly adapted to the needs of the hearers. The Sermon on the Mount was addressed to Jews who were conscious of the importance of the Law of Moses in their religious lives. The central part of this sermon shows the Messiah's approach to the Law.

Before coming to this central theme, Jesus described His disciples as both salt and light — that is, preservative and illuminative. As salt forestalls corruption, so would the disciples exert a salutary effect upon a world of corrupt practices. As light is to be seen and not hidden, so would they shine before men. This was no mandate for withdrawal from the world, for Jesus never advocated monasticism. His people were to have a beneficial, positive effect on society as a whole.

Jesus asserted two ideas when He spoke on the Law. One is the sanctity of the Law. Whatever else changed, the Law's validity would remain unchanged. The other idea is the true interpretation of the Law. Jesus was the perfect Expositor of the Law. The keynote was development. "The Law says . . . , but I say." Jesus did not present a contradiction of the Law but rather its true interpretation. The Pharisees were convinced that they perfectly understood the Law, but Jesus was not satisfied with the type of righteousness they possessed. Something altogether different was required for the members of His Kingdom.

The Law condemned murder, but Jesus interpreted the command to condemn any critical attitude toward a brother. The Law condemned adultery, but Jesus attacked the intent of adultery and expressed to His followers in the most vivid terms that they were to have nothing to do with anything that led them into sin. "If your right eye causes you to sin, pluck it out and throw it away." The hearers, well-acquainted with figurative language, would not take this literally. The Law allowed divorce on certain grounds, but Jesus forbade it except for unchastity. Some have considered His approach too stringent, but since He was speaking to those who were "poor in spirit," He was assuming that they were capable of receiving it.

He also spoke about oaths because at that time the Jews made many subtle distinctions concerning them. He instructed His followers to be so transparently truthful that oaths would be irrelevant. This was another example of His bringing out the true meaning of the Law.

The Law was specific on retaliation, summed up in the words, "An eye for an eye and a tooth for a tooth." This was originally intended as a rough kind of justice to prevent more punishment from being inflicted than the offense demanded. The

"... he went up on the
mountain, and when he sat down his
disciples came to him"
— MATTHEW 5:1

The majestic view toward the Sea of
Galilee from the Horns of Hattin.
This elevation is generally known
as the 'Mount of Beatitudes'.

teaching of Jesus on this theme was revolutionary. He advocated nonretaliation. Let the striker be allowed to slap the other cheek, and let the burden-bearing laborer walk a second mile on the road. Could not this policy lead to chaos, offering a perfect opportunity for the slackers to escape their responsibilities? The teaching of Jesus on this matter, however, was not intended as a blueprint for industrial relationships. It was intended rather as a positive contribution to the reduction of personal feuds. Of course, men would take advantage of such an approach, but the members of the Messiah's Kingdom must be more concerned to show reconciliation so that they may better reflect the attitude of their King. They later had a perfect example in Jesus when they saw Him at the time of His passion.

Such a pattern is even more vividly seen in Jesus' words about the right attitude toward enemies. It is natural for one to hate his enemies. For most men, enemies by definition are those one hates. Thus Jesus demanded something unnatural. Enemies are to be loved, He said. If this seemed impossible, the disciples were reminded that their heavenly Father makes no distinction between the evil and the good when He bestows His gifts upon all men. The disciples were challenged to make God their pattern. His perfection was to be their goal. Those who have never known true poverty of spirit may pronounce Jesus an impractical visionary, and His teaching as having no relevance for the tough world outside the circle of His friends. The impracticability, however, arises solely from the unwillingness of men to face the stringent conditions needed for its perfect operation. The teaching of Jesus — no easy sop to popular opinion — was a tremendous challenge based on revolutionary principles.

Some matters of personal piety

Matthew 6 and 7

The latter part of the sermon emphasizes personal piety. As men listened, they became increasingly aware that Jesus was unlike their usual teachers. The commanding tone of His voice gave unmistakable authority to His teaching. He charged His hearers not to make religion a matter of mere outward show.

Real piety springs from secret communion between the individual and God. The same rule of privacy applies to almsgiving. The Pharisees believed that charitable acts were meritorious. By advertising their almsgiving they therefore displayed their merit. Jesus advocated a less ostentatious charity, which may very well be seen by no one else but God the Father.

Jesus knew the human difficulties in praying; thus He provided in the course of the sermon a pattern prayer, the much-used "Our Father." In it He taught men first to think of the greatness of God and the need to do His will before making specific requests for daily sustenance, forgiveness, and deliverance from the power of evil. Jesus was the best fulfillment of this prayer. His life was never cumbered with a concern for accumulating material things. He did the Father's will continually. He had no need to pray for forgiveness; on the other hand, He had already demonstrated the power of God in resisting evil.

On fasting, Jesus used the same pattern as in the teaching on almsgiving and prayer: it should be private, not public. This advice seems less relevant to modern man than to the first-century pious Jew who regularly practiced fasting. Nevertheless, it cannot be wholly dismissed on that ground, since it is an example of self-denial which is important now as it was then. Even self-denial can become a snare, however, when it is too much publicized.

True piety affects practical life, and Jesus cited instances of this. Treasure must have spiritual content rather than material. Most important is one's attitude to money. "Where your treasure is, there will your heart be also." Jesus maintained that it is impossible to serve both God and mammon (money). Some have criticized Him for a "pie-in-the-sky" philosophy, but this charge arises from a misunderstanding of His teaching. He intended that men should have fulfillment in this life, the experience of spiritual well-being that comes from life unaffected by the "rat race."

The most disruptive threat to peace of mind is worry. Centuries have passed since Jesus taught, but man's ingenuity has not reduced anxiety. The rapid pace of modern life makes anxiety neuroses commonplace. The simple and yet profound remedy that Jesus gave, can be summed up in the words, "Your heavenly Father knows." Nature testifies to His care. The birds and the flowers are unaffected by worry. Some may object that the analogy fails for the reason that man alone is capable of worry because he is capable of thought. Jesus, however, seized the latter fact to show also that man alone is capable of entering into filial relationship with God. This thought was new to the Jewish listeners. Jesus wanted His followers to get their priorities right. The interests of the Kingdom must be placed first, and the rest will be the Father's concern. This seems unrealistic, but the "poor in spirit" know its truth by experience.

Jesus next changed the subject, from anxiety to criticism. Humorously, He pictured a man with a log in his own eye, who was concerned about a speck in another man's eyes. Those who criticize are often those deserving greater criticism. Then Jesus spoke again of trust and prayer for daily needs. The heavenly Father would certainly not be less concerned about His own than an earthly father would be about his children. In fact, Jesus affirmed, "Much more will your Father who is in heaven give good things to those who ask him!"

Jesus reduced to capsule form the Law and the prophets with what has come to be known as the Golden Rule — "Whatever you wish that men would do to you, do so to them." The Jewish teachers taught a negative version, but the positive formulation as Jesus gave it throws the whole emphasis on practical well-being toward others. After pointing out that men are known by their fruits, that is, by the way they live and how they react to others, Jesus made a distinction between merely saying "Lord" and the doing of His will. The doing of righteousness summed up the close of the sermon as it had characterized its beginning. The address closed with the story of two builders, of whom one chose a rock foundation, the other sand. The difference between the two illustrates the difference between doing and not doing the commands of Jesus. The rock foundation in this parable represents a life that not only hears but also does the will of the Lord.

No wonder the listening people were astonished at this kind of teaching; some, because it was too idealistic; fewer, because it preserved the noblest form of ethics. The Messiah did not intend to restrict this teaching to His own time. Its basic precepts are valid for any age, though only for those who fulfill the basic requirement — humility of heart.

Home again in Capernaum

Luke 5:17-26 (Mark 2:1-12; Matthew 9:1-8)

The people of Capernaum soon heard that Jesus had returned. They crowded into the house to hear Him. Probably, they occupied some of the rooms off the courtyard and even filled the street in their eagerness to hear Him. They left no path for anyone else to try to enter. House meetings were not unknown, but on this occasion no meeting had been planned. The proportion of the people who had a genuine desire to hear to those who were stirred merely by curiosity cannot be known. The incident that day centered on another paralyzed man, who was not even in the audience. Four friends carried him to seek healing from Jesus, but they could not reach the doors. However, they were not easily put off by seemingly insurmountable difficulties. They determined to let their friend down through the roof. They somehow noted the spot where Jesus was standing, possibly under a veranda covered with a tile roof. It would be a relatively simple matter to climb onto the flat roof and make an opening in the tiled section large enough to allow for the lowering of the paralyzed man in his bed suspended on ropes. A desperate plan it was, but it was born out of the conviction that Jesus not only could but would do something when He met the paralytic face to face. Access to the roofs of eastern houses was gained by an outside stairway, and the ascent to the roof would therefore be the easiest part of the operation. They quickly removed the tiles before the people beneath became aware of their purpose.

Jesus immediately noted the faith of the men who had brought their friend to Him and assured the paralytic that his sins were forgiven. This unexpected turn of events caused opposition among the scribes present. It was a Pharisaic tenet that God alone could forgive sins. What Jesus said was in their minds nothing short of blasphemy. They did not say so outwardly, but they thought it inwardly. A further testimony to the insight of Jesus is that He knew their thoughts and rebuked them because their thoughts were evil. It is disturbing to realize that even a man's inner thoughts cannot be kept hidden. Jesus knew the scruples of the men before Him, and He said, "Which is easier, to say, 'Your sins are forgiven you,' or to say, 'Rise and walk'?" Without waiting for an answer, He justified His authority to forgive sins by commanding the afflicted man to walk. As with the lame man in Jerusalem, He connected the ailment with the deeper problem of sin.

Various theories about the connection between illness and sin were prevalent among the Jews (cf. John 9:2). Some held all disease to be a direct result of sin and thought those afflicted must be worse sinners than others. It was also thought that suffering was an expiation for sins. There is no reason to suppose that Jesus held either of these current beliefs. No one would deny that sin sometimes leads to illness, but this is very different from affirming that all illness comes from sin. The point of this healing was not that a direct relationship existed between the man's paralysis and his sin, but rather that this man had a twofold need. Jesus again showed His concern for the entire man. He evidently regarded the moral paralysis as more pressing than the physical.

Most of the people present were amazed. They saw the healed man walk away and heard him glorifying God. They remarked that they had never seen anything like this before. It was a spectacular feat, but they failed to recognize the uniqueness of Jesus.

The call of Levi

Matthew 9:9-13 (Mark 2:13-17; Luke 5:27-32)

Four disciples had left their occupations to follow Jesus thus far. All four were fishermen. The next man who followed was a professional man, a tax collector. His profession was not regarded as honorable by most people in Palestine because of the system of tax farming. Men who collected the taxes had bought the franchises from the tax farmer. Unscrupulous men extorted from taxpayers more than was due, and by this means they lined their own pockets. This made them objects of hatred among the populace, and Levi was one of those who sat at the tax office.

The gospels contain no clue whether Jesus had previously met Levi (also called Matthew). The records simply state that Jesus challenged Levi to leave his profession to follow Him. Levi had a lucrative job, but he obeyed. He had a high regard for

Jesus. He saw that He was different from conventional rabbis. He had heard of His many miracles. His mind was ready to respond to Jesus' authoritative challenge. That Levi became widely known as Matthew suggests that the latter name may have been specially given to him by Jesus. It may, however, have been his second name, which he himself preferred. In Matthew's gospel he is named Matthew at the time of his calling, but in both Mark and Luke he is named Levi.

It is significant that Jesus numbered among His followers a representative of one of the most despised classes of Israelite society. If one tax collector could find hope, so could his colleagues. Levi wanted them to meet Jesus. He hastily arranged a banquet for the purpose, but Pharisaic scribes were watching the developments. They saw the chief guest arrive with His disciples and noted the "type" of other guests. Most were tax collectors. Some were among those whom Pharisees contemptuously called "sinners." To them, tax collectors and sinners were highly undesirable company for a respectable rabbi. Jesus' action marked Him, in their eyes, as less than respectable. He was no different in their opinion from the despised common people. Nonetheless, they were still curious to know why Jesus chose such company. They asked His disciples.

The answer of Jesus distinguished Him clearly from the Pharisees in this particular incident, and it also gave a clue to the pattern of His ministry. His words were, "Those who are well have no need of a physician, but those who are sick; I have not come to call the righteous, but sinners to repentance." The miracles that Jesus had already performed showed Him to be the great Physician. Here, He emphasized moral healing. The Pharisees were "bad physicians" in that they not only lacked any remedy for the needy, but they virtually refused to have any concern for them. As physicians are not needed for people who are well, so the Messiah would not be "needed" among people who claimed they were righteous. The Messiah alone has the remedy for those who recognize their sickness. The sneer of the Pharisees survives into the twentieth century. Social distinctions have much too often hindered the work of the Gospel.

7

Jesus and a Cross Section of People

Jesus' views about fasting

Luke 5:33-39 (Matthew 9:14-17; Mark 2:18-22)

All three synoptic gospel writers placed the discussion about fasting after the account of Matthew's feast. A link between the two incidents was obviously intended. Social fellowship may in some quarters be considered unspiritual. This was the Pharisees' approach to the practices of Jesus and His disciples. Rather than feasting in Matthew's house, they should have been fasting, according to the Pharisees' opinion. John the Baptist as well as the Pharisees made much of fasting, but Jesus did not. This confused the common people, who had been led to believe by the Pharisees and John the Baptist that fasting was highly meritorious. The attitude of Jesus was judged to be altogether improper.

Jesus answered His critics with an illustration. He said, "Can you make the wedding guests fast while the bridegroom is with them?" The guests would naturally rejoice in honor of the bridegroom. The friends of Jesus were like guests at a wedding. He told them that the time to mourn would not be until the bridegroom was snatched away from them. None of His hearers knew what was in Jesus' mind when He said this. He was the Bridegroom, and He knew He must die. His mission could not be accomplished without it. Nevertheless, while He was still with them there was no place for sorrow.

Jesus continued with two further illustrations. He had often

93

seen poor people patching their rough garments. It was common sense to use old patches, for cutting a piece from a new garment would unnecessarily ruin the new clothing. The new patch, of unshrunk cloth, would readily tear the old material in the first washing. The second illustration was also drawn from domestic life. No one seriously would consider pouring new wine into old wineskins — the shriveled leather would not survive the vitality of new wine. The obvious practice was to use new skins for new wine.

What was the meaning of these illustrations? The old clothes and the old wine represent the approach of John the Baptist and the legalistic Pharisees with their fasting, and the new garment and the new wine represent the approach of Jesus. Did Jesus declare here that fasting was an outworn religious practice? This cannot be, since Jesus sanctioned fasting on another occasion. Rather, He was condemning, as outworn and cramping, the stubborn viewpoint that no new approach can improve upon the forms of worship of the past. When certain religious rites became sanctified by long use and stultified by custom, there was also the strong body of conservatism to oppose any reform. A moment's reflection would show that the unique teaching of Jesus could not possibly be poured into the same old molds that had made Pharisaism thoroughly legalistic. New molds were needed. The essential message was more important than the outward shell of formal religious observance. The wine was more important than the skins. Fasting had its uses, but it was not to be regarded as indispensable. The approach of Jesus to this practice illustrates His approach to many features of the old order. His mission was not intended to be a patching-up process, but was an entirely new and productive way of life. No one who advocates new approaches, as Jesus constantly did, can avoid conflicting with the "sacred cows" of the *status quo*.

The centurion's servant

Luke 7:1-10 (Matthew 8:5-13)

The incident that follows is one of the few narratives that Matthew and Luke include but Mark omits. It took place at Capernaum, already the scene of notable incidents. The main interest focused on a Gentile's faith. The story is representative of the relationship between the Gentiles and Israel's Messiah.

A detachment of Roman soldiers was stationed in the town. It was commanded by a centurion who was highly respected by the town's inhabitants. Normally, the general Jewish public despised the Roman army, but there was something different about this man. He had provided the synagogue building, which showed his sympathy for the Jewish faith. Remains of a later synagogue still stand at the site of Capernaum. This synagogue

The synagogue at Capernaum. Built in the second century, this structure was erected on the ruins of the earlier, first-century building.

"After he had ended all his sayings in the hearing of the people he entered Capernaum"
—LUKE 7:1

was erected on the foundations of the earlier, first-century building, and in its ruins are inscriptions that show a curious mixture of Jewish and Gentile emblems, which some think were preserved from the earlier building. A Jewish community deeply indebted to a Gentile for the provision of a center of Jewish worship was certainly rare. It reflects something of the unusual character of the centurion. He may have been a proselyte, a Gentile convert to the Jewish faith, but the details of the story do not support this. Evidently he was a man of considerable piety. As the Jewish elders spoke well of this Roman centurion, it is not surprising that the man showed evidence of real faith.

The circumstances are simply stated. The centurion's servant (Luke calls him a slave) was critically ill with paralysis. The officer had heard of Jesus' power to heal, for he requested His help. As a Gentile, he hesitated to go personally to the house where Jesus was living, for Luke states that he sent the Jewish elders to ask Jesus to come and heal his servant. Matthew omits intermediaries and describes Jesus in direct conversation with the centurion. Luke brings out more clearly the nature of the centurion's faith and humility. Both writers, however, emphasize the contrast between the Jews' lack of faith and the faith of this Gentile in the claims of Jesus. The Jewish elders recommended the centurion to Jesus as a worthy man. He was a man of at least moderate wealth, for he had servants and he had provided a synagogue. It is significant that the man himself disclaimed worthiness. He may have been simply respecting Jewish scruples against entering a home of a Gentile.

As an officer he was habitually snapping out orders to his subordinates and expecting prompt, unquestioning obedience. A strong man of commanding and authoritative bearing, he nonetheless submitted to the higher authority of Jesus — allowing Jesus to give the command that his servant would be healed. He had implicit faith that Jesus' authority over disease was just as real and efficient as was his own authority over men and that at Jesus' command the healing would instantly occur.

Jesus marveled at the centurion's faith. It was superior to any He had found in Israel. There was no magical element in it. Many in the future with the same kind of faith as this Gentile would outstrip those who thought that they possessed hereditary right to sit with the patriarchs Abraham, Isaac, and Jacob at the messianic banquet. It was the Jews' firm belief that such a banquet would inaugurate the messianic age, but they never conceded that the Gentiles would share in such a privilege. Jesus stated that even the "sons" (i.e. Israelites) would forfeit their right to be present because of their unbelief. The only alternative for them was outer darkness. This may at first seem harsh, but Jesus was not suggesting that the believing sons would be excluded. Since the Messiah had come to bring light, those who rejected Him rejected this light, and spiritual darkness must follow. This was no easy reasoning for a Jewish audience that took for granted that all the children of Abraham would have passports to the blessings of the Kingdom.

In the narratives, the healing itself is almost incidental. Matthew specially notes that it occurred at the moment when Jesus spoke His command. The extraordinary power of Jesus again came into focus. It was not merely a power to heal, but also a power to inspire faith. Some reason may be suggested for the greater depth of faith in a Gentile than in most of the Jews. Jewish minds were at that time so bound by a variety of theological prejudices that they considered it essential to be doubly sure before entrusting themselves to one making such claims as Jesus made. Gentiles, on the other hand, were less enchained by tradition and could react more readily to any powerful demonstration of authority. This is amply illustrated in the early history of the Church, where Gentile expansion far outstripped the acceptance of the Gospel among the Jews.

A funeral at Nain

Luke 7:11-17

Probably the next day after the centurion's servant was healed, Jesus and His disciples journeyed from Capernaum to Nain, a distance of about twenty-five miles. Since it was a good day's journey on foot, they would not arrive much before evening. Other travelers joined them on the way, and by the time Nain was reached, a sizeable crowd was with them. On approaching the city, they were met by a funeral cortege. Few in the crowd paid much attention to it, for such a procession was a

common sight, but Jesus noted it at once. As the crowd with
Him mingled with the funeral crowd, He thought especially of
the sorrowing widow mourning the loss of her only son. He was
moved not so much by a desire to display His power over death
as He was by His compassion.

Jesus approached the cortege and the weeping woman.
Speaking tenderly to her, He touched the bier — a wholly unexpected action. Neither those carrying the coffin nor the mother
had any idea of what Jesus was about to do. They were utterly
amazed to hear Jesus addressing words to the corpse, "Young
man, I say to you, arise." The young man sat up and began to
speak. It was unbelievable. Jesus had conquered death. Nothing
is recorded of what the young man said. The response of joy by
the mother must be assumed. Luke, however, concentrates on
the reaction of the onlookers, a mixture of fear and wonder.
The sense of awe produced by a dead man's beginning to speak
is understandable, but it is to the credit of the bystanders that
they began glorifying God. Their understanding went no further
than to think that another of the prophets was among them.
Their identification of Jesus as a prophet may have derived from
their recalling the similar raising of young men from the dead by
the Old Testament prophets Elijah and Elisha. Although in Jewish eyes this was no small estimate of Jesus, it did not go far
enough. Others did better as they recognized that the acts of
Jesus were the acts of God. No wonder His fame spread still
further after this incident.

Several features of the event warrant discussion. Certain
procedures were practiced at Jewish funerals that were in marked
contrast to the approach of Jesus. Mourners were hired to chant
a lament. This was designed not as a comfort to the bereaved,
but as a measure of the respect in which the dead person was
held. There was little attempt to relieve the sorrow. Jesus,
however, in His infinite pity and tenderness, told the widow not
to weep. For Him, human sympathy for the sorrowing was more
important than the repetition of traditional ritual. Death would
continue to bring its gloom into human families, but the Christian Gospel, following the method of the Master, would overshadow the sorrow with genuine sympathy and certain hope.

More significant was the way Jesus ignored traditional taboos. A corpse by Jewish law and practice was a source of defilement. Touching one would at once cause a person to be defiled. Jesus did not have to touch the bier to perform the miracle, for, earlier, the centurion's servant was healed with a word. He intended His action to be symbolic. It must have presented an enigma to many of the bystanders. How could a defiled man perform so powerful a miracle? Only two alternatives were possible: either it was not a miracle at all (but no one suggested that) or else Jesus' power overcame ceremonial defilement as well as it overcomes the defilement of sin.

It is futile to conjecture about the reactions of the young man brought back to life. In no narrative where the gospel writers relate a raising from the dead do they give any indication of this. Their reserve is in marked contrast to the free use of imagination by the writers of the apocryphal gospels.

The most important question concerns the historical character of the narrative. Did it happen as Luke reported it? A variety of answers have been given. Some take the view that since raisings from the dead do not occur now, therefore the dead cannot be raised; consequently, the record must be false. Others consider that the dead man only appeared to be dead, but in fact was in a coma, out of which he was roused. It is not unknown for a person in a deep coma to be mistaken as dead. It is highly improbable, however, that the funeral proceedings would have progressed that far without the mistake being discovered.

A miracle of this nature cannot be ruled out in view of the central miracle of the resurrection of Jesus from the dead. This explanation is more credible than that which sees the whole narrative as symbolic, created by the Christian community to illustrate the lifegiving power of Jesus. If the Messiah was as powerful as the early Christians believed Him to be, the incident at Nain cannot be written off as no more than a symbol. Besides, Luke states clearly that "a man . . . had died."

An inquiry from John the Baptist

Luke 7:18-23 (Matthew 11:2-6)

To those who devoted themselves to the mission of John

the Baptist, the success of the ministry of Jesus was a problem. Had they fully recognized the preparatory character of John's work, they would not have been surprised at the greater popularity of Jesus, for they had heard John say, "He must increase, but I must decrease" (cf. John 3:30). However, the main problem arose not so much from John's disciples as from John himself. His initial vision had become blurred, and doubts had arisen. He was beginning to wonder whether Jesus was the Messiah after all.

John's circumstances were an important factor in his doubting. A prison is not an environment conducive to optimism. Ancient prisons were dank and dismal. As a prisoner, John may have wondered why the Messiah, at the height of His popularity, did nothing to alleviate the misery of his faithful forerunner. Such lack of action was contrary to John's notions of the Messiah. Had He been mistaken in identifying Jesus as the coming one? Should he have looked for a Messiah of a different kind? If so, his own mission had been wasted. Such questionings formed the background of the inquiry that John sent to Jesus through two of his disciples. There is no need to suppose, as some have done, that the record of John's earlier recognition of Jesus is unhistorical and that this inquiry was John's first hopeful feeler for an answer to the perplexity of his own mission. Men can at times doubt their strongest convictions.

John, by Jesus' own testimony, was a great man, but he was not exempt from human weakness. Moreover, the doubts that arise in a leader's mind will confuse his followers. John's disciples were no exceptions. In answering the query sent to Him by John through those disciples, Jesus was mindful of these men. While these two disciples watched, Jesus cured many people of diseases, plagues, evil spirits, and blindness. The evidence was indisputable; they were witnessing the signs of messianic power. Jesus, however, said nothing about His claims to messiahship. He simply told the men to go and tell John what they had seen and heard. Matthew and Luke give an identical report of the message that they were to take to John, implying that great importance was attached to its precise form. It linked the healing ministry of Jesus with His preaching ministry. Not only were the healings to be stressed, but also the fact that the poor were hearing the Gospel. Remarkably, raisings from the dead were included in the miracles reported. Luke placed the incident after the raising at Nain, and Matthew after the raising of Jairus' daughter. John the Baptist could not fail to be impressed by the record of miracles performed by Jesus, but the main mission was the preaching of the Kingdom in a similar vein to John's own earlier preaching.

What significance would John attach to the fact that it was to the "poor" that the Gospel was being preached? He may have understood it metaphorically as the "pious," in a sense similar to certain Old Testament occurrences. More likely, however, he took it literally. It was a reminder that the Gospel preached by Jesus was comprehensive, including even the lowest strata of society. Both Greeks and Romans downgraded the poor, but the Messiah's message was directed to them. Jesus evidently expected John to interpret the report as a messianic claim. It has always been the hallmark of true Christian proclamation that none are excluded on social or economic grounds.

Jesus sent a parting word to John, a word of personal encouragement. "Blessed is he who takes no offense at me." Jesus knew the mind of His herald. He detected John's perplexity and doubt. He realized that His methods were a stumbling block to John. The herald had cleared a pathway for the Messiah, but now he was in danger of stumbling. The Messiah was sympathetic and uncritical. Some of the noblest visions become clouded, and great causes that once gleamed with promise can at times become perplexities.

A testimony about John the Baptist
Luke 7:24-35 (Matthew 11:7-19)

The crowds around Jesus probably heard John's two disciples make their request on their master's behalf. Jesus took this opportunity to clarify the connection between His mission and John's. Both Matthew and Luke record a sequence of five questions that in a few words describe the most characteristic features of John. "What did you go out into the wilderness to behold?" The question suggests curiosity, as if John were an exhibition worth an excursion to see. Was he like "a reed shaken by the wind?" Did they expect to find a man who would change his opinion according to popular reaction? John certainly was not that. "What then did you go out to see?" Was it to see someone whose importance was emphasized by his apparel, like the aristocracy in kings' palaces? Such people are not found in desert places, but in kings' courts. Was it then to see "a prophet?" Most of the hearers would assent to this. He looked and spoke like a prophet. Jesus' rhetorical questions show the skill with which He led his hearers to consider an important truth.

Jesus enlarged on John's prophetic function by noting that John had performed a special office that none of the earlier prophets had been called upon to do. He was the Messiah's herald, the one predicted by Malachi (3:1), whose words were cited by Mark at the beginning of his gospel and here quoted by Jesus in testimony to John. Many listening to Jesus had probably attended John's preaching and heard him announce the nearness of the Kingdom, but they also found it difficult to understand the true nature of John's mission. Jesus took this excellent opportunity to make a remarkable comment about His forerunner. "Among those born of women none is greater," was the Messiah's own tribute to John. John was the last and the greatest of the old order. With Jesus the new order had dawned, and the least in the Kingdom announced by Jesus would be greater than John. The seeming paradox perplexed the hearers. How could a man be greater yet less than the least? The difficulty is resolved if one bears in mind that John was himself essentially a prophet of the Old Testament era. The new order of Jesus superseded all that John and the Old Testament prophets had proclaimed. It was based on personal commitment to the Messiah. In His comments about John, Jesus was not detracting from his importance, but was removing any suggestion that John's repentance-baptism was sufficient in itself. That such misunderstandings occurred is evident from the existence of a group of disciples in Ephesus at a later period who knew only the baptism of John (Acts 19).

Luke mentions a divided reaction among the crowd when they heard the comments of Jesus about John the Baptist. Those who had submitted to John's baptism were favorably disposed. They acknowledged before God the rightness of John's mission.

Pharisees and lawyers also were present, who had not only rejected John's baptism, but also the purpose of God. The baptism of John was a testing ground for the mission of Jesus. Those who had already resisted God's purpose for themselves in denying John's mission were not likely to see God's purpose in the mission of Jesus.

There is another enigmatic statement that Jesus made about John. Matthew related it in the above context, but Luke placed it later on (cf. Luke 16:16): "From the days of John the Baptist until now the kingdom of heaven has suffered violence, and men of violence take it by force. For all the prophets and the law prophesied until John; and if you are willing to accept it, he is Elijah who is to come" (Matt. 11:12-14). Apparently something catastrophic had taken place since the proclamation of John the Baptist, which had revolutionized men's approach to the Kingdom. Because of its superior privileges, the Kingdom as proclaimed by Jesus was a prize to be sought. If the least in it are greater than John, entry into it must be highly desirable. Why, however, did Jesus speak of men of violence seeking entry? This has been much disputed but He was probably referring to the numbers spurred on by the dynamic preaching of John to desire entry into the Kingdom. The words could be taken in a hostile sense — of those violently resisting or breaking in — but this does not appear to be the meaning here. The Greek word for violence can also mean strong desire or eagerness. Jesus was revealing that John was the climax of the dispensation or era, represented by the Law and the prophets. In no more emphatic terms could He have declared that His own mission went beyond contemporary Judaism.

Surprisingly, Jesus identified John the Baptist with the expected "second" Elijah. It was believed that Elijah would reappear just before the messianic age, although John himself had emphatically denied that role (cf. John 1:21). Had John failed to recognize the prophecy that he himself came to fulfill (i.e. Mal. 4:5)? Perhaps he had denied the role because his questioners implied the return of Elijah in a crudely literalistic sense, rather than as one coming in the "spirit and power" (Luke 1:17) of the Old Testament prophet (i.e. an "Elijah-type"). Nonetheless, here and also later (cf. Matt. 17:10-13), Jesus asserted the identity of John with Elijah and thus left no doubt that this is the true interpretation of the passage in Malachi. Jesus knew well that some had rejected this view of John, as some rejected Elijah before him.

Jesus illustrated the inconsistency of current attitudes to the contrasting ministries of John the Baptist and His own. He referred to children playing games in the market place, but quarreling over what game to play — whether weddings or funerals. Some wanted one and some the other, until an impasse was reached and they played neither. Both Jesus and John were confronted with an uncooperative audience. John's mission was criticized because of its austerity, and his critics were like those who refused to play funerals; Jesus' mission was criticized because of its joy, and His critics were like those who refused to play weddings. Many hearers would join neither John nor Jesus. Because of John's abstinence, he was said to have a demon; because of Jesus' willingness to eat and drink with social outcasts, He was termed a glutton and a drunkard. What possibility was left? Conformity to current Jewish procedure was all that remained. Those who challenge contemporary opinion are likely to be castigated. Certainly the mission of Jesus demanded a reappraisal of religious conventions. To summarize the matter, Jesus remarked that wisdom is justified "by her deeds" (according to Matthew) or "by all her children" (according to Luke). Wisdom was probably here intended to stand for God the all-wise, in which case Jesus was saying that God is seen to be right through the acts of His children, i.e. through John the Baptist and Jesus. Even without men's cooperation, the mission of God through both would be seen to be justified.

Simon and the sinner

Luke 7:36-50

Jesus was not perturbed by the Pharisees' calling Him a glutton and a drunkard. After His comment concerning this, he accepted a Pharisee's hospitality. This incident shows that Jesus did not exclusively seek the company of tax collectors and sinners. Nevertheless, the gospels do not give the impression that Jesus was a frequent visitor at the homes of Pharisees. The treatment He received in this man's house shows the reason. As a class they considered Him on a lower level than themselves. It was their opinion that those who had not devoted much time to the formal study of the Law were inferior to those who had. In their eyes Jesus was untaught and therefore to be numbered among the common people, however eloquent His teaching. The scene in the house of Simon the Pharisee may therefore be regarded as typical.

The host customarily observed certain formalities when entertaining guests. Water was provided for foot washing, and oil for anointing. Any host failing to observe these common courtesies showed little respect for his guest. When Jesus was invited to Simon's house these courtesies were ignored. It is inconceivable that Simon overlooked them. He avoided them deliberately; he clearly had no respect for Jesus. Jesus did not seem surprised at Simon's breach of courtesy. He did not mention the matter until Simon inwardly criticized Him for accepting the action of a disreputable woman. Jesus was confronted with a deeply ingrained class distinction for which He had no sympathy. He did not inaugurate a social revolution to combat it. He combated it by means of His own gracious attitude toward those whom others treated with contempt.

Other guests shared Simon's meal. Luke mentions their murmurings, but does not identify them. Presumably, they were Pharisaic friends of Simon. They may have been curious to see what Jesus was like at close quarters. The entry of a woman upset the dignity of the meal. Simon was taken aback, for she was noted for her immoral life. He may not have seen her until she had already washed the feet of Jesus with her tears, dried them with her hair, and anointed them with ointment. The odor of the ointment may have first attracted Simon's attention. Luke's narrative gives the impression that at first he said nothing but was nevertheless harboring critical thoughts. Jesus knew what he was thinking. This was another example of His insight into men's minds, one of the several recorded occasions when Jesus answered thoughts that had not been uttered. Simon probably registered his thoughts by the lines on his face. He had become convinced that Jesus was no prophet. Certainly, no prophet would allow Himself to be defiled by a sinner's touch or remain unaware as to who she really was. Surely Jesus' willingness to permit the woman's action showed a lack of the prophetic gift on His part.

Jesus' method of dealing with Simon was characteristic. By a simple story about two debtors, He invited Simon's cooperation in rethinking his whole position. He was asked to express his opinion whether a man who had been forgiven much would love more than a man forgiven little. Simon grudgingly conceded the point. At this, Jesus turned the focus on Simon himself. Simon failed to love because he had never seen himself as a debtor before God in the same way as the woman had. With all her unenviable past, she was at least deeply aware of her need. Jesus' comment, "Her sins, which are many, are forgiven, for she loved much," must not be misunderstood, for God's forgiveness of sin is not based on a person's prior love for Him. Love is not prior to faith, but a fruit of faith. Jesus was confirming what the woman already knew by experience — that her sins were forgiven. Her act of love was evidence that she had found liberation from the chains that had bound her. The tenderness of Jesus toward her is one of the most striking examples of His concern for broken and bruised lives.

The guests were alarmed. A profound theological problem had been raised. They wanted to know what kind of man this was who claimed to forgive sins. Their traditions had taught them that God alone had power to do so (cf. Mark 2:7). They seemed more concerned with the theoretical problem than with the experience of forgiveness. Whereas the woman went away with an inner peace, the critics went away with their quibble. Jesus never answered them. Forgiveness and peace were benefits too priceless to be dissipated by fruitless discussion. Simon and his guests were typical of many who failed to realize that the Messiah had come to meet human need at its deepest level. This was work of a spiritual nature that baffled them.

Ministering women

Luke 8:1-3

After recording the incident of the woman whose sins were forgiven, Luke mentions other women who had come under the influence of Jesus. He makes it clear that women also had a part in the Lord's ministry. The occasion was a preaching tour among the cities and villages. The twelve disciples accompanied Jesus together with a company of women. Some of them had good reason to be grateful to Jesus because He had healed them or cast out evil spirits from them. Luke mentions only three of them by name. Mary, whose home was in Magdala, had been possessed with seven devils, a description possibly intended to indicate the intensity of the possession. Hers had been a severe case, and the completeness of the cure was all the more remarkable. She never forgot her indebtedness to Jesus. She was among those who later prepared spices to embalm His body after the crucifixion. To her the risen Lord first appeared on that first Easter day because she tarried longer at the tomb than the other women.

Joanna, described as the wife of Chuza, a steward of Herod, was another who went with Mary to the tomb that Easter morning. Whether she had been cured of some ailment or not Luke does not say. Her husband evidently held a position of some influence at Herod's court. How she came to be associated with the mission of Jesus it is impossible to say. She nonetheless became a staunch follower. The third woman is named Susanna, of whom nothing further is known. There were "many others," who remain unnamed.

Some of these women were wealthy and considered it a privilege to support Jesus and His disciples on their tours. Other rabbis were provided for in the same way. By their financial support the women contributed an important service to the mission of Jesus.

The mention of these women reminds us of the influence that Christianity has had on the emancipation of women generally. The world of Jesus' day had little conception either of the freedom or the importance of women. In Israel a woman's status was avowedly inferior to a man's. This was true also in most Gentile areas. Macedonia, however, was one of the notable exceptions. It is Luke more than any other writer who focused attention on Jesus' approach to this subject. As a Gentile, he appreciated the different emphasis taken by Jesus in contrast to that of most of His contemporaries.

8

Miracles and Men

Storm on Galilee

Matthew 8:23-27 (Mark 4:35-41; Luke 8:22-25)

Boisterous winds at times swept in from the valleys between the hills and whipped the quiet waters of the Sea of Galilee into a fury in an incredibly short time. A sudden squall engulfed Jesus and the disciples while they were rowing across the lake. The waves lashed the boat, rapidly filling it with water, but Jesus remained asleep on a cushion, oblivious to the furor around Him. The disciples' terror contrasts strongly with Jesus' calm. Seasoned fishermen, as some of the disciples were, could not easily be terrified. It was not the first storm on Galilee that they had weathered. This time, however, the situation seemed desperate. They were compelled to wake their Master, not so much because they feared for His safety, but because they feared for their own. In panic they shouted out above the storm, "Do you not care if we perish?" The words could not hide their consternation at His seeming lack of concern.

Two rebukes were needed: one for the wind and the other for the disciples. At a word from Jesus the wind immediately ceased, and the disciples were filled with awe. The rebuking of the wind was a display of power over the natural world. Who could tame the wind but He who made it? It is possible, of course, to strip the incident of the miraculous — to say that the squall ended naturally as suddenly as it had begun, the end merely coinciding with the command of Jesus. This, however, would leave unexplained the awe of the disciples. They were clearly impressed by the connection between the authoritative voice of Jesus and the immediate calm. They could explain it only by reference to the personal power of Jesus. Nevertheless, it raised problems in their minds. It made them wonder what kind of person He was. They were conscious of having grossly under-rated Him.

Why did the evangelists record the stilling of the storm? Was it just a remarkable event that shows Jesus as a performer of marvels, or is there some deeper meaning? Some find a connection between this incident and what follows, when Jesus cast out demons. There was widespread belief that behind the natural forces were demonic agencies. The fiercer the storm, the more malignant the demon. If this had been in Jesus' mind, the rebuking of the wind would be understandable. It would also illustrate His power to control the spiritual agencies behind the natural world. There is, however, no need to suppose that Jesus shared this common belief. Those who accepted it needed to know of one whose power was great enough to combat even the adverse forces of nature. If Jesus was what He claimed to be and what the early Christians believed Him to be, such power over the natural world is not unexpected. If all things were made by Him, the stilling of a storm presents no difficulties. The rationalist considers any interference with the course of nature as incredible. The rationalist, however, cannot explain the uniqueness of the person performing the action. The storm eventually would have stopped anyway, of course, but it was the time and the suddenness of its stopping that shows the unique power and character of Jesus.

Jesus also rebuked the disciples. The gospel writers each put it in a slightly different way. Matthew records the rebuke in the question, "Why are you afraid, O men of little faith?" Mark puts it in two questions, "Why are you afraid? Have you no faith?" Luke says simply, "Where is your faith?" All three focus on the absence of faith. Fear thrives where faith is missing. If they had believed in Jesus, they would have considered the possibility of His taking action, but it never occurred to them. Jesus had to teach them to expect greater things from Him. They had a long way to go before they would be equipped to further the mission of Jesus.

Demoniacs at Gergesa

Matthew 8:28-34 (Mark 5:1-20; Luke 8:26-39)

Looming into the night sky, a dark mass of cliff face blotted out the moonlight and overshadowed the strip of coast when Jesus and the disciples reached the other side of the lake. On both sides were burial places as they ascended the bank. Suddenly, weird terrifying shrieks rent the night air. Darting from behind the tombs, two demoniacs swiftly bore down on the little group. One of them was notorious and utterly uncontrollable. Men had tried using chains to tame him, but he shattered the links to pieces. His frenzied strength was phenomenal, and no one dared to pass where he lived. The disciples must have been terrified, although the gospel writers do not mention their reactions. Or had their faith grown stronger since the stilling of the storm? If Jesus could subdue the fury of the waves, He could also deal with the fury of demons. Surely the disciples were also overawed by the dignity and authority of Jesus as He stood facing the advancing demoniacs. The scene is parabolic, for the whole mission of Jesus consisted of good facing evil, of light penetrating darkness, of the overcomer confronting the defeated.

Demon possession does not fall into a scientific category, and medical science must therefore explain the phenomenon in other terms. Many similar symptoms occur in classified psychiatric cases. It has been suggested that demon possession was a first-century concept to explain what is now known as mental instability. The question arises, however, whether all instances of demon possession can be identified with mental disturbances. Similar symptoms can be traceable to different causes. Medical science should pay more attention to spiritual factors in the treatment of some psychiatric disorders. The narrative of the Gergesene demoniacs is valuable in showing the close relationship between the personality of the person possessed and the demons. When the demons spoke they spoke through the lips of the man. When the man spoke he did not give his own name but the name of the demon. The possessed man had ceased to act as a self-controlled individual. His thoughts were not his own. He acted incoherently, often against his better judgment.

Mark and Luke concentrate on the more notorious demoniac, but Matthew includes them both. There are other stories where Matthew included two and the other writers mentioned only one (e.g., two blind men at Jericho; two asses at the entry into Jerusalem). Some have seen this as Matthew's tendency to enhance the narrative, as if the miracle improved its value by being doubled. In the present instance, surely the cure of one was impressive enough without the need to duplicate.

Instead of meaningless shrieks, the cry of the demons became rational and specific. "What have you to do with us, O Son of God?" The demons recognized no affinity between themselves and Jesus. He was utterly alien to them. It was as if the demons totally admitted defeat. Their conqueror was unmistakable. The demons expressed their fear of torment and admitted the ultimate triumph of God over the forces of evil.

This act of Jesus was decisive. He commanded the unclean spirits to leave the man. It was never God's purpose that human personality should be distorted. Jesus asked the man's name.

The hills near Gadara were a familiar sight to Jesus and the disciples, looking eastward from the Sea of Galilee.

"They came to the other side of the sea, to the country of the Gerasenes"
—MARK 5:1

His answer "Legion" may possibly indicate the intensity of the demons' sway. There was no connection with a military legion, which numbered six thousand men. A Jew would be familiar with the concept of legions of spirits. Why did Jesus ask the name? It was probably to enable the man to differentiate himself from the possessing demons. It was a distinction between the "I" and the "many."

The request of the demons to be allowed to remain rather than be banished into the abyss (Luke) or sent out of the country (Mark), needs explanation. It apparently was a request to avoid utter banishment, although the demons recognized the power of Jesus to banish them. He agreed to their further request to be sent into the herd of swine at the top of the cliff. The demons immediately left the man. There is no mention of a final paroxysm, only the frenzied stampede of two thousand swine into the lake. The whole herd disappeared. Only the herdsmen were left on the top. At the foot of the cliff Jesus talked with the former demoniac, now a perfectly normal man. The herdsmen fled to the city with the news, and many flocked to the scene. There they heard more details. The untamable had been tamed. The violent man was sitting, quiet as a lamb. The city people, however, wanted Jesus to leave their district. Possibly this was because of the substantial financial loss suffered by the owners of the swine herd. Both Mark and Luke mention that they were gripped with fear, probably overawed at the thought of having so powerful a person as Jesus in their midst. Whatever their reason for begging Jesus to leave, it was characteristic of men's frequent reaction to His mission.

By way of contrast, one of the healed men who had been so notoriously rejected and even feared by society wanted to remain with Jesus. He was the first person he talked to as an integrated personality. The Messiah made clear, however, that the healed man's task lay nearer at hand, among his own people. In spite of their desire to be rid of Him, Jesus would not go without providing a witness. Everyone knew the man's former state. His remarkable transformation would be a powerful witness. In talking of what Jesus had done for him, he could perform a worthwhile mission and prove the power of Jesus more effectively than if he had followed Him. Here in miniature occurred what was to happen throughout the Christian Church after Jesus the Messiah departed at the Ascension — His commissioned followers would remain on earth to testify to the power and love of God in Jesus Christ.

A needy woman and a ruler's daughter

Matthew 9:18-26 (Mark 5:21-43; Luke 8:40-56)

Early that morning Jesus and His disciples left Gergesa. When they arrived on the opposite coast a crowd had already collected. They were probably wondering what marvel Jesus would do next. They may have heard reports of the strange happenings among the tombs of Gergesa. Most were stirred by curiosity. One man had a more serious purpose. Jairus, one of the rulers of the synagogue and much respected in the community, pressed out of the crowd to plead with Jesus to come to his house. His daughter, an only child, was dying. In deep grief he flung himself at the feet of Jesus. It was an unusual obeisance from a synagogue official, but he was desperate. He had faith that healing might come if Jesus laid hands on the girl. He had heard of others who had been healed by Jesus in this way. However, Jesus was interrupted by another case of need.

Milling crowds prevented Jesus and Jairus from making much progress toward the latter's house. A woman was behind Him, a victim of a hemorrhage for twelve years. She had spent considerable sums on doctors' fees but without effect. She had almost given up hope, but she knew that Jesus possessed power to heal. She had faith that He could heal her. She was convinced that all she needed to do was to touch Jesus' garment. Many were jostling Him, but she stretched out her hand to grasp the fringe of His robe. Immediately she felt the surge of new strength as she was cured. The healing did not occur unknown to Jesus. The disciples found it incredible that He stated that someone had touched Him when people were pushing in all around Him. Jesus knew who had done it. The power that flowed from Him as she was healed was with His consent. It was no magic touch, but a touch of faith by which Jesus' power went out to heal her. Luke the physician mentions the transfer of power from Healer to healed. The words of Jesus to this woman are similar to those spoken to the woman in the house of Simon the Pharisee — "Your

faith has made you well; go in peace." The one incident was deliverance from the guilt of sin; the other incident, from the grip
of an incurable disease. In both, the Healer showed concern for
the patients' peace of mind.

Meanwhile, the ruler became increasingly distraught. He
may have reasoned that his daughter's need was more urgent
than the woman's. The latter had waited twelve years; surely
she could wait a little longer. He attempted to hurry Jesus, but
it was too late. One of his servants reported that his daughter was
dead; the Master need not be troubled any longer. Jesus, however, did not take His orders from men. He was not governed by
their conclusions. Although common sense indicated that since
the girl was dead there was nothing more that could be done,
yet He knew otherwise. He alone knew what He would do. His
first move was to reassure the father that his daughter would be
healed. In this miracle of Jesus the element of compassion is
again prominent.

Among the crowd gathered at the house were relatives, mu-
sicians, and wailing women, the latter two groups hired for the
purpose. No time had been lost. There was an impressive outward show of mourning, which provided scant comfort to the
sorrowing father as he returned or to the stricken mother within.
The shallow mourning easily turned to derisive laughter when
Jesus announced that the child was only sleeping. Nonetheless,
with an authoritative action, which spoke more eloquently than
words, He ordered them all from the house. The parents and
Peter, James, and John were allowed to remain inside. Jesus took
the girl's hand and commanded her to rise. Those words of command so deeply impressed the disciples that they remembered
the original Aramaic (*Talitha cumi*), which Mark records. The
restoration was instantaneous, after which Jesus' human concern
is evident in His request that the girl be given some food. Obviously she had completely returned to normal. The parents
and disciples alike were amazed. Mark and Luke both say that
Jesus commanded them not to tell anyone. Was it possible, however, to keep it secret? Would not everyone outside the house
immediately know what had happened? The little girl could not
be kept in hiding from the community. Some have seen this
command to silence as Mark's editing and therefore as not origi-

nal to Jesus. There is no good reason, however, for supposing that
Jesus did not give it. He was guarding against the tendency of
crowds to view His miracles as wonders rather than as signs of
His messianic mission. In spite of the command, however, news
of the event spread throughout the district.

Because Jesus stated that the girl was not dead, but only
asleep, the question arises whether or not she had really died.
Jesus, however, meant sleep in a metaphorical sense. Luke states
simply that "she was dead." Why did Jesus express Himself
ambiguously? Possibly He wished to veil the true nature of the
event from those who lacked the capacity to understand its place
in His mission. Or perhaps He wanted to assure the people that
the girl would soon be raised to consciousness as from sleep.

There had been four outstanding manifestations of the supernatural power of the Messiah within two days. At His word a
storm had been stilled, a demoniac cured, an incurable disease
healed, and a dead girl restored to life.

Further miracles of healing

Matthew 9:27-38

Since many other instances of healing must have occurred,
one might expect that each evangelist would have recorded a
different sample of each type. This is not what they did, however, and some significance must therefore be attached to the du-
plications. At times, repetitions are necessary to make an impact
on minds that are not at first disposed to be impressed. Matthew
is especially liberal in the samples that he provides. The two following incidents have parallels elsewhere, but nevertheless have
some claim to consideration in their own right.

After leaving the house of Jairus, Jesus was accosted by two
blind men crying out, "Have mercy on us, Son of David." This
request could be interpreted only as a plea for healing. The title
with which they addressed Jesus was rare in His ministry. It was
used later by the crowds who heralded His entry into Jerusalem,
and it was also used by two other blind men outside Jericho. In
Galilee, it was used only in this incident and later on by a foreign
woman (cf. Matt. 15:22). These blind men may have heard the
promise that the Messiah would open the eyes of the blind. If

so, they used a messianic title in the hope that Jesus was the promised one. Their faith was quickened by reports of recent miracles by Jesus. With a sharpness of hearing that is common in blind people, they would have picked up snatches of conversation from others who passed by.

Apparently Jesus did not respond at once, for He went into another house. The blind men followed Him inside. Then He turned to them to inquire whether they believed He was able to do what they asked — a clear instance of a demand for faith before the healing. This demand is undoubtedly the focal point of the story. They assented, and Jesus touched their eyes and said, "According to your faith be it done to you." This insistence on previous faith marks such healings as distinct from mere wonders. Again, a command to silence was given. Significantly, Matthew, who did not mention it in the case of Jairus' daughter, mentions it here. Once again the order was not heeded. Two men, with their opened eyes as irrefutable testimony, spread His fame. Theirs was an understandable enthusiasm.

In Matthew's record, this event is linked with another. A dumb demoniac was led to Him almost as soon as the other men had left. The dumb man began speaking after Jesus cast out the demon. The main point of the story was not so much the cure, but the reaction of the multitude. The people admitted that nothing like this had previously happened in Israel. The uniqueness of Jesus was beginning to dawn upon them. The Pharisees, however, had a totally different reaction. They charged Jesus with casting out demons by the prince of demons. This was not the only incident when such a charge was flung at Him. On another occasion He pointed out the inconsistency of it (Matt. 12:24 ff.). Here He did not pursue it. Matthew mentions it to bring out the contrast in the responses to Jesus' miracles.

As He went away continuing His healing, Jesus was moved for the multitudes and urged the disciples to pray for more laborers. Only God could meet the demand for spiritual reapers.

The choosing of the Twelve
Matthew 10:1-4 (Mark 3:13-19; Luke 6:12-16)

The choice by Jesus of twelve men to be trained in His teaching and methods marked an important stage in His ministry. Specific, intensive training could not be given to multitudes. The future success of the mission depended in a large measure on those called apart for the purpose. The evangelists give no exact time and sequence of Jesus' choosing His disciples. Some of the disciples were associated with Jesus from the earliest days of His ministry, such as Peter and Andrew, James and John, Philip and Nathanael, and Levi, all of whom are previously mentioned. It is not known when the others were officially added. It was, of course, before the sending out of the Twelve, since by that time they existed as a separate group. Yet, there apparently was a specific occasion when Jesus appointed the Twelve to be apostles. Both Mark and Luke give a rather general indication of the timing of this event. Luke says, "In these days," which shows that the precise timing was unimportant. It is convenient to discuss the appointment of the Twelve together with the account of their mission, although these may not have occurred at the same time.

Luke includes one feature that is characteristic of his portrait of Jesus. Before appointing the Twelve, Jesus spent all night in prayer. This insight into His inner life is important. All major developments in His ministry were preceded by prayer. That it was so on this occasion shows it to have been a critical event. These men were to be in a special sense His messengers. Luke wanted his readers to know that in choosing these men Jesus was acting in full harmony with the Father's will. Of those mentioned above, all but the last occur in the order given in all the lists recorded in the gospels. In the list in Matthew's gospel, Matthew's own name is placed after that of Thomas. One comment only is necessary. In the lists in the synoptists, Nathanael is called Bartholomew, which may have been his family name. The remaining five names are Thomas, James of Alphaeus, Simon the Zealot, Judas of James, and Judas Iscariot. Thomas later became known as the doubter who came through to glorious faith, and Judas as the betrayer who, in bitter remorse, ended in suicide. The names of the lesser-known given above are from Luke's list, but in place of Judas of James, Matthew and Mark give Thaddaeus (although an alternative reading has Lebbaeus). Matthew and Mark call Simon the Zealot "Simon the Canaanite." "Canaan" does not describe a local district, but is derived from the Hebrew word equivalent to Zealot.

The main problem arising from the choice of the Twelve is the inclusion of Judas Iscariot. More will be said on this in the discussion of the betrayal. The mystery of it must be noted here. Since Jesus knew what was in man, He knew the type of man He had chosen.

The mission of the Twelve

Matthew 10:5-15 (Luke 9:1-6; Mark 6:7-13)

Jesus sent His disciples on a twofold mission — to preach and to heal (including the exorcism of demons). To prepare them, He gave instructions that were colored by the local environment, but which have furnished guidelines for the subsequent mission work of the Church. One particular saying stands as a prelude to Matthew's account of this mission. It also occurs in Luke at the outset of a similar mission undertaken by seventy other people. It uses an illustration that Jesus often employed: "The harvest is plentiful, but the laborers are few; pray therefore the Lord of the harvest to send out laborers into his harvest." Jesus had just prayed before appointing the Twelve. This was to be the pattern also for them. There were boundless opportunities, but few to seize them. The Galilean towns needed the message of the Kingdom, but the Messiah could not visit them all. He delegated the task. This was the strategy that later led to the spreading of the Gospel through Gentile lands. For the present, however, this was not to be. The Messiah had come primarily to the "lost sheep of the house of Israel." Only Matthew notes this. He was specially interested in the Messiah's mission to Israel, as many details of his gospel show. Samaria and Gentile lands would hear later; Israel must hear first.

The theme of their preaching — the same as that preached by John the Baptist and by Jesus Himself — was the nearness of the Kingdom. It is certain that Jesus elaborated on this theme for the benefit of His disciples. These beginnings of apostolic preaching were nevertheless preparatory. Their preaching would deepen when they emerged from the agonizing experience of the passion and had learned the new meaning of the message in the light of the resurrection of Jesus.

Details are given about the procedure the disciples were to follow. They were not to be cumbered with more than the minimum of material possessions. Not even a spare tunic was to be taken. They were to take no money and no food. Jesus considered that a laborer was worthy to receive something in return for what he did. This was a generally accepted principle for itinerant teachers and preachers. One small detail, however, has caused difficulty. Matthew and Luke state that no staff was to be taken, but Mark's record permits it. Perhaps Jesus meant that they were not to procure a staff specially for this journey, and certainly the word that Matthew uses could be so interpreted. Luke and Mark, however, use a different word. Jesus may have intended to indicate that nothing — not even a staff — was absolutely necessary, but those who had them could use them. Some have thought that Luke wanted to make the privations more stringent, but the provision or otherwise of a staff is of little consequence.

Jesus also gave instructions about procedure on the journey, especially in regard to what the disciples were to do when people refused to hear the message. The advice was simple and straightforward. While they were in a city, they were to stay in that home where hospitality was offered, and were not to seek more comfortable quarters. The customary greeting of "Peace" was to be used to show the friendly purpose of the mission. If hospitality was unworthy, the blessing of peace would not rest on the household; if hospitality was not offered at all, the very dust of the city was to be shaken off as a symbol of their unworthiness and of judgment. Cities rejecting the Messiah would incur more serious judgment than the cities of Sodom and Gomorrah, the fated cities that suffered destruction in the time of Abraham on account of their wickedness. A harsh prediction for a Messiah of mercy, it was a solemn reminder of the consequences of rejecting the message.

The way ahead for the Twelve

Matthew 10:16-42 (Luke 21:12-19; cf. Luke 12:1-12)

Looking to the future, the Messiah described the considerable opposition that lay ahead for His messengers. He saw enemies as packs of wolves dangerously searching for prey; in the face of them His people would be like sheep. Humanly speaking, the outlook seemed grim. The wolves would tear the sheep apart. The disciples, however, were to learn that the sheep were never without the Shepherd's protection.

The imagery of discipleship was changed to serpents, and then to doves. The former were symbols of wisdom, the latter of innocence. As serpents quickly sense danger and rapidly move to avoid it, so should the messengers of the Gospel. They must not court disaster. Also they should be quick-witted and know when and how to strike with the Gospel of love. Similarly, they should show an unmixed simplicity of motive that is symbolized by doves. The world's ways were crooked and perverse (cf. Phil. 2:15), but the way of the Messiah was straight and single-minded.

Jesus translated the metaphorical language into concrete situations. The messengers of the Gospel must expect to answer for their faith before hostile courts, sometimes before lower authorities such as synagogue councils, which had power to punish by flogging, and sometimes in higher councils as before governors and kings. The book of Acts, especially in relating the experiences of the apostle Paul, furnishes examples of what the earliest preachers endured in the service of their Master. Paul defended himself before Gallio, Felix, and Festus — all governors representing the Roman Emperor — and also before King Herod Agrippa. The prospect would certainly terrify the timid, but Jesus reassured them. There was no need for anxiety. The Spirit of God would supply the right words for them to speak.

There was, however, a glimpse of future tragedy as Jesus forecast family feuds over the faith, a forecast that has been fulfilled many times in the bitter hostilities that develop when men are faced with the challenge of the Gospel. Jesus did not gloss over the difficulties that lay ahead. He had no delusion that the Gospel would be popular. Persecution must be expected, although it should be avoided as far as possible by moving from one town to another, at least as far as the evangelization of Israel was concerned since there were enough cities to reach. At this point, Jesus said to the disciples: "You will not have gone through all the towns of Israel, before the Son of man comes." This statement presents a problem. What is not clear is the meaning of the coming. Some suggest it meant the coming of judgment to

Israel when Jerusalem was destroyed by the Roman armies in A.D. 70. Others think that the coming must refer to His return at the end of this age, in which case the first part of the statement remains puzzling. Jesus did not intend to confuse. The mind of His hearers was on the present mission to Israel. Later, they would have recognized an allusion to the fall of Jerusalem. The immediate mission, however, was intended to be symbolic of the wider missions to the world; thus, the cities of Israel stand for the cities of the world, some of which are still without the Gospel.

The third part of the discourse provided encouragement. If the way was to be rough for the disciples, it would be more so for the Master. The apostles would be maligned no more than Jesus Himself. Already He knew the vicious Pharisaic accusations, and He warned the disciples to expect the same. Hidden intrigues would be the worst form of opposition, but Jesus gave assurance that all would be made plain at the end. The messengers of the Gospel themselves must avoid the secretive methods of their opponents. They need fear only God who alone has power over both body and soul.

Jesus further assured the disciples that God, who cares for the lesser creatures such as the many sparrows that sold for so little in the market place, has infinitely greater concern for His children. Even the hairs of their head are numbered. Jesus could not have expressed the Father's care more vividly. When messengers of the Gospel must answer for their faith before men, they can depend on the Father's honoring those who honor Him.

Jesus concluded His discourse by returning to the subject of family feuds. He wanted His disciples to understand the claims He was making on His followers. Those claims must take precedence over the closest family ties. Jesus likened His mission to the taking up of a cross. He meant it metaphorically, although He would know it literally. His mission could not be accomplished without it. Real life was to be found in self-giving. This thought led to the subject of rewards, which, according to Jesus, are governed by motives. Those who share the work of a prophet are entitled to a prophet's reward. The same applied to a righteous man. So simple an action as a disciple offering a cup of water to some "insignificant" person would not go unrewarded. This differed from most men's idea of reward. Recompense is normally expected to bear a direct relation to work done rather than to the motive behind the work. Moreover, the most prominent work usually gained the greatest reward. Not so in the message of Jesus. The prophet who preached would not be superior to the host who entertained. The lesson has not always been learned in the Christian Church. It involves a basic subjection of self-interest to the greater interests of the Kingdom.

9

Comments and Clashes

Cities under rebuke

Matthew 11:20-24 (Luke 10:13-15)

It would be expected that the greatest spiritual impact of the ministry of Jesus would have occurred in those places where most of His healing work and other miracles were performed. These cities, however, merely marveled at the miracles, but they saw nothing of the spiritual challenge underlying them. They were interested more in the healing of broken bodies than the restoration of broken spirits. They heard the preaching of repentance but did not repent. They saw no reason to change their ways. In spite of apparent popularity, the Messiah's mission had little success; the measure of the spiritual response of the masses was small. In the three cities clustered at the northern end of the Sea of Galilee — Chorazin, Bethsaida, and Capernaum — there was particular hardness of heart.

Jesus unleashed harsh words concerning these cities. His mission was essentially one of mercy, but He did not hesitate to warn. The message of mercy depended on a simple condition — the willingness to repent. If men rejected that condition and continued to delight in sin, the message of mercy was revoked. Judgment was the only alternative. The Old Testament illustrated the serious consequences of unwillingness to repent. Tyre, Sidon, and Sodom all suffered divine judgments. Compared to Tyre and Sidon, however, Chorazin and Bethsaida were privileged. The Messiah never walked the streets of Tyre and Sidon;

their people never heard His teaching. Had they done so they would have repented in the traditional manner of wearing sackcloth and sprinkling ashes on their heads. Nonetheless, Chorazin and Bethsaida remained unmoved. A day of reckoning would come. In His teaching, Jesus repeatedly referred to a day of reckoning. It presented a challenging picture. A terrible accountability would be required of them at the judgment day — they had squandered their messianic privileges.

Capernaum received a special word of rebuke. It was even more privileged than the surrounding cities. The Messiah had His temporary dwelling there, although Capernaum could claim no special terms on this score. Rather, the opposite was true. Those with the most opportunities to respond carry the greatest responsibilities for failure to respond. The city was puffed up with a sense of self-importance, but it would be brought low, even to Hades (death, destruction). It could descend no lower than that. Its humiliation would be complete.

These severe words are reported by both Matthew and Luke, but in different contexts. Matthew placed them after the words of

"And you, Capernaum, will you be exalted to heaven? You shall be brought down to Hades"
— MATTHEW 11:23

The Sea of Galilee from the site of Capernaum on the northwest shore. This lakeside town was the center of Jesus' Galilean ministry.

Jesus about John the Baptist. They serve as examples of the fact that neither John's message nor the message of Jesus had been received by that generation. In Luke's account, the words appear as part of the mission discourse to the seventy. They record the saying of Jesus that any town that rejected His messengers would have more to answer for than ancient Sodom. The precise order of these "woes" is unimportant. They may have been spoken more than once. If not, they clearly contained a truth that both evangelists saw the need to include in their presentation of Jesus. They did not omit His sterner tones, nor gloss over the fact that even His mission experienced a lack of response.

Praise and comfort

Matthew 11:25-30 (Luke 10:21, 22)

The refusal of these Galilean cities to repent is the backdrop against which a glimpse into the inner consciousness of Jesus is presented. Did anyone suppose, after listening to the pronouncement of the woes, that Jesus was utterly despondent about the success of His mission? If these cities of Galilee, with their high privileges, had refused the message, what reason was there for continuing the preaching mission? Jesus did not despair. With perfect insight into the nature of things, He knew that the Kingdom would never come by popular acclaim — by whole cities yielding allegiance to the Messiah. There was room here for encouragement to the eye of faith. Jesus gave an exquisite gem of praise to God at the very time He deplored the destiny of the cities He had condemned.

His praise was addressed to His Father as Lord of heaven and earth. The quality of all praise is governed by one's concept of God. Those whose "God is too small" will hardly consider it worthwhile to praise Him. The thanksgiving of Jesus sets the pattern for His people. The wealthy and flourishing cities of Galilee could not be compared with Him who controls all of creation. Jesus' evaluation of people differed from that of others. Those who apparently were the wisest and most blessed with understanding were not the most important to Him. The Kingdom would come through channels other than human reason. A childlike simplicity, a readiness to admit to being a mere babe, would be true spiritual understanding. Only then could the revelation of God be received. Jesus was overjoyed that some were responding in this way. The Father had chosen this method of ensuring the success of the mission. Most important to Jesus was His knowledge that this was pleasing to His Father.

Following this prayer of thanksgiving, Jesus made a statement that has caused much debate because of its high claims regarding His relation to the Father. The claims, however, are no higher than would be expected from the kind of Messiah that the gospel writers present. The statement in Matthew's gospel is very similar to passages in John's gospel, since both writers present portraits of the same Messiah. The statement reads:

> All things have been delivered to me by my Father; and no one knows the Son except the Father, and no one knows the Father except the Son and any one to whom the Son chooses to reveal him.

To understand the meaning of these words is to understand the mission of Jesus. He claimed to be the sole means through whom men can truly know the Father. All other means are subsidiary to Him. He is completely qualified to be the sole means because He is, in a unique sense, the Son. Human analogies are imperfect for conveying divine truth, but the father-son relationship is highly understandable and helpful. As a human son shows some of his father's characteristics — infinitely more will the divine Son reflect all the characteristics of the heavenly Father. All justification for studying the earthly life of Jesus is found here. What happened in Palestine centuries ago ceases to be remote when viewed as the revelation from the Father. Truth is eternal, and it shines through the first century into all succeeding generations. External features have changed. Man's progress has been phenomenal. It is nonetheless still true that no one can come to God as Father except through Jesus Christ. Neither before nor since has anyone spoken with such authority about God and the way to Him.

After so categorical a claim, Jesus issued a personal invitation for any with a sense of need to come to Him. The invitation is addressed to those who labor and are heavily burdened

— but why in such terms? Was He thinking of manual laborers? Most likely He meant the words in a metaphorical sense, for those burdened with the requirements of the Law, which they could not fulfill. Nothing crushes the human spirit more than impossible demands. Or He may have been thinking of those burdened with sin; this would make the application more universal and would be in line with the constant call to repentance during the mission of Jesus. Whatever the meaning, the emphasis is on a sense of need. To burdened people there is promise of rest, whether in the first century or in the twentieth. Jesus was the perfect example of calmness, even when He was most active or facing harsh opposition. To give this rest of mind to others was part of the purpose of His mission. He dealt with sin, the basic cause of man's unrest.

The example of Jesus was an inspiration for those willing to learn from Him. If they fulfilled His conditions, they would share His rest. The rabbis used the illustration of a yoke to describe a man's allegiance to the Law, but Jesus used the same figure for allegiance to His person. He thus illustrated His relationship to the disciples. It is reassuring to discover the true character of one's yoke-fellow. Jesus gave a priceless summary of His own character in the words, "I am gentle and lowly in heart." Lowliness was not admired in the ancient world. Nor has the astonishing advance in human achievement put any higher value upon it. Gentleness also was mistaken for weakness. Nonetheless, for a disciple committing himself to his Master, what qualities could be more desirable? Such a yoke would never chafe. The demands would hardly be noticed. The yoke is easy, the burden light.

A clash with the Pharisees in the grain field

Matthew 12:1-8 (Mark 2:23-28; Luke 6:1-5)

When any group maintains strong convictions, confrontation with others is inevitable. It is not surprising, therefore, that Jesus frequently clashed with the Pharisees. Some instances have already been noted. Two more examples are given together in the synoptic gospels — one in a wheat field, the other in a synagogue.

The first clash was over an interpretation of the ritual laws of the Sabbath. The Pharisees were deeply concerned about the correct observance of the various rules. They saw themselves as staunch upholders of Jewish tradition and culture. Their zeal for legal observance, however, led to a rigidity of interpretation that conflicted with the original intention of the Law. Sabbath observance was a notable example. As Jesus and His disciples walked through a grain field one Sabbath, the disciples plucked grains of wheat as they went. In itself, the plucking of wheat was allowed in the Mosaic law, but oral tradition had forbidden such action on the Sabbath on the grounds that it technically constituted work. According to Luke, the disciples rubbed the grains in their hands. He does not say whether this was done in full view of the Pharisees, or whether they were lying in wait. Some Pharisees certainly were at hand and they lost no time in criticizing.

To answer the criticism, Jesus cited the instance from Scripture where David broke the law to satisfy hunger — the occasion when David and his men entered the house of God and took the "Bread of the Presence," the name for the bread set apart for sacred purposes. In this case, a rigid interpretation of the law would have done more harm than good. It might have been argued that David and his men should not have eaten the priests' food — yet, their need justified their action. Jesus phrased His remark as a question, as if the Pharisees ought to have been acquainted with the incident.

Matthew records a second question, "Have you not read in the law how on the sabbath the priests of the temple profane the sabbath and are guiltless?" He alluded to the work involved in attending to the sacrifices and renewing the bread. On Pharisaic principles, this could be construed as a technical breach of the Sabbath, but no one would think of regarding the actions in this way. The real principle on which Jesus justified the action of His disciples is stated by all three synoptic writers — "The Son of man is lord of the sabbath." Some have understood the term "Son of man" to mean man in general, and have supposed that Jesus was conceding that man must make his own decisions about the Sabbath. Since in most instances the same term refers to Jesus himself, it seems clear that He was claiming for Himself the authority to reinterpret the Law. Mark adds a saying that

Wheat field in Palestine
ready for harvesting, in May.

*"On a sabbath, while he was going through
the grainfields, his disciples plucked and ate some
heads of grain, rubbing them in their hands"*
—LUKE 6:1

throws further light on the claim. Jesus said also, "The sabbath
was made for man, not man for the sabbath." This summed up
His criticism of the Pharisaic attitude, in which the Sabbath had
become more important than man. It must not be supposed,
however, that Jesus was advocating a laxness in the observance
of the Sabbath as an institution, for He clearly supported the
view that it was intended for man's benefit. Nevertheless, unnecessary restrictions nullify the essential purpose of the Sabbath.

Matthew's account brings out most clearly the parallel be-

tween David's action and the disciples' action. Jesus claimed that
something greater than the Temple was here and apparently He
was referring to Himself. He then added, "And if you had
known what this means 'I desire mercy, and not sacrifice' you
would not have condemned the guiltless." It would have been
an act of mercy for the Pharisees to allow the disciples to pluck
the grain, and not to regard them as guilty. Some have seen in
this an arbitrary act of authority on the part of Jesus, or else a
misunderstanding of that authority on the part of Matthew.
There is nothing arbitrary, however, in restoring the essential
function of the Sabbath. It was part of the mission of Jesus to
enable men to come to a true understanding of God's laws.

A clash with the Pharisees in the synagogue
Matthew 12:9-14 (Mark 3:1-6; Luke 6:6-11)

On another Sabbath, Jesus came into conflict with the Pharisees during a synagogue service. They knew His views about the
Sabbath and were waiting for further evidence in order to accuse Him. They may have arranged for a man with a withered
hand to be present. They anticipated that Jesus would have compassion on him, although they delayed the healing by asking
whether such an action would be legal on a Sabbath. Jesus posed
a counterquestion. "Is it lawful on the sabbath to do good or to
do harm, to save life or to kill?" To clarify what He meant, Jesus
used an illustration of a man whose sheep had fallen into a pit
on the Sabbath. Should he leave it there until the next day?
The decision was essentially practical. Common sense would
dictate some act to save the animal. Surely common sense should
do more for a person! The disabled man was there for the Pharisees to see. Who of them could deny that there were strong humanitarian reasons for an immediate healing, whatever the legalistic objections? When common sense clashes with legal demands, too often the former is banished. The Pharisees failed
to see that their attempts to protect the Sabbath were actually
undermining its basis.

Mark says simply that they were silent. They dared not
choose either of the alternatives Jesus put before them. They
could not admit that the Sabbath was for doing harm or for de-

stroying life, although they knew that if they admitted that it was for doing good and for saving life, Jesus would point out that this was exactly what He was doing. Mark adds that Jesus looked around at them in anger, being grieved at their hardness. Their silence hid nothing from Him. It spoke more eloquently than words. It stirred His anger. He noted a sheer absence of compassion in the faces of those around Him — religious men as they were. With eyes still fixed upon His accusers, Jesus commanded the man to stretch out his hand so that all in the synagogue could see its full restoration. He had made His accusers too uncomfortable. They left the synagogue resolving to find ways of getting rid of Him. Their scruples were offended, their pride wounded. They cared nothing about the man who could now use both hands. They were so deeply incensed against Jesus that they consulted with the Herodians, whom they normally considered to be traitors to the Jewish cause. Since Herod was a tool of Rome, his supporters were no more welcome to the patriotic Pharisees. What prompted such strange bedfellows to join a common plot against Jesus is not recorded. Apparently, the Pharisees were using the Herodians as means to further their own ends. The alliance shows the strength of opposition that already at this stage was leveled against Jesus.

The Beelzebub controversy

Mark 3:7-12; Matthew 12:15-37 (Mark 3:20-30; Luke 11:14-20)

Following the synagogue incident, Jesus withdrew to the seashore. He did not, however, escape the multitudes. Among those following Him were people suffering from all kinds of diseases or possessed with unclean spirits. Jesus did not ignore this mass of human need. His compassion was again stirred, and healing power flowed from Him. People came not only from Galilee but also from Jerusalem, Judea, Idumea, Trans-Jordan, Tyre, and Sidon. The fame of Jesus was widespread. So many were pressing against Him at one time that He requested a boat to be ready at hand. Their eagerness contrasted vividly with the Pharisees' caviling. Above the clamor was heard the cry of unclean spirits calling Jesus the Son of God, but He ordered them not to make Him known. He did not want His mission to become no more than a medical crusade. Their pressing in to touch Him shows the embryo of a superstitious approach. The crowds must learn that His mission was greater than this. Matthew, when later recalling the healing ministry, saw a fulfillment of prophecy, and he cited Isaiah 42:1-4. This is one of the prophet's Servant songs, and Matthew identified Jesus as that Servant. Other portions of the Servant songs were to be fulfilled by Jesus, most notably in His passion (cf. Isa. 53). Matthew saw the tenderness of the Servant as fulfilled in the tenderness of Jesus. His mission was not based on wrangling or shouting, but on care for those unable to fend for themselves. The prophet used the figure of a reed cut for a quill, which would at once be rejected if it were at all bruised. God's chosen Servant never accepted the principle of the survival of the fittest. He would tend even the bruised reed and make something out of it. Another illustration was that of a smoldering lamp wick, which was easier to extinguish than to revive. The Messiah's approach, however, brought hope to the weakest. The weakest were not beyond help. He would never tolerate injustice. Right would win out in the end.

Against this background of popular acclaim, the Pharisees again appeared on the scene. Jesus was back home, and the crowds were still pressing Him. Mark states that He and His disciples were so busy they had no time to eat. His friends thought Him to be mad, making the kind of snap judgment often made by those who take no time to assess a situation. They saw only the pressing crowds and heard the resultant commotion. They had not witnessed the ministry of mercy that had brought it about.

Two opposite reactions followed the healing of a blind and dumb demoniac. The common people were amazed, but the Pharisees were critical. The common people wondered whether Jesus really was the Son of David. The Pharisees were convinced that He was not. They claimed that He was in league with Beelzebub, leader of the demons. How could such opposing estimates be drawn from the same evidence? The Pharisees were already prejudiced against Jesus, and their prejudice was fertile soil for calumny. Their charge against Jesus was sufficiently serious for Him to answer it and sufficiently important for all the synoptic writers to record it.

When the Pharisees charged Jesus with being linked with Beelzebub (or Beelzebul), they were using a popular name for the prince of demons. Some said that Jesus was actually possessed by him, but others were content to claim that He cast out demons by Beelzebub's authority. Still others wanted some further sign, presumably more startling than any they had so far seen. Mark says that some of them had come from Jerusalem especially to protest. The charges sounded formidable, but were nevertheless illogical and absurd. Jesus used two arguments to expose this. First, Satan would never do anything to weaken his own position. No country ever strengthened its position by civil war. A kingdom's stability is soon shaken by disruptive elements. If Jesus were on Satan's side, why should He cast out demons at all? This should have been obvious to His accusers, who had not thought out the implications of their own charge. Second, the Pharisees' own disciples who practiced exorcism were in the same position as Jesus, and what applied to Him must equally apply to them. They were obviously not prepared to consider their own adherents to be in league with the devil. The hollowness of their accusation is apparent.

Satan meets his match

Matthew 12.28-32, 43-45 (Luke 11:21-26)

The logical source of the power of Jesus over demons was the Spirit of God, since the result was beneficial. Had the Pharisees understood this, they would have perceived that the Kingdom of God had come. Jesus pressed home His point with relentless logic. A powerful man's house can never be plundered unless a more powerful person first overcomes him. Satan will not release his captives until he has met his match. The many cured demoniacs were indisputable testimony that this had happened. Jesus pressed His point home for a decision. There was no room for compromise in this question of deciding whether Jesus was possessed by the Spirit of God or by Beelzebub. Men must make up their minds one way or the other. Those who could not discern the gracious ministry of the Spirit in Jesus' ministry must be opposed to Him. They were driving people away from the Kingdom rather than attracting them.

Both Luke and Matthew include an illustration by Jesus to show how any other way of dealing with unclean spirits except by the Spirit of God is not only ineffective but destructive. He pictured an unclean spirit wandering through desert places to find a habitation after being cast out of a man (it was commonly believed that this was the condition of disembodied evil spirits). In the meantime the man experienced moral reformation. Disorder was replaced by orderliness and cleanness. So attractive had the man become that the unclean spirit not only himself returned but brought seven other spirits with him. The man finished with eight instead of one. The number indicated the intensity of the man's degradation. The conclusion was that the exorcism had been inadequately carried out. The victory had not actually been won. The point of the story is that when a man's life becomes orderly and stays orderly, it is evidence that the unclean spirit has been effectively overcome. The test is in the duration of the cure. Tampering inadequately with evil forces is dangerous. Let no one, however, call inadequate what is performed by the Spirit of God.

Jesus warned sternly against perverting the Spirit's work. Forgiveness was possible for every other kind of sin but this. A man may even blaspheme against the Messiah as Son of Man and still be forgiven, but not against the Spirit.

The saying has been thought harsh by some who think it limits God's power to forgive, but this sin against the Spirit is the deliberate and malicious attempt to deny all true values — to see wrong as right and evil as good. The Pharisees who brought the false charge against Jesus probably had little idea of the serious implications of their suggestion. They were warned lest their present tendency harden into habit, when their condition would become irremediable. The warning has frightened some into fearing that they have unwittingly committed the unpardonable sin, but such a possibility is certainly excluded. Those who are sufficiently concerned about this have not reached a hardened attitude against the promptings of the Holy Spirit. This discussion between Jesus and the Pharisees shows the importance of the Spirit's work in the ministry of Jesus.

Judging by results

Matthew 12:33-37

More than once Jesus used the simile of trees and their fruits to show how men's claims may be tested. While still thinking about the Pharisees' blasphemous charge, He addressed them in terms of an illustration concerning a tree. The challenge was put in a strangely direct way. Make the tree either good or bad, and the fruits will follow accordingly. A good tree cannot produce bad fruits and a bad tree cannot produce good fruits. It was not as obvious as it ought to have been to these Pharisees that the same principles applied to human lives. If their charge that Jesus was possessed by Beelzebub was right, why did His actions not conform? Moreover, they pretended to speak good things about Jesus and yet were maligning His good work. Their inconsistency was exposed. They were challenged to make their position clear.

Jesus then criticized His opponents. He called them "a brood of vipers," one of His most strongly-worded descriptions. Was His charge justified? Vipers are deadly creatures intent on harming their prey. Jesus nonetheless spoke of them to illustrate the vicious character of these Pharisees in their opposition to His ministry. He possessed an unerring insight into men's minds and recognized at once their malicious intentions. There are times when righteous anger is justified and courageous condemnation salutary. John the Baptist had used the same illustration of vipers. Neither he nor Jesus doubted the evil bent of the minds of those opposed to the mission of the Messiah. By these words, however, Jesus was not condemning every Pharisee as evil. The men He was addressing had shown themselves to be so by their remarks; their speech betrayed their character.

Jesus likened the situation to two men with treasures. They can bring out of their treasure only what is already there. The good man's treasure will be good and the bad man's bad. By treasure Jesus meant the store of men's thoughts. Why speak of evil treasures? The mind becomes like an evil treasure when a man cherishes evil as if it were some choice thing worth preserving.

Because words express the inward character of a man, Jesus

challenged, "I tell you, on the day of judgment men will render account for every careless word they utter; for by your words you will be justified, and by your words you will be condemned." It is staggering to realize that such significance is given to words. Words pierce deeper than swords. Many who would do no physical harm to others do not hesitate to attack them with vicious words. Moreover, the comment of Jesus states the lesser but implies the greater. If careless words must be answered for, how much more those evil words which are premeditated? At a later time, James wrote in his epistle concerning the urgent need to bridle the tongue. It is an ever-present problem.

Luke recorded a similar saying about trees and fruit in Jesus' "sermon on the plain" (Luke 6:43-45). Matthew has a parallel in his Sermon on the Mount, which stresses the destruction of the trees that bear evil fruit.

10

Parables, Opinions, and Traditions

Seeking the spectacular

Matthew 12:38-42 (*Luke 11:29-32*)

Most men love something extraordinary and impressive, some sign of greatness, especially in someone claiming their allegiance. It was believed that when the Messiah came, He would perform distinctive signs. Therefore, the scribes and Pharisees looked for such evidence in Jesus because some said that He was the Messiah, and they requested some special sign from Him. Jesus, however, knew the insincerity of their request. They had ignored many of the signs He had already done, and they had criticized others. Would another sign convince them? Jesus' forthright answer to their request was severe. He saw them as reflecting the attitude of their whole generation, which He called "evil and adulterous." These are strong words. Did He have so poor an estimate of His contemporaries? Were not the scribes and Pharisees at least attempting to follow a noble ideal? Were they not thoroughly devoted to the Law? Jesus was using Old Testament words that described those who, while professing to worship God, had been unfaithful to Him.

Jesus offered one concession to their request for a sign, but it was an enigma. He spoke of the sign of the prophet Jonah. The ancient story was well known to them, but the interpretation that Jesus put upon it perplexed them. Jonah's three days and three nights in the fish had been prophetic of the Son of Man's three days and three nights in the earth. The sign was

137

entirely different from what they expected. It required spiritual discernment for interpretation. It was given as a sign, especially to those who were to form the coming Church. It was not a spectacle to cause sensation, for that kind of sign had been rejected by Jesus at His temptation. All men would have to learn that the Kingdom would not come by magical means.

Jesus compared the people of His day with those in Nineveh of Jonah's time. The men of Nineveh were better in this comparison, for they repented when Jonah preached, but there were few signs of repentance among the contemporaries of Jesus. He again referred to the judgment day. Responsibility would be governed to some extent by opportunity. Jonah at best was a reluctant preacher. His mind was not in complete harmony with his message, although the hearers responded better than the preacher deserved. By comparison, the men of Galilee had a preacher unique in human history, with a message that the world had never before heard. They failed, however, to respond. Jesus reminded them that something greater than Jonah was present — an indirect reference to His own mission.

Jesus also pointed out that the journey of the Queen of Sheba (of the South) over long distances to visit Solomon was a judgment on His generation for their failure to recognize in their midst one far greater than Solomon. These allusions to Jonah and Solomon give a further glimpse into the self-awareness of Jesus. He was fully conscious of the superiority and uniqueness of His mission.

New family relationships

Mark 3:31-35 (Matthew 12:46-50; Luke 8:19-21)

As Jesus was addressing a crowd of people, His mother, brothers, and sisters came to the edge of the crowd, wanting to speak to Him. Jesus took the opportunity to illustrate the new relationships He had formed with His disciples. In reply to the request of His family to see Him, He asked, "Who is my mother, and who are my brothers?" Many thought the question strange since they knew His family. Was He disowning them? Was He publicly suggesting that they should not interrupt the progress of His ministry? Possibly they were bent on advising Him, in which case He would have had to make it clear that higher loyalties existed than loyalty to human families.

Mark mentions that the people were sitting around Him, like pupils learning from their Master. These were His disciples, but He called them His "mother" and "brothers." This was the new relationship — the family of God. Jesus left His hearers in no doubt as to what its requirements are. Nothing other is needed than obedience to God's will revealed in His word. The family of God is characterized by the desire to please the Father. Jesus thus presented one of the most characteristic features of His mission, to unite people in an entirely new family relationship.

Jesus did not teach the universal Fatherhood of God and the universal brotherhood of men, as if all men are brothers irrespective of any essential requirements. If everyone actually did the will of God, barriers to universal brotherhood would disappear; but the condition is not fulfilled. Jesus would not claim as His "brothers" any who rejected the will of God as the governing factor for their life.

Many have tried to construct a new society on the basis of a misunderstanding of this teaching of Jesus. The family idea is compelling. Spiritual brothers and sisters of Christ cannot escape the fact that they are in a new relationship to one another. The New Testament epistles are full of the evidence that this concept of Jesus was highly practical. The early Christians found a deeper love for each other than often existed among the members of the same family. This happened to at least two of those who belonged to the human family of Jesus. When James and Jude later wrote letters, neither of them claimed their fraternal kinship with Jesus, but each described himself as His "servant." They were part of His "spiritual household."

Why Jesus taught in parables

Matthew 13:10-15 (Mark 4:10-12; Luke 8:9, 10)

The appeal of the story form is ageless. It is not confined to any one culture. It was not new when used by Jesus. Examples of parables are found in both Greek and Jewish writings, although no other showed such mastery of the story form as Jesus. His parables are superb in the economy of words and depth of spiritual truth.

Nevertheless, when Jesus began teaching in parables, His disciples came and asked why He was doing so. They were surprised, not because Jesus was illustrating His teaching, for every good teacher uses illustrations, but rather because the form of the parables perplexed them. Obviously, they failed to understand their real purpose. Parables were easy to remember, but they left many wondering whether or not they had grasped the point of the teaching.

Jesus gave His own reason for the use of parables, and this reason has been much misunderstood. In what He said about parables, however, He could not have intended anything that was inconsistent either with His mission or His character. He drew a distinction between those who understood and those who did not. The parables were about the Kingdom, which required a certain attitude of mind to appreciate it. Those who were unsympathetic could not be expected to plumb the depths of His teaching. He spoke of the secrets of the Kingdom, by which He meant not something completely hidden, but rather, something generally hidden yet understood by those who possessed the key. The key was faith in the Teacher Himself and an acknowledgment that the Kingdom was bound up with allegiance to the King. It was symbolized in Jesus Himself. The Kingdom was not something that man could build through his own efforts, but something that God was inaugurating through His Son. It was not to be an organization, but an organism; not a Utopian earthly state, but a divine rule in the hearts of men.

This will help to explain the enigmatic saying of Jesus — that He spoke in parables so that seeing they might "not perceive" and hearing they might "not understand." He was using the passage of Isaiah 6:9, 10. There was a fulfillment of this passage in the way that Jesus taught. Did He intend, however, that people should not understand His teaching? The idea is unthinkable. His fame as a teacher had not spread because of the obscurity of His message, but because of its clarity and authority. His teaching could not have conveyed its authority if it had not been understood. He taught to help men to understand, not to prevent them from doing so. What, then, did He mean? The truths of the Kingdom would not become clear until the exaltation of the King. The Son of Man had yet to be crucified; the mysteries of the Kingdom would not be revealed until He had conquered death. His present purpose was to plant the core of His teaching in minds disposed to receive it. It was unavoidable that some would think they understood, who were yet interpreting the Kingdom in a manner wholly alien to the meaning intended by Jesus. On the other hand, most would purposely close their eyes to the light because they had no desire to see the spiritual message behind the words. For the latter, the parables were specially adaptable. If their minds were not disposed to receive the truth, they would not remember the teaching. However, if they remembered the parables, possibly at a future date the meaning would dawn upon them.

So rich are the parables in spiritual illumination that they are always yielding new treasures. The disciples were in a more blessed position than the line of prophets and righteous men who had looked forward to the coming Kingdom. Although many more mysteries were to be revealed after the resurrection of Jesus, the disciples were given some insights into the Kingdom. Jesus never suggested that His immediate teaching was sufficient. Full understanding would come after the completion of His mission.

A series of Kingdom parables

Matthew 13:1-9, 16-52 (Mark 4:1-9, 13-20; Luke 8:4-8, 11-18; Mark 4:26-34; Luke 13:18-21)

Probably all the parables of Jesus were intended to illustrate some aspect of the Kingdom. There is no uncertainty about this in the sequence of parables Jesus told by the seashore. Several of them begin with the words, "The Kingdom of God is like."

The first three parables illustrate growth, the parable of the sower probably being the best known. The sight of farmers scattering seeds was common among an agricultural people. The farmer's intention was, of course, to sow the seed in good soil, but the wind would invariably waft some seed to unproductive parts of the field. The ancient farmer, with no advantages of mod-

". . . what was sown among thorns . . . is he who hears the word, but the cares of the world and the delight in riches choke the word . . ."
— MATTHEW 13:22

A Palestinian farmer. Jesus illustrated His mission by referring to the typical hazards of ancient farming methods.

ern planting techniques, did his sowing in spite of these hazards. Jesus saw this as an illustration of the various responses He had experienced during His mission. There had been fruitless areas. Some of the people had heard without understanding, and the evil one had snatched the truth from their hearts, just as birds snatch away seeds lying on hardened paths. Others had made some show of response but had drifted away like shoots in soil too shallow to sustain roots. Others had received the teaching enthusiastically, but it had soon taken second place to their more dominant interests, like seedlings choked by thorns. Nevertheless some fruit had grown in the many who had believed, like the fruitful plants that had grown in fertile soil. Indeed, the returns were astonishingly good. Even thirty percent returns would have been considered a good harvest. From sixty to a hundred percent would certainly have been a bumper harvest. The mission of Jesus encouraged hope, but the greatest harvest was not to come until the mission was completed.

The parable of the tares serves a different purpose. A man sowed good seed only to find many weeds coming up with the good shoots. He concluded that an enemy was responsible, and yet refused to allow his men to pull up the weeds until harvest time. It would have been folly to remove the weeds, since both good and bad shoots looked alike. Jesus used this as a picture of the difficulty His followers would have in discerning between the children of God and the children of the evil one. Yet, there is a clear division between the two. Some restraint must be exercised when the temptation arises to judge the faith of others. When Jesus interpreted His parable, He spoke of the angels as

A threshing floor in Galilee. Jesus spoke of angels as reapers, and He pointed out the burning of weeds as a vivid picture of coming judgment.

". . . Gather the weeds first and bind them in bundles to be burned, but gather the wheat into my barn"
—MATTHEW 13:30

reapers and pointed out the process of burning weeds as a vivid illustration of the coming judgment.

The third parable of sowing points to the rapid growth of the Kingdom. The mustard seed — an extremely small seed — grows to be a tree of considerable size, capable of supporting nesting birds. The small group of disciples faced with a great task might well have despaired. The forecast, however, was for rapid and extensive growth, and it was fulfilled in the phenomenal expansion of the early Church. In spite of its small beginning, the Kingdom was never small in impact.

Four other brief parables belong in the same sequence. One parable compares the invisible growth of the Kingdom to the action of hidden leaven in a lump of dough. No part of the dough remains unaffected. This does not mean that the Kingdom will leaven the whole world, for there is nothing to equate the dough with the world. The intent of the parable is not to teach the extent of the Kingdom, but rather, its permeating effect in the world.

Two parables compare the Kingdom to treasure. In one, a man found a treasure in a field. He apparently was a tenant. He bought the field to gain ownership of the treasure. Some have considered his action to be unethical. Jesus was not, however, commending the action but illustrating, rather, the great value of the treasure. All else took second place, and no lesser estimate of the Kingdom was considered adequate by Jesus. In the other parable, a merchant found a pearl of such value that he considered it to be worth all that he had. In both stories the treasure is costly but worth paying for. Before men can be motivated to sacrifice everything for the sake of the Kingdom, it is essential for them to appreciate its worth.

The final parable is drawn from fishing. The familiar dragnet that enclosed a great variety of fishes is symbolic of the Kingdom. Within the Kingdom there would be the good and the bad; the time of separation, as in the parable of the tares, is the end of the age. Again, the note of judgment comes into prominence. Judgment is inescapable. The Kingdom brings men to decision and distinguishes between them. There can be no middle way. Men are either for or against the Messiah.

A royal view of Jesus and of John the Baptist

Mark 6:14-29 (Matthew 14:1-12; Luke 9:7-9; cf. Luke 3:19, 20)

Various opinions about the Messiah had been expressed by different groups. The focus then turned to Herod's view. Only after a period of time, apparently, did he hear of the fame of Jesus. He had been living in Perea, east of Jordan, whereas Jesus' mission was in Galilee, in the western part of his domain. On hearing the reports, his first thought — springing from a guilty conscience — was that John the Baptist had risen from the dead. There was good reason for his uneasiness. John had been executed after months of captivity in the wretched prison of Machaerus. Herod had feared John the Baptist and could only think that the mighty works of Jesus proved Him to be a reincarnation of John.

It is necessary to review why John was cast into prison and why Herod executed him. The sordid story discredits both Herod and his wife, Herodias. Herod had previously been married to the daughter of the Arabian king, Aretas. His rejection of this wife caused friction between the two rulers, and war had broken out between them. Herod was decisively defeated. He had not only treated his first wife shamefully, but he showed contempt for his half-brother, Herod Philip, by robbing him of his wife Herodias. The fiery John had courageously denounced this action and other evils committed by Herod. True to the tradition of Old Testament prophets, whose line ended with him, he did not fear the consequences. He knew that neither Herod nor Herodias would take such criticism without reprisal. Arrest was inevitable, for Herod could justify his action from political motives. He was unconcerned about the moral issue. Josephus reports that he was afraid of John's great popularity and feared for the security of his own position. He had refrained, however, from executing John because many of the people held him to be a prophet. This accounts for John's long imprisonment. It was during this period, that John had sent his inquiry to Jesus.

The circumstance surrounding John's death was Herod's birthday and the lavish banquet for the occasion in the magnificent palace at Machaerus. Wine flowed freely, and Herodias's daughter danced before the drunken guests. Prompted by his delight in the dance of the princess, Herod, in the hearing of all present, offered her up to half of his kingdom out of an extravagance that can best be accounted for by intoxication. Overwhelmed, the girl sought her mother's advice and acted upon it even though it involved the demand for the head of John on a platter. Even the callous Herod was taken aback at such a request, but he thought more of his oath than of any humanitarian concern for John. Many times he had listened to John and, in spite of his criticism, had been glad to hear him. He knew John was a just man. However, he decided that because the courtiers had heard it, he must keep his oath. In a more sober state he might never have made such an oath over so trivial a matter as an exotic dance. The gospel writers leave to the imagination the scene in which the head was brought to the girl who in turn gave it to her mother. They conclude their narratives by noting that John's disciples arranged a decent burial for their master. Nothing is said about their own reactions. Did John's death cause them to turn their allegiance to the Messiah whom their master had announced? It is well known that some did not become followers of Jesus, since there were still some of John's disciples later on at Ephesus (cf. Acts 19).

Why did both Matthew and Mark include this sordid story? The part of the herald in announcing the mission of the Messiah has already been noted. His was a noble office, and his tragic death set the stage for the even more poignant death of the Messiah. There was nevertheless a fundamental difference. John's death occurred after the completion of a noble task. The Messiah's death was in itself His noblest task — He came to invest death with redemptive significance.

Direct criticism of Pharisaic traditions

Mark 7:1-13 (Matthew 15:1-9)

No one would doubt the value of traditions that have proved helpful in the experience of others. Nevertheless, tradition can become a hard taskmaster. Periodically, tradition needs reexamination and reassessment. Such a process, however, is seldom welcomed by those who consider it their sacred duty to guard the traditions. The Pharisees were in this position. In their zeal for upholding traditions, they paid insufficient attention to their effect on human life.

One such tradition was ritual handwashing with its many regulations. Before meals, ritual cleansing was essential, whereas after meals, it was desirable. These requirements no doubt originally served a useful hygienic purpose, but the Pharisees had added to the basic requirements of cleanliness many other reasons for ritual cleansing. For instance, the books of Scripture could defile the hands. This theory was pushed to such an extent that things that came into close proximity with the sacred writings could themselves defile the hands that touched them. Some of the more stringent restrictions were probably not introduced until after the time of Jesus. The failure to observe this ritual cleansing by some of the disciples of Jesus constituted a serious transgression in the eyes of the Pharisees. From rabbinical sources it is known that breaches of ritual requirements were regarded as serious.

The most famous of the Jewish elders who had formulated traditions were Shammai and Hillel. The former was conservative in his interpretations of the Law, whereas the latter was liberal. On most major questions they disagreed, but on the question of ritual hand-washing they were united. Any traditions supported by the elders commanded such respect that their opinions were placed on a level with the Law itself. Against this background, the scribes and Pharisees wanted to know from Jesus why His disciples failed to walk according to the tradition of the elders by eating with defiled hands. In answer, Jesus criticized His critics, using a passage from Isaiah 29:13. The prophet had described a people whose outward religious lives honored God, but who inwardly honored men; a people who thought more highly of human precepts than of God's commands. Thus they deserved to be called hypocrites because they professed to be what they were not.

This criticism was considered serious by these Pharisees because they sincerely believed themselves to be the major custodians of the Law of God. To be told that they were doing the opposite required some justification. Jesus cited the case of Corban. The Mosaic commandment to honor parents by making provision for their support was circumvented by this means. A man could evade his liability by declaring his resources to be Corban, that is, given to God. Rabbinical rules laid down certain restrictions on the use of Corban, but the type of case cited by Jesus can be verified from rabbinical sources. When a vow was once made, it was binding, even if it involved a breach of the Mosaic law. The Pharisees could not defend themselves against the criticism that they were in such cases nullifying the Word of God.

Comments to the people about the Pharisees

Mark 7:14-23 (Matthew 15:10-20)

Having leveled a basic criticism against the Pharisees about their attitude to the Law, Jesus addressed the crowd. He told a parable to show the shortcomings of the Pharisees' teaching about defilement. He made a double statement, partly positive and partly negative. The Pharisees would agree with the statement that what comes out of a man defiles him, for they admitted that all men had both good and evil thoughts. They would not however agree with the other statement that nothing outside a man could defile him. This would hit against all their taboos concerning food. The Jew could not consider all foods as "clean," but this in effect is what Jesus was demanding. No doubt the disciples themselves had not yet realized the radical nature of this teaching. Both Matthew and Mark report that the disciples asked for an explanation. According to Matthew, they brought a report to Jesus but phrased it as a question. "Do you know that the Pharisees were offended when they heard this saying" (i.e. about what defiles a man)? They possibly had some sympathy for the Pharisees, since they had been brought up to respect the Pharisaic interpretation of the Law.

Jesus answered by assessing the Pharisees as unworthy religious leaders. He pointed out that in a garden the owner plants his own plants. So in Israel, God the Father planted His own teaching, enshrined in the Law. The Pharisees' "plants," which were not in harmony with the Father's purpose, must be uprooted. Moreover, leaders who were themselves blind were of no use for leading others, since both the leaders and those whom they led would sooner or later fall into a pit.

According to Matthew, Peter asked for an explanation of the illustration that Jesus had given. Perhaps he was specially resistant to change in the traditional food laws. Later, a special vision was given to him to teach him what God considered "clean" (Acts 10). Defilement that came from the heart was more serious than ritual defilement. Jesus made His meaning clear by citing examples. Evil thoughts, murder, adultery, fornication, theft, false witness, and slander were samples of real defilement, totally different from ritual uncleanness. Lesser matters are too often observed with greater meticulousness than weightier matters. The disciples needed this teaching to prevent them from making the same mistake as the Pharisees.

11

Miracles Again

Jesus at Nazareth

Matthew 13:53-58 (Mark 6:1-6; Luke 4:16-30)

Luke recorded the incident at Nazareth at the beginning of the ministry of Jesus. Jesus' own people showed Him no honor on that occasion. Both Matthew and Mark relate a similar experience, but as a later occasion. Jesus went to the synagogue and taught. As before, the congregation was astonished and, as before, the people started asking questions. Are the two occasions to be identified as one incident? Many scholars say that they are; and if so, Luke's order is usually regarded as less probable than the others. There is much to be said for this view, especially since the same question is asked in both accounts, and the same proverbial saying is given in reply. Moreover, if there had been two such visits, it is difficult to believe that the astonishment experienced on the first occasion, which was natural enough, was repeated on the second. On the other hand, the setting is different. If Luke's placing of the incident at the opening of His ministry was his own choice, the reason was probably symbolic. He wished to make clear that Jesus was rejected at Nazareth, before relating the reactions of people in other parts of Galilee. The incident occurs in Mark after the healing of Jairus' daughter, and in Matthew after the parables of the Kingdom. In both, the reference to time is general. This is an example of an incident where chronological order is less important than the

150

tragic fact that the people who knew Jesus best had the least regard for Him. Familiarity bred contempt.

Matthew's and Mark's narratives include three details that Luke does not give. In Mark, Jesus is called "the carpenter" and in Matthew, "the son of the carpenter." Did Matthew for reasons of reverence prefer not to call Jesus "the carpenter"? This may be, but Mark's description is certainly authentic. Every Jewish boy learned a trade, and nothing would have been more probable than for Jesus to learn the same trade as Joseph and later succeed him as the village carpenter at Nazareth. The hands that were often stretched out to bless and that were later to be stretched out to die were hands that were not unsoiled with honest toil. The Messiah made no distinction between manual work and a teaching ministry, although it apparently amazed the people at Nazareth that wisdom and manual work could be so united in one man.

The names of the brothers of Jesus are given, along with the mere mention of His sisters. Significantly, the only two brothers of whom the New Testament makes later reference are both referred to in writings outside the New Testament. James is mentioned by Josephus as a man whose piety in prayer caused his knees to become hard like camels' knees. Jude is mentioned indirectly, as his grandsons were brought before the emperor Domitian to answer for their views. These brothers of Jesus could never forget what they had heard in their home at Nazareth, even if at first they saw nothing messianic about Him.

The third detail mentioned by Matthew and Mark, although in slightly different ways, relates to the fact that Jesus did not do many mighty works in Nazareth because of the unbelief of the people. Mark says, "And he could do no mighty work there, except that he laid his hands upon a few sick people and healed them. And he marveled because of their unbelief." Matthew's version states, "And he did not do many mighty works there, because of their unbelief." Both writers are agreed about the paucity of results. Unbelief imposes limits even for the Messiah. The point is important, for the gospels do not present a Messiah who forces Himself upon those unwilling to receive Him.

Feeding a multitude: the setting

John 6:1-7 (*Matthew 14:13, 14; Mark 6:30-34; Luke 9:10, 11*)

The one miracle of Jesus that is told by all four evangelists must have special importance. It involved more than five thousand people. The basic details are similar in all four accounts, but special points of interest emerge when they are compared.

Mark and Luke both mention that the incident happened when the twelve apostles returned from their mission. Matthew shows it to follow the report that Jesus received of the death of John the Baptist. The sequence of events seems to be as follows. Jesus heard about John while the apostles were still on their mission. The apostles then returned and reported to Jesus what they had done and taught. Jesus needed time to talk to them alone, and for this reason He withdrew with them, intending to find some quiet place. Luke says that they went to a city, Bethsaida, but this must describe only the general location. Matthew and Mark mention a lonely place, whereas John describes the direction as across the sea. It is important to note Jesus' desire for solitude even though on this occasion the quest for it was not fulfilled. When responsibilities press, quietness and seclusion are essential, and even the Messiah needed such provision. His example is salutary for those activists who consider it a waste of time to stop working. Many have cracked under the strain who would not have done so had they followed this example.

Crowds, however, thwarted the intention of Jesus and His disciples, for multitudes followed them. Matthew and Mark tell us that Jesus and His disciples went by boat, but the crowds streamed along the shore, reaching the landing place before the boat arrived. Jesus did not rebuke them. He welcomed them and spoke about the Kingdom. His quest for solitude was temporarily interrupted. Three gospel writers show that later, after Jesus had dismissed the crowds, He withdrew to the hills to pray. For the present, He was stirred by compassion toward the people and His compassion led Him not only to teach but also to heal. John comments that the crowds followed because they had seen the signs that He had done. They no doubt wanted to see more.

It was the Passover season. The fact that many pilgrims were preparing to leave Galilee for the annual journey to Jerusalem may account for the large numbers on this occasion. According to John, it was from a ridge in the hills to which Jesus and His disciples had climbed that Jesus first noted the crowds approaching Him. Only a few had apparently preceded their arrival, and these had presumably followed them to the ridge. As Jesus watched the rest straggling along the shore, He saw them as sheep without a shepherd. His own heart was moved as a true Shepherd concerned for His sheep. John says that He knew what He was about to do.

Jesus put a question to Philip. It is not clear why Philip was singled out. He may have been the nearest to Jesus at the time. Nevertheless it is reasonable to conjecture that this particular disciple was a literal, down-to-earth type, for he later earned a rebuke from Jesus for his lack of spiritual perception (John 14: 8, 9). The question was, "How are we to buy bread, so that these people may eat?" Philip made a hasty, rough calculation of the size of the crowd. The men numbered about five thousand, not including women and children. He probably knew the current state of their limited funds. The whole sum — about two hundred denarii — would not be nearly enough. The denarius was approximately the amount earned by a farm laborer in one day, and it barely provided subsistence. Obviously, the word must have spread to the others about the strange question. Meanwhile, Jesus was teaching the multitudes, but it was getting late. As evening approached, the disciples decided it was time for Jesus to send the people away. They had concluded that it was impossible to provide for them.

Feeding a multitude: a miracle

John 6:8-14 (Matthew 14:15-21; Mark 6:35-44; Luke 9:12-17)

In a crisis Jesus always knew what He would do. Faced with a hungry multitude, He was not baffled. He challenged the disciples to feed the people, fully aware of their inability to do so. Andrew, on behalf of them all, ventured the information that the total food supply consisted of a young lad's lunch of five barley loaves and two fishes. It was poor diet, the basic food of the poorest. The sea of Galilee abounded in small fish of the kind the boy had taken with him. None of the disciples could have guessed what Jesus would do. They had already seen Him perform some notable miracles, but to use so small a quantity of food to satisfy the needs of a multitude seemed impossible. It has also perplexed men since then to such an extent that various rationalizing theories have been proposed to explain it away. Nevertheless, the fact that all four writers record it, and two of them record a similar event later, is difficult to explain if the incident has no basis in truth.

The disciples organized the crowds to sit down without knowing what was to happen. Surely something in the bearing of Jesus inspired the confidence of both the disciples and the crowds. One eyewitness remembered the greenness of the grass. It was a colorful scene. Jesus first blessed the loaves before they were multiplied by being broken. A blessing was similarly offered before a Jewish household began a meal. The distribution was so well organized that everyone shared the food, and no one was left hungry. Twelve baskets of left-over food remained to be gathered. The baskets were the kind used by poor people for carrying provisions. There would be no difficulty in finding twelve such baskets on this occasion. John alone notes the reaction of the people. They saw the miracle as evidence that Jesus was "the prophet to come." Nevertheless Jesus knew their thoughts. Their intentions were political. They wanted to make Him king. This would have ruined the mission. John says that Jesus withdrew to the hills, but he leaves untold the crowd's frustration at having their intentions thwarted.

This is a clear example of the inability of the people of Palestine to avoid a political idea of messiahship. So great was the general desire for effective leadership that the people were susceptible to any possible candidate. The attempt to seize Jesus as their political leader was prompted by His wide popularity, which would insure considerable support. The power to perform miracles such as mass feedings was naturally an appealing quality in any prospective demagogue. The kingship of Jesus, however, was of a wholly different kind. The Messiah's mission would not bow to violence. Men must come by the way of faith, to acknowledge voluntarily that the Messiah's reign was greater than all nationalistic and political ideas of sovereignty.

Walking on water

Matthew 14:22-33 (*Mark 6:45-52; John 6:15-21*)

The event following the feeding miracle was a miracle of a different kind. Jesus remained behind when the disciples embarked in their boat to cross the lake. They soon found themselves in adverse conditions. Strong winds thwarted their progress. Nothing was unique about this setting, but certain features made that particular evening notable.

Both Matthew and Mark state that Jesus compelled the disciples to get into the boat, as if they were somewhat reluctant to do so. He left them with no option. He may have recognized too much willingness on their part to yield to the crowds' enthusiasm to make Him king. This would have boosted their feeling of self-importance.

Jesus was confronted with a real threat to His mission and desired to deal with it alone. Moreover He wanted to pray alone in the hills before rejoining them. From this vantage point He could see the difficulties surrounding the little boat. He saw in the scene a picture of the contrary currents surrounding His mission. Possibly, the men in the tossing boat were the subject of His prayer just then, a prayer not confined to their present difficulties. It surely concerned also their unpreparedness for the continuation of the mission.

In the early morning Jesus moved out toward the boat. The disciples must have been in an agitated state of mind. The form of Jesus suddenly appeared, probably through a mist, a short distance from the boat. They were startled. They were sure they were seeing a ghost. Even rugged fishermen, well-equipped through much experience to cope with contrary winds, were nevertheless terrified at the thought of confronting a ghost. When they heard Him say, "It is I; have no fear," they were no longer afraid.

Mark reports that they were utterly astonished, but he does not say what caused their astonishment. It may have been the result of seeing Jesus walking on water, or of seeing the immediate cessation of the wind when He got into the boat. They would not, however, have been unaccustomed to the sudden dropping of the wind on the Sea of Galilee. Mark did not spare the disciples, for he says "their hearts were hardened." They had witnessed the miracle of the loaves. If Jesus could multiply loaves, He could surely walk on water. The two miracles illustrate His undisputed sway over the natural world. The sequence of events shows that more than external miracles are required to convince men of the true nature of the Messiah, even those closest to Him.

Matthew introduces an incident that some have considered to be of doubtful authenticity because he alone mentions it and because it has the appearance of a heightening of the miraculous. If the main story is true, however, there is nothing intrinsically improbable about Matthew's addition. It concerns Peter, who seemed still to have been uncertain about the identity of the shadowy figure. Peter challenged that if it really were Jesus, He should bid him come to Him across the water. Matthew does not tell us the distance involved. It could not have been far, for Jesus was able to stretch out His hand to grasp Peter as he began to sink. The wind had intimidated Peter, for a gale was still blowing until Jesus got into the boat. Peter was to be commended for venturing, but he earned a rebuke for doubting. He had again failed to recognize his Master's true nature. Not until Jesus got into the boat did all of them catch a new glimpse of that nature. Their conclusion was, "Truly you are the Son of God." This declaration was only another shaft of light. It was to be a slow process before the full light dawned.

A small detail in John's account deserves notice. The disciples were glad when Jesus was in the boat, and almost immediately the boat was at the shore. This was not a second miracle, but indicates that they were nearer the shore than they thought. If the boat was already near the shore, why did Jesus not wait for it to reach the shore? None of the gospel writers gives an answer. At any rate, the miracle may be regarded as one of the steps whereby Jesus was teaching His disciples that His spiritual power is greater than natural forces. There is still need for men to learn the same lesson.

Satisfying food

John 6:22-71

Jesus next returned to Capernaum, where He was met by various people. He knew their intentions. They were expecting another miracle like the feeding miracle. It suited them to be miraculously fed. Jesus instead began talking to them about more satisfying food. John gives a fairly full account of the subsequent discussion, part of which appears to have taken place outside and part in the synagogue.

The Son of Man came to give another kind of food. He was specially commissioned to do this by the Father. Although Jesus spoke of this spiritual food as a gift, His hearers immediately asked, "What can we do?" This is characteristic of man in search of spiritual truth. He wants to do something for a sense of achievement that satisfies his pride. But Jesus required only faith in Himself as the sent one. Such a challenge as this prompted His questioners into evasive action. They asked for a sign. This would leave them with the initiative, for it would give them the opportunity of deciding whether the given sign was adequate. They wanted something at least as impressive as Moses' provision of manna in the wilderness. Perhaps they were implying that the feeding of the five thousand did not compare with Moses' provision of manna for a far greater multitude during the forty years in the wilderness. Jesus knew the drift of their thoughts, and He reminded them that it was God, not Moses, who provided the manna. The heavenly food that He was talking about was no different.

By this time they were intrigued about this heavenly bread and desired to have it. This made the time opportune for Jesus to say outright that He was the Bread of life. The need for faith was again underlined. They must understand that Jesus Himself had come to do the Father's will. It was His will that everyone who believes on the Son should have eternal life.

Such profound spiritual lessons perplexed the hearers. They knew Jesus as Joseph's son. They could not understand why He was speaking about coming down from heaven. They needed to be taught of God. Unless He drew them to Himself they would never come. It is difficult for men to recognize their own inability to come to God. Jesus nonetheless demanded nothing less than such recognition. At this point, He returned to the manna illustration, demonstrating the weakness of the parallel, since the manna had no power to bestow life. Those who ate it died.

Jesus, as the heavenly Bread, however, has power to give vitality. This heavenly Bread is essential for eternal life.

The Jewish hearers were completely baffled at the thought of eating the bread of life if that bread was Jesus' flesh. But Jesus said again that it was necessary for men to eat His flesh and to drink His blood, to have life that was eternal. He was, of course, speaking symbolically. He had in mind the Last Supper, which He intended to eat with His disciples. The form of the supper would enshrine this truth. It was valuable for men to have some preparation for the meaning of the act that was to become a central feature in the subsequent life of the Church.

John gives no further hint of the reactions of the hearers generally, but he commented on what the disciples thought. He remembered how difficult they found these statements of Jesus. Jesus had showed them that the key to life was the spirit, not the flesh that represented human effort. Moreover He pointed out to them that not all of them would believe. One of them would betray Him. He described him as a devil, but the disciples did not understand.

Faith from beyond Israel

Matthew 15:21-28 (Mark 7:24-30)

In His mission charge, Jesus had forbidden His disciples to go to Gentile districts, since He Himself was sent to the house of Israel. Both Mark and Matthew, however, record an occasion when Jesus went into Gentile territory, around Tyre and Sidon. But neither of them give any indication that Jesus pursued His mission there. Matthew says that He withdrew, whereas Mark says that He entered a house but did not want anyone to know that He was there. His withdrawal to Gentile territory was for personal reasons. It is essential to note this distinction in order to appreciate the attitude of Jesus toward the woman who pleaded with Him on her daughter's behalf.

She was a Grecian from the district of Syro-Phoenicia. She had a young daughter possessed by demons. Reports of Jesus had spread as far as Tyre and Sidon (cf. Mark 3:8). The woman had probably decided what she would do if Jesus ever came into her vicinity. The main feature of the narrative concerns her meeting with Jesus and begging Him to do something. Matthew

Tyre. The circular structure in the foreground was an oven used to manufacture glass. Other ruins, from Roman times, are visible in the distance.

"And from there he arose and went away to the region of Tyre and Sidon"
— MARK 7:24

gives her urgent plea, "Have mercy on me, O Lord, Son of David; my daughter is severely possessed by a demon." It is strange that a Gentile should use the title "Son of David," but she obviously knew something about Jewish affairs.

Matthew notes the silence of Jesus that greeted her request. Did He feel no compassion for her? Surely He could not remain unmoved by the desperate plea of the mother. Or was He so conscious of His mission to Israel that the needs of non-Israelites must be ignored? The sequel shows that compassion was not lacking. The reason for the silence was in the Messiah's purpose; He wished to avoid further publicity. It was hard on the woman, but His mission must take precedence. The disciples, watching the scene, feared lest the woman would cause a commotion. They urged Jesus to send her away. According to Matthew He said that He was sent only to the lost sheep of the house of Israel. Some believe that Matthew inserted his own Jewish bias since Mark makes no mention of it. It seemingly accords with other instances in Matthew of the Jewishness of Jesus' mission. There is no reason, however, to suppose that Matthew presents a biased picture. The sayings that appear to be specifically Jewish must be balanced against others that show the worldwide character of the mission, as for instance the farewell commission to preach in all parts of the world (cf. Matt. 28). The Gentiles were to be reached, but not until the Jewish Church had been launched. For Jesus to have extended His mission at this stage would have impeded it, but He was no narrow nationalist.

The woman cried, "Lord, help me." It was a cry from the heart, but Jesus' answer amplified His previous statement: "It is not fair to take the children's bread and throw it to the dogs." She understood His meaning. The "children" were the Jewish people, and the "bread" was their privileged position. "Dogs" was a common Jewish designation for Gentiles. Jesus did not use the common word for dogs, but the more familiar word meaning "household pets." Most eastern dogs were scavengers and such a term would have implied Jewish contempt. Jesus' words, however, did not suggest contempt. His purpose was to draw out the woman's faith. With quick wit she exploited the illustration. Not entitled to the "bread," she would be satisfied with the crumbs that little dogs eat from their master's table; the scraps were better than nothing, and a master would be hard indeed if he forbade the children's pets to be fed. Her answer delighted Jesus, for it showed a true appreciation of His purpose. Acknowledging her great faith, He assured her that her desire was granted. According to Mark, Jesus told her that the demon had already left her daughter. Returning home, she found the little girl in bed, fully restored.

This incident is recorded in the gospels to illustrate the response of Jesus to the faith of a Gentile. Although beyond the scope of His immediate mission, the incident anticipated the later ministry of the Church to the Gentiles. Most of the "lost" sheep of the house of Israel preferred to remain "lost," and greater faith would be found among Gentiles, whom the Jews labeled as "dogs."

More healings in Galilee

Mark 7:31-37; 8:22-26 (Matthew 15:29-31)

Leaving the district of Tyre and Sidon, Jesus returned to the Sea of Galilee, which became the setting for more miracles of healing. Matthew briefly summarizes the type of people who were healed — the lame, maimed, blind, and dumb. Obviously impressed by the effect that the healings had on the multitudes, Matthew noted that they glorified the God of Israel. Evidently the populace generally believed that the power used by Jesus was divine, and therefore they should have acknowledged His claims. Matthew, however, reports that they glorified God only so long as they saw the effects of Jesus' power. He does not relate what happened when the effects were no longer visible. It is a fact of history that the Jewish people ultimately rejected their Messiah. Their desire to glorify God because of Jesus was short-lived.

Mark concentrates on one particular instance of healing. A deaf man with impeded speech was brought so that Jesus could lay His hands upon him. Mark says that Jesus took the man aside from the multitude, perhaps because He wished to minimize the idea of mere wonder-working. Mark tells about Jesus' use of means of healing. Jesus placed His fingers into the man's ears and His saliva-moistened finger touched the man's tongue. Some times Jesus healed with a word; at other times, even in the absence of the patient; and at still other times, with physical contact. Probably the method was varied to avoid any magical significance being attached to it. The physical contact may have been desirable to give reassurance to the patient. With this deaf man the sigh and the prayer of Jesus were more important than the touch. The sigh conveyed compassion for the pathos of human suffering as Jesus saw it, and became His inarticulate prayer for the healing of the afflicted man. Mark preserves the Aramaic form of the command, "Be opened" (*Ephphatha*). The authoritative nature of the command so impressed the hearers that it was vividly recalled at a later time when Mark heard the story.

At the conclusion of the incident Jesus again commanded that no one should be told about it. Mark comments that the more He charged them the more they proclaimed it. The people were understandably astonished at the completeness of this and other cures, but why did Mark relate the command to secrecy? Also, why did Mark omit to mention that the people glorified the God of Israel? Is this evidence, as some have maintained, that the commands to silence were Mark's idea and not original with Jesus? Could Jesus ever have imagined that such remarkable cures could be kept secret? He knew human nature better than to suppose this. If He knew the people would not heed Him, however, why did He give commands of this nature? The problem is not easily solved. Most likely it was part of the Messiah's mission to deflect attention from the merely marvelous, knowing how deeply ingrained man's quest is for the sensational.

Mark relates another healing in which a blind man's sight was restored in two stages. First he saw dimly and then clearly, which illustrates another aspect of the variety of healing techniques used by Jesus. The healed man was ordered to go straight home, presumably again to avoid unnecessary publicity.

12

Testimony and Transfiguration

Another feeding miracle

Matthew 15:32-39 (Mark 8:1-10; cf. Matthew 16:5-12; Mark 8:15-21)

As already pointed out, the action of Jesus in feeding five thousand or more people was so remarkable that all four evangelists recorded it. In addition to this, two gospel writers included still another such incident, which has remarkable parallels. So similar is the story of the feeding of the four thousand told by Matthew and Mark that many scholars regard this as a variant record of the same miracle. For various reasons, this view is unsatisfactory. Matthew and Mark had a purpose in relating two similar events and they obviously regarded them as distinct. A Messiah who could feed five thousand people could certainly feed four thousand.

Not only was the crowd smaller, but the number of loaves and fishes differed. In the former event there were five loaves; in this, seven. In the former there were two fishes; in this, a few small fish. In the former, twelve baskets of leftover fragments were collected; in this, seven. Furthermore, the description of the baskets differs, for in the former event the word used describes the small food baskets that most people carried with them, whereas in the latter event the word used indicates much larger baskets. Differences in detail to this extent would not have arisen from repetition of the same event. If repetition had occurred, there would have been the tendency to exaggerate details. In this case, however, a smaller crowd is fed from a larger original supply — the tendency toward enhancement is missing. Nor is this eased by supposing that the feeding of the five thousand is a developed version of this account, for then the difficulty arises over Luke's and John's retention only of the later version. Obviously the view that there were two mass feedings meets fewer difficulties, and this view cannot be said to be either impossible or improbable.

Further incidental differences lend support to this conclusion. In the feeding of the five thousand, special mention is made of the green grass, but by the time the four thousand were fed, sometime later in the same year, the grass would be scorched. Both Matthew and Mark refer only to the ground. Nevertheless, one such incident would sufficiently illustrate the power of Jesus over natural resources and the compassion of Jesus toward the multitudes; the question arises why the evangelists included a second incident. One answer perhaps is found in the significant difference of location and therefore a probable difference in the character of the audience. The five thousand were Galilean Jews, but the four thousand were fed in the area of the Decapolis and may well have been a mixture of Galilean Jews and Gentiles.

Matthew mentions that after the miracle, Jesus left for Magadan, whereas Mark refers to Dalmanutha. Neither place, however, can be identified.

One objection sometimes given to treating the two feeding narratives as separate events is the improbability of the disciples' question, "How can one feed these men with bread here in the desert?" so soon after the earlier miracle. Did they so soon forget? This is hard to believe. It does not, however, necessarily follow from this that there could have been only one such feeding miracle. Doubts arise easily in human minds. The disciples may have been influenced more by uncertainty over the willingness of Jesus to feed a multitude twice than by unbelief over His power to do so. The event that immediately followed shows however that unbelief was not beyond them. They had forgotten to take bread with them when they were boating to the other side of the lake. Jesus asked whether they also forgot the *two* occasions when multitudes were fed. Their memories were evidently short. They had not yet measured the marvelous potential of the Messiah.

In both mass feedings, there are deeper truths than the provision of material needs. Although the concern that Jesus showed for physical needs must not be underrated, His own mind was on spiritual issues. In the following incident He contrasted His own teaching to the "leaven" of the Pharisees. If miraculous reproduction of food was all that man needed, the Messiah could have provided it, but it was not His mission to do so. The spiritual challenge was of far greater importance.

More sign-seeking

Matthew 16:1-4 (Mark 8:11-14)

The two main Jewish parties, the Sadducees and the Pharisees, found Jesus to be a considerable problem. His remarkable powers bewildered them, but they could not regard these as evidence that He was the Messiah. In the Jewish world, anyone claiming special authority must be able to produce special signs. This prompted the two parties to send representatives to Jesus to seek a sign from heaven. They would draw a distinction between a miracle like the feeding of the multitudes and a specific sign produced on demand. They could not, or would not, bridge the gap between the two. The root of the trouble was their pride. If Jesus had acceded to their request, it would have inflated their vanity. Moreover, the Messiah had not come to give signs on demand. He had no need to do so. They should have been able to discern His authority without special miracles to satisfy their curiosity.

Their quest for a sign drew from Jesus a blunt challenge. He reminded them that men frequently forecast the weather with very limited powers of foresight. An evening red sky foreshadows a fair day to follow; a morning red sky, a stormy day ahead. These predictions resulted from experience, but men failed to discern the signs of the times. Mark notes that Jesus sighed deeply in His spirit. He was faced with man's obstinacy. If signs already given were insufficient, how could any more prove effective? The very desire for a further sign displayed unbelief in His former signs. Jesus did not merely charge them with unbelief. He called them "an evil and adulterous generation" — strong words intended to shock. Their approach was so warped that nothing would be a "sign" to them. In Mark's account, the saying of Jesus stops there; in Matthew's account an addition is made — no sign except the sign of Jonah. Some have supposed that Matthew added His own words to Mark's account since the hearers of Jesus would not have understood the allusion to Jonah. It must be remembered, however, that Jesus was conscious of His coming passion (as Matt. 16:21 shows). Whether or not the hearers understood the allusion could not affect the truth that the passion and resurrection of Jesus would be the only signs given. In Matthew's record, an explanation of the sign of Jonah had earlier been given to some of the scribes and Pharisees (12: 39 ff.). Jesus therefore repeated what He said before in answer to a similar request. It may have happened on other occasions also.

Caesarea Philippi — the turning point

Matthew 16:13-16 (Mark 8:27-29; Luke 9:18-20)

Caesarea Philippi lay at the foot of Mount Hermon, near the headwaters of the river Jordan, an area of exceptional natural beauty. The city had been built by the Herodian king, Philip the tetrarch, and named in honor of Caesar Augustus. The citadel stood on a rocky prominence near a shrine dedicated to the Greek god Pan (the modern Banyas). The impressive rocky protrusion, part of which formed a section of the ancient structure, may well have suggested the figure of speech that Jesus used in His important discussion with the disciples on this occasion.

Jesus asked the leading question, "Who do men say that the Son of man is?" Reactions to the mission of Jesus had varied. Official religious groups did not treat His claims seriously, and He had refused their demand for a sign. The common people wanted to make Him king, and this had caused Him resolutely to withdraw from them. He knew His mission would meet with a lack of response; its spiritual nature was alien to the politically and materially minded people. Would He find the right response from those closest to Him? A direct challenge was needed.

Jesus asked for the opinions of men in general and of the disciples in particular. The sequel shows that He was not asking for information but teaching a profound truth. Summarized are various popular ideas about Him. Everyone was agreed that He

The Jordan River near its source,
in the area of Caesarea Philippi.

*"Now when Jesus came into the district
of Caesarea Philippi, he asked his disciples,
'Who do men say that the Son of man is?'"*
—MATTHEW 16:13

was no ordinary man. He stood out like a John the Baptist, to cite a contemporary example; or like Elijah or Jeremiah, men who long before had challenged their generation. There was no assertion of the uniqueness of the person and mission of Jesus. He was one among a number, even though the number was a select and illustrious group. The whole mission would have failed if Jesus had conformed to popular ideas about His identity.

He then asked the disciples for their own opinion of Him. "But who do you say that I am?" The "you" is emphatic. Jesus was distinguishing His disciples from people in general. Their estimate was most important, for they were involved in the mission. Simon Peter spoke for the rest. When Peter said, "You are the Messiah," it was more than a personal spontaneous outburst. It represented the growing conviction of the disciples, although still very imperfect. Many rude shocks awaited them before this conviction would deepen into an unshakable faith. It is not altogether certain what Peter meant by "Messiah." Matthew and Luke record variants of Peter's answer. Matthew has, "You are the Messiah, the Son of the living God," whereas Luke has more briefly, "The Messiah of God." These variations introduce a thought that is only implicit in Mark's wording. The Messiah could not be an ordinary man. He must be divine. A public acknowledgment of Jesus' messiahship, however, would be premature, which accounts for Jesus' strict command that the disciples say nothing about it.

Jesus tells Peter about the Church

Matthew 16:17-20

Of greater significance than the disciples' confession is Jesus' reply, reported only by Matthew. There was a special blessing for Peter because of the confession. Jesus knew that Peter had not arrived at his conclusion through logical processes, for mere human wisdom could not have yielded this confession. Recognition of the true nature of Jesus came by revelation from the heavenly Father, true for Peter as it would be for all who would later come to acknowledge Him. Peter's confession was the first fruit of multitudes to follow. Jesus' heart must have been gladdened. It came at a significant moment in the course of His mission. His mind was focused on His coming passion, which He was about to reveal to the disciples.

When Jesus said to Peter, "You are Peter (*Petros*), and on this rock (*petra*) I will build my church," the disciples could not have understood the full meaning. As Peter and others pondered this after the passion, the words became increasingly meaningful. So far, no Church was in existence. What, then, would the word *ecclesia* (church) have conveyed to Peter? It may have been familiar to him since the term was used in the

Greek version of the Old Testament to describe the congregation of Israel. Because of this unusual use of the word *ecclesia* some have reckoned the saying to be unauthentic. Such a view, however, credits Jesus with no insight into the future of His mission. His work of incomparable self-sacrifice would not fizzle out through lack of forethought. It would need to be a community effort. If this is granted, no difficulty remains in the use by Jesus of the word "church." Moreover, because the word came to be universally used to describe the Christian community, it must have had an authoritative basis. There is no validity to the objection that the saying is suspect because Matthew alone recorded it. Truth is as effectively conveyed by a single reliable witness as by many. It can confidently be assumed that Jesus Himself used the term.

What did Jesus mean by the whole statement? The crux of the problem rests in the meaning of the word "rock" (*petra*). In the Greek the play on words is unmistakable and obviously intentional. It must have represented a similar play on words in Aramaic. Is the rock therefore to be identified with Peter? Was Jesus saying that the Church was to be built on Peter? It is incredible for Jesus to imply that the future success of His mission depended upon one man. Peter was merely the spokesman for the rest. "This rock" therefore had a wider basis than Peter alone; it referred to Peter as the representative confessor of the true nature of Jesus, without which there could be no Church. This is not to equate the "rock" solely with Peter's confession, but with a combination of confession and confessor. Peter was never more true to his name than when he openly acknowledged the messiahship of Jesus. Such a decisive experience could be compared to a rock in contrast to the shallow estimates of Jesus held by the multitudes. A Church built by Christ Himself of people who accepted a high view of the nature of Jesus would prove impregnable. Nothing would shake it, not even "the gates of Hades" — the worst opposition to which Jesus could refer. This remarkable confidence has been amply justified by the course of history; in face of the most intense opposition, the Church has survived.

The figure of a building led on to the reference to "keys." Still addressing Peter, Jesus promised him the keys of the Kingdom of heaven. These "keys" invested Peter with the power to bind and loose. A Jew would have understood these terms to mean "prohibit" and "permit," as the rabbis used them of enforcing or relaxing their laws. As the disciples were to be the Messiah's representatives on earth, there was need for some relationship between what was allowed or prohibited on earth and what was allowed or prohibited in heaven. Peter's representative character again comes to the fore. Later, similar words were addressed to the disciples collectively (Matt. 18:18); thus the present statement must be interpreted in that light.

A strong rebuke for Peter

Matthew 16:21-23 (Mark 8:30-33)

Immediately after Peter's confession and his commendation by Jesus, it was necessary for him to be rebuked. It shows the kind of human material that the Messiah was shaping for His purpose, like a potter molding vessels of honor from imperfect clay.

This was the first time that Jesus spoke of His coming passion. All the synoptic gospels place His remarks immediately after the confession at Caesarea Philippi, and they must be treated as the natural sequel. Although His coming passion was constantly on the mind of Jesus, He could speak of it only to those who knew something of the real character of His mission. It was not easy to speak of suffering and death. He knew it must come, and He knew that the people responsible would be the chief priests, elders, and scribes. They had already shown their hostility toward Him and His mission. The disciples as yet had no clue of the consequences of that hostility. They could now be expected to be more perceptive.

In mentioning His coming death, Jesus also told the disciples of His resurrection on the third day. For Him the rising was the major focus, but for men unaccustomed to the thought of resurrection it is understandable that the death element of the prediction loomed largest. Three occasions are recorded when Jesus mentioned the matter, but it was too much for even the closest disciples to grasp. The Messiah's path was lonely.

According to Matthew, Jesus foresaw that Jerusalem was to be the place of His passion. This was the logical place, since the religious leaders were to be responsible for His death, as He had predicted. Jerusalem had a special place in His mind at this time.

Luke says nothing about the reaction of the disciples to this prediction of Jesus. Matthew and Mark confined themselves to Peter. The thought of Jesus' suffering and dying was so alien to him that he grabbed his master's arm and rebuked Him, as Matthew recorded, "God forbid, Lord! This shall never happen to you." It did not occur to Peter how audacious it was to rebuke the one he had just acknowledged as Messiah and Son of God. He was doing a strong man protective act, as he later did at the arrest of Jesus. His words are an example of impetuous inconsistency hard to equal. Did he really think he had the right to pronounce the destiny of Jesus?

Jesus' reply was swift and trenchant, a spontaneous revulsion to what opposed the very spirit of His mission: "Get behind me, Satan!" He saw beyond the inept Peter; this was Satan's artifice — a repetition of the basic temptation that recurred at intervals.

Peter's attitude reflected the human viewpoint — the avoidance of suffering and death. Without question, however, he was doing the devil's work. With this incisive rebuke, Jesus commanded the adversary to get behind Him and then said to Peter, "You are a hindrance to me; for you are not on the side of God, but of men." The language, uncommonly stern for Jesus, reflects the conflict between spiritual forces. This was a crisis in His ministry — a clash with the powers of darkness. The severity of Jesus' reaction testifies to His strong resolve to pursue at all costs His God-given mission.

Terms for discipleship

Mark 8:34-9:1 (Matthew 16:24-28; Luke 9:23-27)

After rebuking Peter, Jesus set out His terms for those who would follow Him. Peter had misconstrued things and clarification was needed.

The three accounts of this charter of discipleship are almost identical in wording. The conditions laid down evidently made a deep impression on the minds of the early disciples. As a first condition the disciple must deny himself, that is, refuse to put his own interests first. All honest people admit this to be a most difficult challenge. Self-interest is deeply ingrained in human nature. Those first disciples had still much to learn. There was a large element of self-interest in Peter. The others were equally at fault, for not long after this, they squabbled over who was the greatest. The disciples could expect no easier conditions than those faced by the Master who in His whole mission denied Himself.

As a second condition, the disciple must take up his cross. The symbolism would not be lost to the hearers. Crossbearing at this time was a familiar sight to the Jews. It meant suffering and death. After the disciples would see their Master bearing His cross of wood, the saying would gain new meaning. Following Him might not include a literal fulfillment in martyrdom, but it would involve a willingness to follow His example. Some early Christians did literally bear a cross of suffering under the various persecutions which afflicted the Church. Most, however, had lesser crosses to bear. Jesus was stating that His followers were to expect hardship, but the mission was worth all that, and more.

The Master knew that His terms reversed the usual assessment of values. To most men, "gain" was associated with material things and had nothing to do with their life as related to God. Jesus used the illustration of a profit-and-loss account to teach that the value of an individual life outweighs everything material of the world. This reflected His own determination in pursuing His mission, which was concerned with redeeming the lives of men. His rhetorical question to the disciples was as if to say, "What exchange-equivalent could be found for a life?" He was using the familiar language of barter. Jesus might have been thinking of Himself, since He later spoke of giving His life as a ransom, or exchange-price, for many (Mark 10:45).

Some suppose that following Jesus is a negative action, involving loss in this life, since Jesus mentioned that the Son of Man would recompense men when He came in glory with His angels. They dismiss this assurance as a "pie-in-the-sky" approach that provides a poor substitute for the loss of present material amenities. This is to misunderstand the real meaning of the words of Jesus. He wished men to know that a time of reckoning according to true values was unavoidable. This is plain justice, which demands that everyone accept responsibility for his own actions.

As Jesus contemplated the Kingdom of God He said that some standing before Him would not taste death before they had seen it come. This is how Mark and Luke relate it. Matthew, however, has "the Son of man coming in his kingdom" for Mark's "coming in power." Some have found difficulty in Matthew's account, since it appears to make Jesus place His future coming in the lifetime of His contemporaries. If this is the meaning, the saying was unfulfilled. A possible explanation is that the Kingdom refers to the Church, and its "coming" refers to the establishment of the Christian community at Pentecost, in which the spiritual presence of the Son of man came in the midst of His people. The difficulty of this interpretation is that the meaning of "kingdom" in this saying does not link up with the thought of the Son of Man's coming in glory in the previous saying. Others have seen an allusion to the transfiguration of Jesus, which took place immediately after this, when His glory was seen by three of the disciples. Surely, however, Jesus was thinking further ahead than just a few days. Most likely He wished to avoid the impression that the promise of recompense was so remote that the present disciples could ignore it. Some of those same men would see the coming of the Kingdom, even though they would not see the coming in glory. Since Jesus at other times used the word "kingdom" in more than one sense, it seems best to suppose that He did the same here. Both future consummation and immediate coming were probably in His thinking.

The transfiguration

Matthew 17:1-8 (Mark 9:2-8; Luke 9:28-36)

A week after the disciples' confession at Caesarea, Jesus took three of His disciples up on a mountain presumably in the same district. The purpose was known to Jesus but not to the disciples. Nothing is known of the reactions of the disciples left behind. They may have thought it was favoritism on the part of

"... Jesus took with him Peter and James and John ... and led them up a high mountain apart. And he was transfigured before them ..."
—MATTHEW 17:1, 2

A view by telephoto lens of snowcapped Mount Hermon in the distance, looking northeast across the Sea of Galilee.

Jesus. This impression would have been strengthened when the three returned, had not Jesus charged them to keep quiet about their experience until after the resurrection. Great revelations usually do not come to crowds, but to men when they are alone. Jesus had a purpose in choosing three witnesses for this unique event. When the story could be told, its truth would be supported by three witnesses, conforming to the Law's requirement that statements should be authenticated by two or three witnesses.

The three men — Peter, James, and John — were no better than the rest. They were simply representatives. What they saw bewildered them. If, as seems most probable, they were ascending the slopes of Mount Hermon they were surrounded by panoramic vistas. The ascent could not have failed to impress them. There is no reason to suppose that they reached any of the summits, but they were high enough to be far away from other people.

Luke tells us that Jesus went there to pray. When He stopped, the disciples, wearied with the climbing, were on the point of sleeping on the ground. For them it was no strange sight to see Jesus in the attitude of prayer, but this time they noticed a remarkable difference. He became radiant with an unearthly glory, which even included the clothes He was wearing. The disciples could only compare it with the brilliance of the sun. This brilliance, however, was coming from the face of Jesus. No wonder the disciples were confused. They were alert enough to notice the presence of two others, whose appearance was equally unearthly. By some means they identified them as Moses and Elijah, perhaps from the conversation that they overheard. Luke alone notes the topic of that conversation — the departure of Jesus and what He was to accomplish at Jerusalem. The word used for "departure" (*exodus*) is significant, since it shows that death was not regarded as the finale. The departure involved also the resurrection. Why did Moses and Elijah participate in the transfiguration? They were the most notable representatives of the Law and the prophets respectively. This visually demonstrated their essential unity. Both pointed to a Messiah whose fulfillment of His mission involved triumphant death and resurrection.

The symbolic meaning of the transfiguration completely by-passed the disciples. They were conscious only of the fact that something extraordinary was happening. Their first confused re-action was to think of some way to retain the experience. They could think only in physical terms. Peter suggested building booths to house them, a clear indication that he utterly failed to see the spiritual implications of the vision. Mark and Luke com-ment that Peter really did not know what to say. All three were overawed and terrified. There came no answer from Jesus to Peter's suggestion. The disciples suddenly became aware that the vision had vanished. A brilliant cloud remained and enveloped them. Out of it came the voice of God bearing witness to His Son and exhorting them to listen to Him. The precise wording differs in the three gospels. Matthew and Mark have "This is my beloved Son," whereas Luke has "This is my Son, my Chosen" (although some texts have the same as the other gospels). Mat-thew adds the words "with whom I am well pleased." This di-vine testimony to Jesus made a profound impression on the dis-ciples, coming as it did so soon after the first intimation of the approaching passion. It showed that the mission of Jesus was not merely one of His own choosing. It had the backing of the heav-enly voice. All that Jesus had said was to be heeded. Later, however, the memory of that unique witness to Jesus did not prevent one of the three disciples from denying Him and the others from forsaking Him.

Matthew alone relates the disciples' reaction to the heavenly voice: "They fell on their faces, and were filled with awe." He also recorded the encouraging words of Jesus: "Rise and have no fear." Jesus understood their bewilderment. He also knew that after His resurrection, the meaning of the testimony would be-come clear. At this point, the disciples became aware that they were once more alone with Jesus. The situation returned to nor-mal. Or had it? Could things ever be the same following an ex-perience of such spiritual magnitude? The disciples must have realized in a new way something more of the uniqueness of Jesus.

Although baffled by the vision, it would have been natural for them to spread reports about the sheer wonder of it. Jesus, however, commanded them not to do so "until the Son of man is raised from the dead." Mark alone notes that they questioned among themselves what the raising of the dead meant. Luke does not mention that they were commanded to keep silent, but he reports that they told nobody in those days. How much clearer the whole matter would become when Jesus' glory would again be seen after He had risen from the dead.

13

Quests and Queries

The question about Elijah

Matthew 17:9-13 (Mark 9:9-13)

Following Jesus' warning that they should tell nobody about
the transfiguration, the three disciples posed a question concerning Elijah: "Why do the scribes say that first Elijah must come?"
They were wondering why they had seen Elijah with Jesus. His
presence prompted their thinking about the traditional teaching
of the scribes concerning Elijah. On the basis of Malachi 4:5
("Behold, I will send you Elijah the prophet before the great
and dreadful day of the LORD comes), the scribes maintained
that Elijah would precede the coming of the Messiah. The disciples, having seen the momentary appearance of Elijah on the
mountain, were naturally perplexed. If Jesus was the Messiah,
why had not Elijah come before this, and why did he vanish
now? They had misunderstood the prophecy. Their question to
Jesus involved His own mission.

The three events near and at Caesarea Philippi all feature
Elijah, which unmistakably links them together. At Caesarea
Philippi, the popular view that identified Jesus with Elijah was
reported. At the transfiguration, Jesus was seen engaging in conversation with Elijah. On the descent from the mountain, Jesus
replied to the disciples' question that Elijah should be identified
with John the Baptist. The answer is not altogether free from
ambiguity. Jesus agreed that Elijah would come before the Messiah, and then added that the prophet would restore all things.

If Elijah was to restore all things what mission would be left for the Messiah Himself? Why would the Messiah have to suffer? It would seem unnecessary. The statement is not totally enigmatic if it is recognized that Elijah had already come in the person of John the Baptist. Men, however, had done with him what they pleased, and he certainly had not restored all things. What then is the explanation?

Possibly a confusion persisted in the popular exposition over the role of Elijah in the two advents of the Messiah. In Christian expectation of the future, Elijah was included, as Revelation 11:3, 6 shows, although there is no mention in that passage of the restoration of all things. More likely, Jesus was implying a distinction between the coming and the restoration. The scribes were right in supposing that Elijah must first come, but the restoration was connected with the Son of Man and His suffering. It was too early for the disciples to grasp the idea of a suffering Messiah, but it was constantly in the mind of Jesus.

Failure and faith

Mark 9:14-32 (Matthew 17:14-23; Luke 9:37-45)

As the three disciples and Jesus had nearly completed their descent from the mountain, in the valley below they noted a crowd and discovered the other disciples in the throes of an argument with the scribes. The contrast with their exhilarating experience on the mountain could not have been more striking. Left to themselves, the nine disciples appear to have failed miserably.

The trouble had begun over their inability to heal an epileptic boy at the urgent request of his father. The father had come seeking Jesus, but he found only the disciples. He must have accepted them as second best, since the boy's condition was desperate. All the evangelists recorded the severity of the convulsions from which the boy suffered: the foaming at the mouth, the grinding of teeth, the uncontrolled falling — all symptoms of an epileptic fit. The writers all go beyond the description of physical symptoms and mention spirit possession. As if to illustrate the reaction of the demon world to Jesus, a convulsion occurred just as they were bringing the boy to Him. From the glory of the mountain the Messiah had returned to the conflict of the valley. The pathos of human suffering could not have been more tellingly set before His eyes, nor could the pathos of unbelief.

Mark gives the most detailed account of the encounter. Jesus asked the disciples about their discussion with the scribes, but the boy's father answered the question for them. The disciples were thoroughly frustrated at their own failure to effect a cure, and the scribes were no doubt rejoicing at this. They probably thought that the disciples' inability revealed the weakness of their Master. The father, with a crushing burden on his mind, was uninhibited: "I begged your disciples to cast it out, but they could not" (Luke 9:40). The disciples probably winced at this public announcement, but they had no opportunity to make excuses. Jesus did not at first mention their failure. He was moved with compassion for the boy. "How long has he had this?" The father may have considered the question irrelevant, but he told Jesus it was from childhood. It was clearly a chronic case. The father further pleaded impatiently, "If you can do anything, have pity on us and help us." His "if" implied doubt. In his despair he hardly dared to hope that Jesus would be any more successful than His disciples.

Jesus used another "if" in reply to the father's "if." "If you can! All things are possible to him who believes." There was no questioning of Jesus' ability to heal, but there was doubt about the man's ability to believe. The father at once saw the point and uttered the words — paradoxical as they are — which have many times been used by others, "I believe; help my unbelief." A blend of faith with an awareness of faithlessness is a true response of the heart to the challenge of Jesus. Faith must be there, but with human nature as it is, this faith can never totally exclude doubt. The father took the only possible course in asking Jesus to deal with his doubt. There remained no barrier to the healing. The demon was rebuked and forbidden to return. A final convulsion left the boy seemingly dead, but he was lifted up by Jesus, completely cured. This majestic authority of the Master highlighted the dismal failure of the disciples. Luke records that all were astonished at the majesty of God. The Messiah's bearing distinguished Him from all others. A healing had again symbolized the triumph of Jesus over the forces of darkness and vividly illustrated the place of faith in His mission.

Once more alone with Jesus, the disciples had but one thought — their failure. It was a shattering and humiliating experience, and they asked Jesus why they could not cast the demon out. The reason for failure is worth knowing if it leads to constructive self-examination. Jesus' answer implied that the quality of faith, rather than the quantity, was most important. A minute faith like a grain of mustard seed could remove the massiveness of a mountain. The exaggeration was intentional. Faith, if it works at all, is limitless; nothing is impossible. The figure of moving mountains to illustrate the overcoming of difficulties can be paralleled from rabbinical writings and was probably familiar to the disciples. The Messiah was expounding on the quality of faith that could do the impossible for the success of His mission. For the moment, however, He was proceeding along a lonely path. His closest associates had hardly approached the most elementary reaches of true faith, which, according to Jesus, comes only through prayer.

Tax money from a fish

Matthew 17:24-27

Matthew alone mentions this incident, which happened at Capernaum. Formerly a tax collector, his interest in it is understandable, for it concerned the payment by Jesus of the Temple tax money. Levied by the authorities in Jerusalem, it amounted to a half-shekel per person in the Temple currency. Every male was expected to pay it as a patriotic as well as a religious duty. The tribute money was used to defray the expenses of the morning and evening sacrifices. The tax collectors had approached Peter asking whether his Master paid the tribute. The form of the question suggests that an affirmative answer was expected, which Peter's reply confirms. There must have been a reason, however, why Jesus had not made the current contribution. This is brought out in His conversation with Peter about the whole matter.

Matthew brings out a remarkable feature of Jesus' dealings with His disciples, in that Jesus knew what was in Peter's mind before Peter said anything to Him. He forestalled any comment on Peter's part. Jesus read the recesses of Peter's mind and recognized that he wanted to know his Master's present attitude toward tax. Presumably, Jesus had paid the tax in the past, but Peter wondered why He had delayed to do so on this occasion. The Master, however, intended to teach the disciple a lesson. If Peter had really seen Jesus as the Messiah and as the Son of God, would this not, in his mind, have raised the problem of the obligation to pay the Temple tax?

The Messiah was a master teacher of men. He used the technique of a counter question, "What do you think, Simon?" Jesus wanted Peter to think about the matter himself. It would have been easier but less satisfying to present a ready-made answer. The question to Simon was simple enough and required little intelligence on his part to answer it, "Do kings tax their own children?" Peter gave the obvious negative answer. He had just recently confessed that his Master had greater dignity than an earthly king by calling Him "Son of God." What justification was there to extract from Him tribute for God's own Temple? Jesus left Peter in no doubt that the Messiah was not obliged to acknowledge any such claim upon Himself, for His own relationship to the Temple was entirely different from that of the people of Israel.

Jesus, however, would cause no offense in the matter, even to assert His authority. It would serve no present purpose, for His Kingdom was not to be built on such methods. He would settle the tax for Himself and Peter. His way of doing this has caused offense to some. The command that Peter should cast a hook in the sea and take up a fish from whose mouth a shekel would be taken seems strange. To many, its strangeness proves that the incident cannot be genuine, especially since Jesus performed it in His own interest. Others have suggested that Jesus meant Peter to catch a fish and then sell it, and pay the tax from the proceeds. Nonetheless, the story as Matthew tells it gives no support to this theory. It would have required a remarkable fish to sell for a shekel in the marketplace. Moreover, Peter normally used nets, not hooks. Some have regarded the story as a myth, but Matthew presents it as fact.

The miracle was an act of foreknowledge in that Jesus knew

that the fish had swallowed the coin, and it was an act of supernatural power in that this fish and no other was directed toward
the hook. The purpose of the incident was to teach Peter a
deep lesson. Having acknowledged the divinity of Christ, Peter
had then impulsively committed His Master to paying a tax
which was not really required from the Messiah, who was God's
Son. The payment, however, was Jesus' gesture to avoid misunderstanding. This event was no mere marvel, but rather has
the character of a sign. Jesus had declined to perform a miracle
to meet His own bodily needs at the first temptation in the wilderness. He was prepared, however, to perform a miracle to meet a
demand which, in view of His position, should never have been
made.

Ambitions

Matthew 18:1-6 (Mark 9:33-37; Luke 9:46-48)

Now that the idea of Jesus as the Messiah came more clearly
into focus, the disciples began to think of their future prospects.
Their imaginations were fired by the idea of the messianic
Kingdom. The Messiah, to their way of thinking, would need
high-ranking officials in His Kingdom, and the literal-minded
among them concluded that the most favored positions would
be shared among His closest followers. Apart from the funda
mental error in their notion of the Kingdom of heaven, their
weakness also lay in the assessment of their own part in it. The
visions of power that come to the human mind can destroy all
thought of humility. It was incongruous that the disciples could
dispute over which of them should be the greatest so soon after
Jesus had twice informed them of His coming passion. It shows
how thoroughly permeated with human failings these associates of Jesus were. They still did not appreciate the mission of
Jesus. Clouds of sorrow were gathering about Him, but they were
concerned only with their personal ambitions.

Jesus knew what they were discussing en route. He said
nothing until they had reached a house in Capernaum, where
they met together. To draw them out, He asked, "What were you
discussing on the way?" According to Mark, nobody said a word
in reply; they were probably ashamed of their quibbles over
such matters. Matthew, however, states that the disciples came

and asked, "Who is the greatest in the kingdom of heaven?"
Luke, giving no indication of the drift of the conversation, says
that Jesus perceived their thoughts. Perhaps the disciples' question was an attempt to turn the conversation away from the
personal level, to make it less invidious by discussing the "greatest" in the abstract rather than to discuss their personal claims.
The symbolic action of Jesus in reply to the question is mentioned by all the evangelists.

A child whom Jesus selected from the street or from an ad-
joining courtyard where children were playing became an object
lesson. Or possibly the child belonged to the master of the house.
Jesus saw in the child the very opposite of what He saw in the
disciples. The child was too young to be ambitious for authority,
trusting, rather, those who cared for him. The child was an excellent example of the attitude that Jesus required for the establishment of the Kingdom. Men ambitious to be the greatest were
not qualified for leading others into the Kingdom, or even for entering themselves. In the ancient world humility was not a virtue.
The Jewish contemporaries of Jesus were notorious for exalting
their own achievements, and the Grecian world had contempt
for humility. In contrast, the attitude of Jesus toward His coming humiliation was most striking. Those around Him who had
opposing standards of value added to the pathos of Messiah's
mission. The contemporary world of Jesus was not ready to accept the teaching that the meek inherit the earth. Even the disciples were not ready to admit the principle that the humblest
men are the greatest.

Following the object lesson, Jesus gave His high evaluation of
children. He pointed out that those receiving children in His name
would be receiving Him. It must have amazed the disciples
that Jesus was concerned about the welfare of children. Such attitudes had no place in their reveries about the Messiah and
His Kingdom. The ancient world was notorious for its lack of
care for children, although more concern existed among the
Jews than among most other peoples. Even the Christian Church
took too much time to learn the simple lesson of the Master. As
for those who cause children to sin, the words of Jesus are un-
compromisingly severe. Let a millstone drag them to the bottom
of the sea.

As the disciples pondered the child illustration Jesus used, they could not have failed to realize how alien their squabbles were to the spirit of their Master. Although they may have preferred that the story of their vanity would not be told, a threefold account of it has been preserved to remind others how utterly incongruous personal ambition is in the Kingdom of heaven.

For and against

Mark 9:38-50 (Matthew 18:7-9; Luke 9:49, 50)

In many groups, the members develop a sense of privilege, which all too often fosters an exclusive approach. The disciples had already shown themselves to be fertile soil for such exclusivism, and an incident of it soon came to light. One of them, John, reported to Jesus what turned out to be a choice instance of officiousness. The disciples had come across a man casting out demons in the name of Jesus. In their judgment, this could not be allowed, for he did not belong to the privileged circle. Only the authorized few should be permitted to exorcise in the name of Jesus. The disciples felt they had no option but to forbid him. They were convinced that they had performed a commendable service. They saw no need to obtain the sanction of Jesus. They would only need to inform Him. They assumed without question that they had the right to judge the validity of the man's action. They were totally unconcerned that they had forbidden a work of mercy. No compassion was felt for those who needed deliverance. Their one thought was to preserve their exclusive right.

The Master's reply was unequivocal. Anyone doing a mighty work in His name could not be diametrically opposed to Him. The disciples had been too hasty, for not all the followers of Jesus had to conform to the same pattern. This man was also a supporter of Christ. This is a lesson that many in the Christian Church find difficult or impossible to learn. Too often the zeal to preserve a select community results in the exclusion of those who were helping rather than hindering. Such an attitude contradicts the approach of Jesus.

Jesus continued on the subject of offenses. If offenses come through a hand, a foot, or an eye, the only action to take is to remove them and cast them away. To be without them is less serious than the offenses they caused. The remedy seems disproportionate to the disease, but the illustration must not be pressed beyond its intended limits. The physical aspects are symbolic of a deeper cause. Hands, feet, or eyes do not act independently of the person, and it is the person who is responsible for the offenses. The vivid and drastic character of the illustration impressed on the disciples how serious it was to cause others to stumble. Jesus did not, however, envisage a world from which offenses would be banished, for He understood men's motives only too well. Nonetheless, He made clear that woe is the inevitable result of such offenses.

Mark recorded another saying of Jesus about offenses, based on the metaphor of salt, but the connection is not at once evident. Jesus had just mentioned the terrible consequences of hell fire, and then added, "For every one will be salted with fire. Salt is good; but if the salt has lost its saltness, how will you season it? Have salt in yourselves, and be at peace with one another." Perhaps Jesus was pointing out that those who consider themselves blameless over the matter of causing offenses should first examine themselves. The figure may refer to Levitical sacrifices, which had to be salted before being offered. The rock salt of Palestine, however, could lose its flavor. The words are a solemn warning against complacency. Anything that causes strife among the followers of Jesus is not true salt. Those who have true salt will be at peace with one another. This is not peace at any price, but peace based on a true understanding of the mission of Jesus.

Teaching about relationships

Matthew 18:10-20 (Luke 15:3-7)

Jesus was concerned about people, and much of His teaching was directed to aid people in their relationships with others. Matthew collated some examples of this teaching into a discourse. The sayings are a continuation of the teaching about the right treatment of children. The importance of the individual was presented by Jesus in the story about a lost sheep. The same story occurs in Luke, in a grouping of stories about lost items. In Matthew's account, the shepherd's decision to leave his ninety-nine sheep to search for his one lost sheep illustrates the heavenly Father's care for the young.

The importance of individuals is also emphasized in Jesus' teaching about brotherly reproof. If a cause of offense exists between two people it ought to be possible for them to resolve it in a mature way. Human nature being what it is, however, provision must be made for a lack of cooperation from the offender. If a man-to-man talk fails, one or two others should be included for a stronger testimony to the offense. These others would witness that every effort has been attempted to put things right. If this fails, the matter should then be referred to the church. Some consider it strange that Jesus should mention the church, which at that time did not exist. He may have referred to the synagogue. It cannot be doubted, however, that He foresaw His followers grouped in communities. The word "church" (*ecclesia*) was to become a commonly-used word to describe them and the full significance of His teaching would dawn upon them when local groups of Christians came to be known as "churches."

The important function of the community in this instruction was to discipline the offender. Jesus said that a man who will not listen to the church is to be regarded as a Gentile or a tax collector. These words may seem harsh and out of character, but His comment is expressed in thoroughly Jewish terms — for in Jewish eyes both Gentiles and tax collectors were despised. Did Jesus share this Jewish contempt? It is difficult to believe that He did. How then is the saying to be explained? Some attribute it to Matthew's own intense Jewishness, but the author would not have attributed an alien idea to Jesus. It is better to regard the words not as a literal expression of contempt for Gentiles or tax collectors, but rather as an example of those who were irreligious in the Jewish sense of not being devoted to God. If a man refused to listen to the church, he should be regarded as not belonging. The severity of discipline shows the high esteem Jesus held for the membership of the future community.

Jesus next spoke on two further aspects of the Church. The first reference was an extension of the binding and loosing statement previously addressed to Peter but now applied to the disciples collectively. This community approach offsets an over-emphasis on the authority of Peter. The saying was, of course, addressed only to the disciples, and could for that reason relate only to the apostles. When immediately afterward, however, Jesus spoke of the community, He apparently had a wider group in mind.

The teaching of Jesus about the coming Church is all the more striking because so few comments concerning the Church are recorded in the gospels. He was not obsessed with massive organizations, but He was concerned with individuals. If no more than two or three agreed together about any matter affecting the Kingdom, such fellowship would be honored in heaven. Followers of the Messiah have too often found it surprisingly difficult to accept His high rating of individual action. It runs counter to the authoritarian approach that has so largely dominated the Christian Church throughout its history.

Jesus assured His disciples of His continued presence. Matthew records a similar promise given by Jesus after His resurrection (Matt. 28:20). The distinguishing feature of this promise is that it is valid for the smallest possible community — one consisting of no more than two people. The individual is important when closely linked with the Messiah. The Church was to be the community in which He would dwell. The disciples who heard this saying must have often recalled it when small groups of Christians were scattered over wide areas of the ancient world. The strength of these communities lay not in numbers, but in the spiritual presence of the Head among them.

Forgiveness

Matthew 18:21-35

Another important theme in the sayings that Matthew preserves is forgiveness. Peter addressed a pointed question to Jesus: "How often shall my brother sin against me, and I forgive him?" Peter may have been debating this with the other disciples, or it may have arisen from his own personal experience. His reckoning was that seven times was sufficiently generous. Jesus at once saw the weakness of Peter's approach — that forgiveness could be measured quantitatively as if it amounted to a mathematical sum. Jesus' answer was shattering: "Not . . . seven times, but seventy times seven." No one would count the times he had forgiven another up to four hundred and ninety before deciding to stop. Forgiveness is not a matter of quantity but quality. One should be filled with the spirit of forgiveness.

Jesus told a story to illustrate this point. A king decided to settle accounts with his servants. One servant owed ten thousand talents, a fantastic sum in excess of a million pounds. Unable to pay, he and his family were ordered to be sold into slavery. He pleaded for another chance, and the king forgave the whole debt. In contrast, the wells of gratitude in this servant dried up when a fellow servant owed him only a paltry sum. The same pleading approach found no response, and the servant cast his debtor into prison. The other servants reported the incongruity to the king, who reversed his pardon and punished the man. The king preferred an attitude of mercy to one of judgment, but he also expected to find a similar attitude among his subjects.

The spiritual application was not left to conjecture, but Jesus pronounced, "So also my heavenly Father will do to every one of you, if you do not forgive your brother from your heart." Such forgiveness is urgently needed in human relationships. It challenges the modern world both individually and nationally. It is easier to receive forgiveness than to show it, and those unwilling to forgive others revoke their own right to be forgiven. No wonder Jesus included in His pattern prayer the words, "Forgive us our debts, as we also have forgiven our debtors."

14

Service

Toward Jerusalem

Luke 9:51-62 (cf. Matthew 8:18-22; John 7:1-13)

Jesus set His face to go to Jerusalem. It was a major turning point in His life. Luke noted the importance of the event and reported a number of incidents and sayings belonging to that journey. He did not, however, confine himself to a straightforward journey narrative, for this part of his book cannot accurately be termed a travel document although he left the overall impression that Jesus was moving on toward Jerusalem. He especially emphasized the significance of Jerusalem for Jesus. Most likely during this period Jesus made more than one visit to Jerusalem. If so, Luke's narrative would allow for those incidents, recorded by John, that happened in Jerusalem before the final entry. It is convenient at this point to include the discussion that took place between Jesus and His brothers just before the Feast of Tabernacles (cf. John 7:1-13).

Jesus' brothers did not share His vision. They did not believe His claims. Their suggestions were colored by their inability to understand Him. They imagined that He was in need of advice and did not hesitate to give it. If He really wanted to make a name for Himself, it seemed obvious to them that Jerusalem, not Galilee, was the place to do it. Common sense apparently supported the brothers, but the Messiah's mission was to be accomplished according to divine timing. The brothers' suggestion echoed the wilderness temptation to use sensationalism.

190

The brothers, however, failed to appreciate the true nature of the mission of Jesus and the deep-seated hostility of the world toward Him. Moreover, His timetable was in other hands.

At the start of the journey, Jesus decided to go through Samaria. The people of the towns and villages of Samaria were not well disposed toward any Jews traveling to Jerusalem for the feast. Jesus was not unaware of this. To one of the villages that they were approaching He sent representatives from His small company to test out the reactions of the people. The report was

A panorama of Samaritan countryside looking to the north from the top of Mount Gerizim.

"And he sent messengers ahead of him, who went and entered a village of the Samaritans, to make ready for him . . ."
— LUKE 9:52

unfavorable. The feud between Jews and Samaritans excluded generosity from either side. The villagers probably relished the opportunity to show their hostility by refusing a safe passage for the pilgrims. They did not know that the Messiah was among them. The disciples, however, regarded their hostility as a direct affront to their Master. James and John boiled with indignation. They felt that drastic action was warranted, in fact, nothing short of divine judgment. In their opinion, these people deserved the judgment of fire from heaven. They may have had in mind the story of Elijah on Carmel and were seized with a sudden desire to emulate the prophet. Their anger led them to the false conclusion that they had power to command fire from heaven as Elijah had done, although they had the good sense to ask Jesus' permission before trying it out. They were not on the same wavelength as Jesus, for His mission was not to destroy. He had no alternative but to rebuke them for their folly. The story reveals the loneliness of Jesus as He set His face toward Jerusalem. The disciples would need much more training before they qualified as ambassadors of peace in a world of strife.

Whereas the disciples misunderstood the mission of Jesus, others were fired with the desire to join the company. One man whom they met along the road offered to follow Jesus wherever He was going. It was a magnanimous and zealous offer. Little did he know what was involved. The foxes and birds had more settled dwelling places. Moreover, the man was unaware that Jesus was moving toward a cross. Another man was invited to follow, but he declined to do so. He thought he had a good excuse. He must remain to attend to his responsibility toward his father. After his father died, he would be willing to follow. Jesus would not tolerate such an excuse. Those who waited for such a reason as this were themselves spiritually dead, unaware of the urgency of the task. Immediate action was required in proclaiming the Kingdom. The mission must take first place.

Another man made what appears to be an even more reasonable excuse. All he wanted to do was to go home and say farewell. Again, the Messiah recognized the danger. The man was really turning away from his responsibilities, like a man plowing a field without keeping his eye focused ahead to the end of the furrow. Such men would never endure the stern demands of the Kingdom. The Messiah insisted on self-denial and utter devotion to His cause. No wonder many found the way too hard.

Teamwork with seventy

Luke 10:1-20

Shortly after setting His face toward Jerusalem, Jesus appointed seventy people in addition to the Twelve. Their special task was to go ahead of Him and prepare the way. His instructions to them were very similar to those already delivered to the Twelve. However, a few differences are noteworthy. Since the mission of the Twelve was distinctive, they were given special authority. No such authority was granted to the seventy, although in the course of their mission they discovered that they possessed extraordinary power. Their job was, however, of a temporary nature.

They were warned before they set out that they could expect the same kind of treatment as the Twelve. They, too, would encounter hostility. They, too, would be as lambs surrounded by a pack of wolves. There was special instruction over procedure. They were to go in pairs, a method that sets the pattern of service best suited to the Messiah's purpose. He did not encourage individualism in the work of the Gospel. Later the Church followed the same principle. The church at Antioch, on instructions from the Holy Spirit, sent out two — Saul and Barnabas. So urgent was the present preparatory journey that the seventy were forbidden to exchange the usual casual but involved salutations, to prevent lengthy delays by irrelevant conversations on the road. For the messengers of Jesus, nothing must impede their immediate mission. Social exchanges were right enough in their place, but they were no asset when urgent business needed to be done.

Before Luke gave the result of this mission, he inserted the denunciation of certain cities — Chorazin, Bethsaida, and Capernaum — earlier referred to by Matthew. The condemnation of the cities was intended by Luke to provide the background to the mission of the seventy. Of the three cities, Capernaum had been the most favored, since the Messiah had made His home there. Nevertheless, it had no reason for pride, since Jesus predicted its downfall. It would be brought down to Hades. All three of the cities have long since ceased to exist.

The thirty-five two-man teams returned overjoyed. The dominant theme of their report was the subjection of demons to them. This impressed them more than the response of the people to their announcements about the Kingdom. To subdue evil spirits was more spectacular. It fired their imagination, and their exuberance is understandable. They knew that the imminence of the Kingdom meant defeat for the kingdom of darkness. This was confirmed by the comment of Jesus — "I saw Satan fall like lightning from heaven." No more vividly could He have revealed His acute awareness of the spiritual conflict in which He and His disciples were so deeply involved. What surprised them did not surprise Him. He knew that the hour was approaching when He would defeat the prince of this world. He already had a mental picture of it. Every exorcism was a token and proof of Satan's fall. Jesus, however, issued a mild rebuke to His followers. They should have been rejoicing far more that their names (and those of others) were being written in heaven, for this was a spiritual triumph of greater proportions than exorcism.

Good neighborliness

Luke 10:21-37 (cf. Matthew 11:25-27; Matthew 22:34-40)

Luke connects the rejoicing of the seventy with the rejoicing of Jesus. The latter was in the form of thanksgiving to His Father. The words are recorded in almost identical form by Matthew for an earlier stage in the ministry, but in both gospels the report follows the rebuking of the Galilean cities for their refusal to believe. The thanksgiving of Jesus reveals a much deeper reason for rejoicing than the seventy had had for their rejoicing. In His mind the victory was already won. Some might have had very different opinions, but so close was the fellowship between the Messiah and His Father that there was no doubt where the initiative lay. The Father was in control. The seventy were no more than "babes," although even to them was given something of the thrill of victory. They were more favored than kings and prophets who had wanted to see the dawning of a better age, but had to be content with their anticipations. At this point, however, it was not possible for the disciples to share Jesus' consciousness of the symbolic importance of the break-down of Satanic power. That would come later.

There was probably no connection between the preceding events and the lawyer's question that led Jesus to tell the incom-parable story of the Good Samaritan. Both Mark and Matthew re-late a similar question, but in different forms and contexts. The lawyer, whose life was devoted to the interpretation of the Jew-ish law, both written and oral, was naturally interested in the basic problems connected with such interpretation. One was the problem of destiny and the means for obtaining an eternal in-heritance. He decided to test Jesus. He commendably framed his question in a personal way, "What shall I do to inherit eternal life?" It need not be supposed that he was seeking to trap Jesus, as others had sought to do. He wanted to test the ability of Jesus to apply Himself to some of the basic problems of Jewish theology. He may have thought that he could reveal some weakness in Jesus. He was probably confident of his own intellectual superior-ity. The counterquestion by Jesus may have been a mild rebuke. "What is written in the law?" As a lawyer he should have known the answer to his own question.

His answer was ready. In the habit of reciting daily the statements from Deuteronomy 6:3 ff.; 11:13 ff., the words came easily to his mind. It was a matter of loving God with the whole heart. He added a quotation from Lev. 19:18 — the command to love one's neighbor as oneself. Linking these two statements sug-gests that the lawyer had been musing on the meaning of the second statement. Some definition of "neighbor" was needed. Perhaps he wanted to ask Jesus about this. His answer was com-mended by Jesus. However, the problem arose for the lawyer when Jesus urged him to act on his own advice.

Good neighborliness in principle is a highly desirable qual-ity. Its practice, however, raises problems. In contacts with His Jewish contemporaries, Jesus must have often felt their tensions. He knew that the common interpretation of "neighbor" was narrow. Tensions existed between Jews and Samaritans and be-tween Jews and Gentiles. Jesus' own interpretation of "neighbor" transcended the boundaries of nationalism, as the story of the Good Samaritan shows. This story was told with a remarkable economy of words. It presented the different attitude of three men faced with the same critical human need. The road from Jerusalem to Jericho was infamous for its brigandry. Galileans would know of its dangers. On the stretches of lonely road exposed to highwaymen's ambushes travelers had been killed or left half-dead. Jesus chose this highly topical setting to illustrate His point. He was interested in the reactions of other travelers toward a man who had been left beaten by the roadside.

The story reveals sharp differences in the attitude of three main classes of contemporary society — priests, Levites, and Samaritans. The Samaritan alone showed concern. The others, who were fellow Jews, passed by on the other side. These two, moreover, were committed to religious observances, and their failure was a failure to live up to their own professions.

The details of the story are less important than the principle it teaches. The first-aid given, the transporting of the injured man on the Samaritan's own beast, the arrangement made at the inn for him to be cared for at the Samaritan's expense, are all details to illustrate the principle of compassion. At the close of

"Jesus replied, 'A man was going down from Jerusalem to Jericho, and he fell among robbers . . .'"
— LUKE 10:30

Geological folds along the Jericho road reveal the tortuous structure of the land along the descent to the Jordan Valley.

the story the lawyer could not escape the application. He was shrewd enough to see that Jesus' concept of neighborliness was considerably wider than his own narrow view. When he was challenged to choose between the three, he found that he could not do so on nationalistic grounds. The only valid criterion was mercy. Love is never far removed from mercy. Luke does not report the lawyer's reactions when commanded to emulate the Samaritan. But his recording of the story has inspired many to emulate the Samaritan's compassion.

A home in Bethany

Luke 10:38-42

As He commissioned the disciples for their tasks, Jesus stressed hospitality, for this practice was to be important in the subsequent mission of the Christian Church. He had advised His team members to concentrate on those houses where they were received, but to waste no time on others. He followed His own advice. One house where He was specially welcomed was that of Mary and Martha at Bethany. Luke describes one occasion when He was entertained there. Hospitality is never without its problems, as it inevitably increases the household chores. On this occasion, Martha was among the pots and pans preparing a meal, while Mary sat and listened to Jesus. Seemingly, Martha had just cause for complaint. Before she said anything to Jesus, she inwardly stewed over the indolence of her sister, who was leaving her to do all the work. Moreover, resentment spreads when it has once begun. If Mary had not sufficient consideration for her, at least Jesus should have. In her mind even He did not seem to care. At length she spoke her thoughts: "Lord, do you not care that my sister has left me to serve alone? Tell her then to help me." A domestic squabble had erupted.

Jesus' method of dealing with it is significant. He said nothing about Martha's unwarranted criticism of His own lack of action. Nor did He imply that Martha was wrong in doing her work. He perceived and commented on her attitude. When common duties cause anxiety, it is time for self-examination. Perhaps to Martha domestic routine was more important than enlightened conversation. Perhaps Mary would willingly have helped after spending time listening to Jesus. Apparently Martha had not recognized the importance of listening to her guest of honor, whose teaching had astonished multitudes who had hung upon His words. This was the "one thing" that she needed. She was probably highly efficient at organizing the household, but she left for herself no time for spiritual instruction. She needed to learn that man does not live by bread alone.

Other occasions would arise when Martha's home would provide a haven for Jesus, especially during the events of the passion. The Messiah, who commented on another occasion that He had nowhere to lay His head, found refreshment in this home. The early Church recognized the importance of hospitality to assist the spread of the Gospel, in the same way that Jesus appreciated its value in the hour of His destiny.

Request for instruction in praying
Luke 11:1-13 (Matthew 6:9-13; 7:7-11)

Luke records more on prayer than the other gospel writers do. He frequently mentions the prayer habits of Jesus. He notes that Jesus prayed before all the major crises. Prayer was crucial in the life of the Messiah. Luke, moreover, mentions the disciples' request, "Lord, teach us to pray, as John taught his disciples." The disciples were conscious of their need. They had watched their Master and wondered at the ease with which He communed with His Father, but it did not come easily to them. John's disciples had obtained instruction from their leader, although there is no knowing what form this took. It was enough incentive for the disciples of Jesus to request similar help from their Master.

He acknowledged the usefulness of a set form of prayer. Why was this necessary? Why did not Jesus use a psalm, or take over the same forms that John had taught his followers? Moreover, Judaism had its set forms as in the Eighteen Benedictions, which may have been in existence in the time of Jesus. The disciples seemed to expect the Messiah to teach them new ways of prayer. The answer of Jesus came in the form of what is generally known as "The Lord's Prayer," but which should more correctly be called "The Disciples' Prayer." Matthew has the same prayer in a longer form, but he included it in the Sermon on the Mount. There is no reason to think that Jesus did not repeat it several times, in which case there would be no problem about its appearance in different contexts. Many have discussed whether Matthew's or Luke's version is the original one, and many prefer to think that Matthew has enlarged Luke's version. It is by no means certain that one was indebted to the other for his material, or that both were using a common source. If the prayer was repeated, it is easy to see how some hearers would recall a shortened version. Luke has "Father" in place of Matthew's "Our Father who art in heaven." Matthew's third statement, "Thy will be done on earth as it is in heaven" is also omitted, as are the concluding words beginning with "Deliver us from evil." Moreover, where Matthew has "debts," Luke has "sins." The gist, however, of the two prayers is the same.

Jesus intended the prayer to be a pattern for the disciples rather than a liturgical recitation. The principle of approach to God that it illustrates is more important than the form it takes. Each part could have been enlarged, but simplicity and conciseness were always major characteristics in the teaching of Jesus. Of greatest importance is the address to God as "Father." This follows Jesus' own practice. The form "Abba" that He used was preserved in the early Church, as is shown by several instances where it was preserved together with the Greek translation, *Pater*. This approach to God marked a real advance, for the Messiah was teaching men to think of God no longer as a tyrant or as an unapproachable monarch, but as a Father — an analogy to the most intimate and familiar of human relationships. The prayer in Luke's form concentrates on man's right relationship to God.

Other teaching about prayer was given by Jesus. He told a story of a traveler arriving unexpectedly at his friend's house at midnight. The friend was put in an embarrassing position because he had no reserve of food. His only course of action was to awaken a neighbor to borrow some loaves of bread. The neighbor's reaction was not unreasonable. He did not want to be bothered, especially as it would disturb the whole household. His displeasure is understandable, for the request could strain even the strongest friendship. The man outside, however, had no other course but to continue to plead for food. His persistence made the neighbor change his mind. The application of the story was left to the hearers. They would note that prayer was not an insistence on rights — as if a man could demand anything of God, nor was it a matter of relationship — for even a close friend will draw the line somewhere. It was essentially a matter of need. God responds not to man's status but to his state of need. As creatures, men must approach the Creator with a sense of inadequacy. Such an approach sharply contrasted with the contemporary Jewish approach to God with its constant stress on human achievement.

The invitations, "Ask, seek, knock" with their corresponding promises, are other words that Jesus must have often repeated. He pointed out that as human fathers would not deceive their children but would give them good things, so, infinitely more, the heavenly Father would give good things to His children. In Luke's record, Jesus summed up the good things as being that gift which is the Holy Spirit. Luke, in the course of his narrative, several times mentions the activity of the Holy Spirit in the life of Jesus. The same gift was available for all His followers.

A story about the folly of wealth

Luke 12:13-21

A misguided person who was having a dispute with his brother over sharing the inheritance came to Jesus for help, as a client appealing to a solicitor, but he soon realized that he had come to the wrong person.

Jesus quickly reminded the man that He was no legal umpire. His mission did not include arbitrating over disputed legacies. Quarrels over material things were outside His purpose, for life was bigger than that. The man was typical of those who live only for what they possess or would like to possess — homes, cars, purchasing power. The wealthy find it hard to bow to a Messiah who reminds them that man's life does not consist in the abundance of possessions. For many, however, it is sadly true that life consists of nothing else.

Jesus told a story of a prosperous farmer. Success came and storage problems arose. The old barns bulged. The astute farmer decided to build new barns. It was not foolish of him to prevent his crops from spoiling. His fault lay in his motives. The man was more than shrewd — he was selfishly complacent.

He said to himself, "Soul, you have ample goods laid up for many years; take your ease, eat, drink, be merry." He never thought to use his possessions for the benefit of others. His concern was wholly for himself. Furthermore, he made plans as if he was able to decide his own destiny. Covetousness led to conceit. He recognized no power other than his own. He thought himself wholly self-sufficient.

There is a striking contrast in the story. The man addressed himself as "Soul," but God called him "Fool." He thought himself wise, but God showed how hollow his wisdom was. His calculations were all wrong. His destiny was in the hands of Another, to whom his riches were of no account. The man was after all a spiritual pauper. The nemesis came quickly, with no time for redress. The same night that his plans were conceived, he died.

Man's love of possessions can be so strong that nothing less than the power of God can take it away. Jesus brought out an astonishing antithesis. Anyone wanting treasure for himself is "not rich" toward God. Man was meant to be rich toward God. Jesus did not imply that His followers should have no possessions; this was not the point of the story. Rather, He was talking about the "abundance of possessions," the amassing of wealth for its own sake. No one who succumbed to such a practice could be His follower.

If men had taken seriously the attitude of Jesus toward amassing wealth, gross inequality could have been avoided. Covetousness, however, is not solely the sin of the rich. Materialism has pervaded society to such an extent that it has become a god for many people in all segments of society.

Another feature of the story is significant. The farmer may have worked hard for his harvest, but he was responsible for only part of it. God had given the increase, but apparently he made no acknowledgment of this fact. In other spheres God blesses the labors of a man, but all too often the creature thinks himself as much a god as his Creator. He, too, fully merits the title, "Fool."

Watchfulness and loyalty

Luke 12:35-48 (cf. Matthew 24:43-51)

Jesus challenged His followers to be ready for immediate action. This naturally imposed restrictions upon them. They could not please themselves and at the same time be constantly ready for the Master's command. Such readiness was inconsistent with indolence or with engaging in business other than the Master's. The stringency of the Messiah's demands could not be watered down. There was no place for halfheartedness. It must be all or nothing.

The service of Christ involves unknown quantities. The biggest unknown is the time of His return. Jesus several times mentioned this and clearly considered it important to alert His disciples to the unexpected character of His coming. A night watchman is of no use if he stays awake for only the first half of the night. He must be alert the whole time. The faithful man is the happiest, for he is ready for the Messiah's return. He will not need to be awakened. The Messiah's followers were so to live that they would be prepared for His Second Coming at any time. In view of that coming, what manner of men ought they to be?

To illustrate this urgency, Jesus used another simile. No householder would go to sleep if he knew that a thief was coming. He would be prepared, but a thief would never announce his plans in advance. The coming of a thief illustrated the unexpectedness of the Messiah's movements. Why should there be such secrecy? Why could not Jesus have explained His plans so that everyone could be prepared? The answer is twofold. Jesus once said that even He did not know the time of His Second Coming. Only the Father knew. The second consideration is more important for Jesus' followers. The mission of Jesus was so taxing that only those whose loyalty would never flag, whose self-interests would never supplant His service, and who would live in constant expectancy, could measure up to His demands. The service of Jesus the Messiah was never portrayed as a soft option, but as the sternest task that any man could undertake.

It was not surprising that Peter, after listening to this, wanted to know whether it applied only to their small group of disciples or to everybody. It was a good question. The teaching of Jesus was designed to challenge men to inquire whether it applied to them alone or to others as well. The answer was given by another parable — that of a steward whose responsibility was to look after the welfare of the other servants. If he was doing this when the master returned from an extended journey, the steward would be held in higher esteem and would be entrusted with even greater responsibility. It was good common sense for the steward to see that he did his job well. The same attitude should mark the servants of the Messiah who share responsibility in His mission. Leadership demands even more rigorous loyalty than humbler service.

The steward who acted irresponsibly by beating the servants because he thought that his master would be delayed in his return is a solemn warning. Jesus applied it in two ways — to those who do wrong acts deliberately against the Master's will and to those who contravene His will inadvertently. The degrees of punishment to which Jesus referred would fit the offenses. The whole teaching is summed up by the statement that much will be required from those to whom much is given. Increasing responsibility brings with it increased demands. To lead others astray is more serious than to stray alone. Leaders are not only answerable for themselves, but for those whom they lead.

15

More Teaching and Healing

The relevance of repentance

Luke 13:1-9

Jesus had begun His preaching with the theme of repentance. With the same theme John the Baptist's preaching had prepared the way. The need for repentance was stressed more than once in the ministry of Jesus. His mission was based on right relationships; wrong relationships — especially man's relationship with God — must be made right before men could engage in that mission.

Some people reminded Jesus of certain atrocities committed by Pilate, the Roman governor. Pilate is renowned in history as the judge who condemned the only completely righteous man who ever lived. Pilate, who was no lover of the Jewish people, was abruptly removed from office because he had alienated himself from the Jews.

The informants on this occasion probably expected Jesus to blaze with anger against the governor's infamous action in mixing some Galileans' blood with their sacrifices. Jesus, however, did not react with anger. He would not give vent to indignation when He himself stood before the governor on trial for His life. He was concerned with the moral problem — not of Pilate, but of the Galileans. There were those present who treated adversities as an indication of the displeasure of God against the individuals who suffered. Whenever men are faced with calamities, they tend to ask why God has allowed these to happen. Although there are times when calamities are the direct result of man's folly, there are many occasions when this is not so.

The problem of suffering is as old as man. That the contemporaries of Jesus were perplexed because a few Galileans were made to suffer more than the rest is understandable. The same perplexity arises in any age and place where tyrants oppress. Jesus anticipated the problem. He was emphatic that in this instance, the suffering was not related to the Galileans' guilt, but He did not pursue the discussion. His mind was on His own mission, which was affected by the attitude of the nation as a whole. Jesus would not countenance a discussion of the guilt of others unless men also faced the problem of their own guilt. He knew the whole nation would perish if it did not repent. To illustrate His point Jesus cited the calamity in Jerusalem when the tower of Siloam fell, killing eighteen people. This contrasted with the Pilate incident in that the blame could not as easily be laid on individuals. In both cases, Jesus gave the same challenge to His hearers — "Repent."

The Messiah had come, but He found no fruits of repentance among His own people. Jesus explained the problem in picture form. A vineyard owner went on an inspection tour of the vineyard with his manager. He noted a fruitless fig tree and remembered that this was the third year that it had borne no fruit. In some settings it might have been regarded as worth retaining for ornamental purposes. The Jewish vineyard owner, however, had a pragmatic approach to trees. A tree producing no fruit was fit only to be cut down, for it was using good soil to no purpose. Jesus used this as a parable of the Jewish people. Throughout His ministry He had looked for fruit but had found none. Common sense suggested that the nation be cut off. This did happen, forty years later, at the hands of Roman forces. Those able to discern saw it as the judgment of God.

The main point of the parable is its conclusion. The manager advised delay in the hope that with proper treatment the tree might produce fruit the following year. This symbolized the forbearance of God toward the rebellious people of Israel. There was still a brief time remaining, during which the Messiah would work among them and teach them the true ways of God. Before judgment came, however, they filled the cup of wrath to overflowing by crucifying their Messiah. Even after that, the cutting down was delayed for many years. God is sovereign, and He holds the right and power to decide when judgment will come. This is a challenge to any nation at any time. None is exempt. Where righteousness and justice are at a premium and men make unholy practices their norm, that nation is in peril.

"And he told this parable: 'A man had a fig tree planted in his vineyard . . .'"
—LUKE 13:6

A fig tree bearing early green figs. These spring figs normally indicate that the tree will bear the later, edible fruit of the summer crop.

The healing of a bent woman

Luke 13:10-17

Whenever Jesus saw those with twisted bodies or distraught minds His compassion was stirred. Luke relates a case when Jesus took the initiative. Teaching in a synagogue, and facing the audience, He saw a woman in the gallery unable to straighten herself. She had "a spirit of infirmity," by which Luke probably meant that a spirit had caused her infirmity. Although Luke was a physician, he did not attribute the illness to physical causes, but to spiritual. Modern medical practice might diagnose the complaint differently, although spiritual causes are factors in more illnesses and infirmities than many would admit. Luke told the story, however, to illustrate the weakness of legalism in its approach to human problems.

Jesus called the woman, laid His hands on her, and at once she was made straight. Following so notable a cure, it might be expected that the whole synagogue audience would have rejoiced — but official legalism stepped in. Jesus had committed a technical breach, which caused the synagogue ruler, with the enthusiasm of a demagogue, to become indignant. To heal on the Sabbath was taboo except where life was endangered. To officialdom, rules can become more important than people. The extension of the woman's misery for another day was less important than the keeping of the Sabbath. Enthusiasm for the law is admirable, but when religious observance becomes more important than human needs, decay has set in. Jesus did not advocate slavish devotion to legalism. If most Christians had always followed Him in this, much of the tragic acrimony in church history would have been avoided. Cherished forms, liturgies, and church order need re-examination so that we may discover whether or not, in our enthusiasm to retain them, we are preventing "bent" lives from becoming straightened.

At times, Jesus spoke with incredible bluntness, as He did on this occasion. He addressed His remarks not only to the ruler but to all who shared the ruler's point of view. He called them "hypocrites," a word that literally means "play-actors" — those who pretend to be what they are not. The legalists were pretending concern about the Sabbath, but they were nevertheless inconsistent. Everyone knew that the most ardent legalist would work on the Sabbath to preserve the life of one of his animals. Such a man surely had no right to object to the healing of a human being.

Man is strangely inconsistent about religious matters. He will demand of others what he is not prepared to demand of himself. He will draw arbitrary distinctions without recognizing that they spring from self-interest. Even the care of animals can be rated higher than the welfare of people, without the inconsistency being noted — especially when the animals are one's own and the people are not. The approach of Jesus is profoundly disquieting because it is transparently consistent. The synagogue ruler would have been a better man if he had seen his own attitude in truer perspective. He might have been criticized if he had made no protest, but that would have been a small matter, for he had witnessed the shattering of one of Satan's chains. Perhaps some glimpse of truth dawned on him as he and others suffered the sharp rebuke of Jesus. The common people, less bound by convention, rejoiced over all that Jesus did. It is not infrequent for common people to see more clearly than their leaders.

Dining out with the Pharisees

Luke 14:1-14

Some Pharisees had a secret regard for Jesus. Luke records more than one occasion when one of them offered Jesus hospitality. Although Jesus was aware of the hostility, He did not refuse such invitations. He loved the company of men, even that of the misguided who opposed His mission. One Sabbath, He was a guest in the home of a Pharisee who was the ruler of a synagogue. In all probability Jesus had been to the synagogue to worship. The gesture seemed friendly, but the account suggests that this Pharisee had ulterior motives.

Among the lawyers and other Pharisees who had been invited as guests was a man diseased with dropsy. He may have come uninvited in the hope of finding healing at the hands of Jesus, or, more likely, he may have been brought in by one of the guests — or planted by the host — to provide a trap for Jesus. If this was a device, Jesus saw through it and answered their unuttered thoughts, "Is it lawful to heal on the Sabbath, or not?" He stole His critics' thunder, for no one had an answer. This disappointed those who had attended the banquet for the purpose of criticizing Jesus. Why were they unwilling to answer? They would certainly have objected if the healing had been performed first. Why not now? They probably feared that some challenging word of Jesus would show them up. Jesus did challenge them further by asking a more specific question, "Which of you, having an ass or an ox that has fallen into a well, will not immediately pull him out on a Sabbath day?" The comparison was obvious. The poor fellow with dropsy deserved better treatment than the domestic animals.

Jesus rather than the host commanded the situation. He led the table talk by telling a particularly candid parable. He had noted the scramble for the places of honor, and He was constrained to give nobler advice. He urged the need for humility, a quality never abundant, particularly among the Pharisees. Most honest men would admit to a good dose of self-esteem. It does not come naturally to think others better than oneself. The higher positions look the most inviting. Two of the closest disciples of Jesus — James and John — had learned so little of the spirit of their Master that they desired to sit on each side of Him in His kingdom. The teaching of the parable was for all men, not simply for the Pharisees. Jesus needed for His mission men who would choose the lower seats until the host should bid them take the higher. It is the humble who attract and the self-important who repel. Jesus had once again taught that the meek inherit the earth.

After this challenge to the guests, Jesus did not spare the host. The feast was a status symbol. The guests did not need the host's generosity, for they were in positions to put on banquets of their own. Jesus challenged His host to invite the poor and the physically handicapped instead. It was a disquieting challenge for the host. He was horrified at the thought of sharing his table with the poor and the incapacitated. One case of dropsy was enough. His notion of fellowship was table talk with his Pharisaic colleagues. He would have little to share with the lower classes. The challenge, however, is still necessary for all who share the Pharisaic spirit. The most blessed are those who are a blessing to others less fortunate, provided they have a genuine desire to share with them. Many of the disciples of Jesus still need to overcome class barriers. In this case, the host was assured of a reward at the resurrection of the just if he followed this social program of Jesus.

The parable of the great banquet

Luke 14:15-24

The table talk continued. Jesus' mention of the resurrection of the just set one of the guests thinking about the Kingdom of God. It was widely believed that the messianic age would be introduced by a great banquet. All true Israelites cherished the hope of sitting at the table with the Messiah. The guest in question may have been embarrassed at Jesus' remarks to the host and decided to turn the conversation to more speculative issues. He declared a platitude about the blessedness of those who would participate in the Kingdom banquet. His manner suggested complacency about his own part in the banquet, for he was oblivious to the fact that at that very time he was dining with the Messiah. Such smugness required correction, and provided the setting for another parable of Jesus.

This story concerned invited guests who made excuses. None of those originally invited attended the feast, which left the host in a dilemma. The story was intended to shake the complacency of Jesus' fellow guests. The Pharisees were convinced that they would be the main guests at the messianic banquet. In the parable, the servant sent to call the guests was met with three main apologies for absence: the first concerned real estate; the second, possessions; the third, matrimony. Although the arguments were specious, they did not ring true. They were typical of the attitude of many to the Messiah's claims. The folly of those who bought either land or oxen without examining them is apparent, yet some were quoting this as a reason for not attending the banquet. If the deals were already complete, a slight delay would not be serious. No doubt Jesus intentionally made the excuses sound hollow to focus on the need for examining any excuse for evading the challenge of the Kingdom. The third man was more blunt. He had married a wife, and he declined to go without even offering an apology. Would a wife keep him from all his obligations?

Too often, domestic affairs have kept would-be followers from the fellowship of the Kingdom. The point of the story is clear; no excuses are good enough. The Messiah demands complete commitment.

The second part of the story reveals a rejection of current ideas about the messianic banquet and the substitution of a revolutionary concept. The host's anger on hearing the lame excuses of the guests symbolizes this rejection. The Messiah's Kingdom was not to be tied to the existing social structure. A radical change was needed. New invitations were sent into two areas — urban and rural. There is no significance in the fact that they were sent in that order. The importance lies in the type of people who were invited to attend. They were the social misfits, the same class of people whom Jesus had already urged his host to invite — the poor, maimed, blind, and lame. All these represented people with a sense of need, as contrasted with the self-satisfied Pharisees. Jesus dealt ruthlessly with complacency. The thought of the Messiah's banquet graced by the poor and infirm is disturbing for the tidy-minded. The Pharisaic method was based on conformity to a recognized religious pattern, but Jesus' approach made havoc of this. In his story, the people who finally shared the banquet were those who never expected to do so, but who were nevertheless prepared to accept the gracious invitation. The Kingdom of God requires a personal decision.

Still another lesson is to be learned from the parable, viz. the place of constraint in the mission of Jesus. The host first sent his servants to bring people in, and when there was still more room, the servants were sent to compel still others to come. The servants did not have to convince those wandering the streets or taking shelter by hedges that they had a need, but the needy were unaware of the promise of a good meal. The servants were prepared for some reluctance — the kind of reluctance or hesitation by those who are faced with something too good to be true. Strong persuasion was required. Jesus, however, was not suggesting violent measures. No one has truly responded to the Gospel under duress. Nonetheless, those most conscious of their need will not necessarily respond at once. The servants of the Gospel must be prepared to persuade men of the genuineness of the invitation extended to them.

A similar story is set in a different setting in Matthew. Many scholars regard the two stories as two versions of one incident, but the differences are so great that it is more reasonable to suppose that the stories were told on separate occasions. Because of the wide use of banquet imagery at that time in descriptions of the age of Messiah, it is to be expected that Jesus frequently repeated similar stories about banquets.

Two parables of searching and finding
Luke 15:1-10 (Matthew 18:12-14)

The Messiah was an enigma to the Pharisees, but not simply because He was unorthodox. The major problem was His attitude toward the common people. Whereas the Pharisees regarded them as distinctly inferior, Jesus never did. In fact, He was more in their company than with those whom the Pharisees considered to be the cream of society. They seemed incapable of imagining that any of the common people could inherit the Kingdom of God. They conceded that such people should repent, but not for this purpose. Jesus dealt with this fundamental mistake in the Pharisees' approach by three parables: the first two focus on searching; the third, on restoring. They all concern lost things or lost people.

The Pharisees extended their contempt for the common people to anyone who associated with them. They therefore regarded Jesus on a level with the tax collectors and sinners because of His dealings with them. Jesus' first story reveals His deep compassion. It is the story of a straying sheep. Most shepherds would know what to do when a sheep strayed. They would not lightly write off the straying sheep as a loss, although it represented no more than 1 percent of the flock. Those who had true shepherd hearts would not argue that time would be better spent with the ninety-nine. Such shepherds would endure many hazards to find the lost sheep, and would treat it with great care and tenderness when they found it. Their reward would be the joy of finding and restoring, and of sharing their joy with neighbors.

Jesus Himself applied the parable. The shepherd's joy symbolized the joy of God over one repentant sinner. He implied that the Pharisees, for all their religious observances and their claims to superior righteousness, never brought joy to God. The challenge is for all time. Religious leadership that has no time for sinful men is out of touch with God. This story describes the mission of Jesus well. He claimed to be the Good Shepherd, the perfect pattern for all shepherding. He later taught men another truth — He would lay down His life for the sheep.

A similar story is that of the lost coin. It was a silver coin, which represented 10 percent of a woman's wealth. She had lost it but knew that it was somewhere in her house. She swept the house thoroughly until she found the coin. The joy of finding and the desire to share that joy is again emphasized. This parable, like the other, illustrates the heavenly Father's joy in receiving back a repentant sinner. The searching illustrates the determination of the Messiah to pursue His mission.

The spirit of the two parables strongly contrasts with the Pharisaic approach — and of any approach where religious profession shows no compassion. By word pictures, Jesus laid bare His own heart. The Pharisees never plumbed the depths of His compassion. They never understood the true nature of repentance because they never saw themselves as sinners. No wonder Jesus remained an enigma to them.

The prodigal son

Luke 15:11-32

The third parable of the trio is more personal. The story's main point is not the lostness but the restoration; not the folly of a runaway son, but the love of a father who received him back. It cannot be understood apart from its setting. The murmuring Pharisees are the occasion for the story.

The son had a right to a share of his father's inheritance. However, he requested to have it before his father's death. The meaning of the parable, however, is not centered in the reason for the request, nor in the father's granting the request, nor even in the son's decision to leave home, but in the father's forgiveness.

The foolishness of the son draws attention to his desperate need. Because he spent all his money, he became victim to the severe famine that afflicted the country to which he had gone.

The famine was a natural calamity, but Jesus made it clear that the son's plight was his own fault. His situation was so desperate that only a swinekeeper would employ him, in work which was anathema to any self-respecting Jew. He was not even offered the carob pods that the swine ate. The contrast of this treatment to the way his father treated his employees struck home. He would be better off sharing their lot. His resolve to return was conditioned by what he knew of his father's character.

The Pharisees would have condemned the sinfulness of the son, but Jesus included no such condemnation in His story. When the focus shifted from the son to the father, the contrast with the Pharisaic spirit became increasingly evident. The father waited for the son and rushed to meet him. In the reconciliation, the father took the initiative. The son had prepared a speech of humiliation, but he never completed the delivery of it. He got as far as confessing his wrong and his utter unworthiness of sonship, but the father's action forestalled his request to become a hired servant. The father treated him as a son. He commanded the servants to fetch the robe, which at once showed the son's status, together with the signet ring and other clothing. Also, festivities were ordered. Apparently, the father had reserved a special fattened calf for such an occasion. No word of rebuke passed the father's lips. There was only the joy of restoration, undoubtedly the whole point of the story. The Pharisees might murmur over Jesus, but the God of Jesus is a God of joy.

With the Pharisees still in mind, Jesus introduced another character into the story. With a few descriptive words, He made the elder brother come alive as a vivid symbol of the Pharisees. This brother not only had a poor opinion of the younger brother, but he also could rationally justify his opinion. The ne'er-do-well had disgraced the family. He was a discredit to a good father. The elder brother felt righteous indignation over the festivities, which in his view were thoroughly undeserved. This approach typified the Pharisees' attitude toward tax collectors and sinners. They could see no reason to rejoice when such men turned back to God in repentance.

A touching aspect of this story is the father's leaving the feast to plead with his elder son. Again, the character of love is demonstrated. Nonetheless, the resentment of the elder son was too bitter to soften under the father's entreaties. No festivities had ever been arranged for him. On the surface his reaction seems justified. The father pointed out, however, that there was nothing that he could not share, and the brother's return had not imperiled this. The Pharisees had a wrong view of God if they thought that He was or should be unwilling to forgive sinners. They were sincere in thinking that they were upholding His honor, but they had not caught the message of His love. They could hardly have missed the point of the parable.

Although this parable reveals the pleasure of God in a sinner's restoration, no doctrine of reconciliation can be built on this teaching alone. At the heart of the Gospel is the love of God, but this cannot be divorced from the demands of God. In the context of the parable, it was necessary to bring out the aspect of God's character that was most obscured by Pharisaic teaching, i.e., His love.

The sacred and the secular

Luke 16:1-13

The parable of the prodigal son is silent on the attitude of Jesus toward the wasting of material possessions. Because the parable was aimed at the Pharisees, however, no comment was made to condemn the younger son's action, although his wretchedness was sufficient evidence of the disastrous consequence of such waste. Jesus next turned His attention, through another parable, to the problem of secular affairs, or as He called it — "unrighteous mammon." This was addressed to the disciples who had already committed themselves in allegiance to Him. It must be interpreted in that context.

The parable is followed by a passage that draws out its meaning, which is invaluable for understanding some aspects that would otherwise be difficult. Three characters are in the story — a rich man, his business manager, and his debtors. The manager did what the prodigal had done, i.e., he wasted money. In the one parable it was the father's possessions; in this the master's. It is easier to waste other people's belongings than one's own. The rich man believed that the reports he had received of his manager's irresponsibility were true, for he dismissed him without receiving an account from the man himself. The manager, since he could see no hope of reinstatement, turned his attention to his future prospects. He planned to give massive discounts to his master's debtors to win their support when he was out of a job. One man was given a 50 percent discount; another, 20 percent. On hearing of the action, the master commended the man's shrewdness, although he recognized its unjustness. It was a worldly-wise thing to do. If this world's concerns are all that matters, it would be foolish not to make the most of all opportunities. The followers of Jesus, whom He called "children of light," are not as "wise" as this, i.e., in the sense in which a materialist counts wisdom.

In considering the saying that concludes the parable, which many label enigmatic and difficult, it must be noted that the point of the story is not the ethics of the man's action, but rather, his prudence. This throws light on the saying, "Make friends for yourselves by means of unrighteous mammon, so that when it fails they may receive you into the eternal habitations." By "unrighteous mammon," Jesus apparently meant not merely money, but the whole way of life dominated by money. This was the world in which His followers were living, and they could not be free of it. They were, however, heirs of another kind of existence, which would not be dominated by mammon. Jesus intended His followers to imitate not the unrighteous action of the manager, but rather, his shrewdness in dealing with the affairs of this world. By this means, mammon can become a friend rather than an enemy, as it had been to the prodigal son. There is an intentional contrast in the parable between "eternal dwellings" and temporary reception into houses. Jesus was saying in effect, "Why not use the same quality of wisdom to secure what is infinitely more durable than the manager's attainment?"

The application throws light on the parable. The quality of service can be gauged as much in small things as in large. What a man does in insignificant issues determines what he does in matters of great responsibility. Jesus applied the principle to unrighteous mammon. If His followers did not show fidelity in handling the affairs of a world ruled by unrighteous principles, neither would they handle aright true riches. Jesus was speaking of the relation between the sacred and secular. Men of this world are dominated by the secular. The Christian's attitude toward the secular reflects his attitude to the sacred. No one can serve two opposing principles at the same time. He cannot fully devote himself to both God and mammon. Most ignore the first and serve only the second, but the followers of Jesus would have to learn to serve God even when dealing with the secular. Money is to be no more than a servant and never an overlord. Many rich men are spiritual paupers because they think more of money than they do of God. It is not, however, only the rich who are so affected. The people whose one ambition is to emulate the rich are in no better state. Their life is equally devoted to mammon — both in ambition and in their resentment of others' wealth. This teaching of Jesus is of fundamental importance, for it balances the sacred and the secular.

16

Duty, Gratitude, and Prayer

The abuse of wealth

Luke 16:14-31

The Pharisees, overhearing Jesus advising His disciples to serve God rather than mammon, scoffed at Him. Luke comments that this was because they were lovers of money. Some modern Jewish writers deny that the Pharisees were covetous and claim that almsgiving was one of their most noted characteristics. Luke's comment, however, agrees with the fact that Pharisees saw no conflict in serving both God and mammon. Jesus first challenged their approach to the service of God. They justified themselves on their pious devotion to the Law and the prophets. They should have left the justification to God, who judges motives rather than actions. They had overlooked that the Gospel of the Kingdom had now been preached and many were entering, although in a manner regarded by the Pharisees as "violent." That social and religious outcasts were becoming disciples of Jesus contradicted their established ideas of the coming Kingdom. Moreover, Jesus pointed out that the Pharisees' attitude toward divorce was an example of how they were not fulfilling the Law of Moses. This dialogue formed the setting for the parable of the rich man and Lazarus.

This story highlights the vast differences in the social and economic position of two men in this life and the complete reversal of their positions in the afterlife. The character of each man is vividly sketched. The rich man dressed extravagantly, and he dined sumptuously every day. He used his wealth mainly on himself. The poor man is presented in a grossly wretched condition. Without possessions, he could only sit begging at the rich man's gate. He was too weak to drive away the scavenger dogs that came to lick sores that covered his body. No contrast between two men could be greater.

The parable next describes the same two men in the afterlife, where again the contrast is marked. Lazarus, the poor man, is in Abraham's bosom, a typical Jewish picture of blessedness. The rich man, however, is in Hades, tormented by fire — a traditional picture of punishment. A dialogue begins between the rich man and Abraham. The rich man is aware of the disparity between himself and Lazarus and requests Lazarus' services to sooth his present position. The request is modest and receives from Abraham a comment tinged with some compassion. This part of the parable has caused perplexity to some, as if Jesus were presenting the view that the afterlife would be a reversal of the present state of affairs irrespective of moral responsibilities. Was the rich man's anguish because of his riches and the poor man's blessedness the result of his poverty? Such an interpretation is alien to the real meaning of the parable. It was not his riches but his love of riches that caused the rich man's distress. Moreover, Abraham pointed to the gulf between him and Lazarus; what the rich man was asking was impossible. As a result he made another request — that Lazarus be sent to warn his five brothers. This led to the climax and interpretation of the story.

Abraham's answer to the rich man's second request would have pleased the Pharisees. "They have Moses and the prophets; let them hear them." The rich man had been so devoted to serving mammon that he had had no time to listen to Moses or the prophets. His answer contains an admission that his brothers were not likely to listen to Moses and the prophets unless something extraordinary happened. He was wrong, however, in thinking that repentance could be induced by extraordinary means. Later, when another Lazarus was actually raised from the dead it was not long before some men plotted to kill him. The extraordinary event had hardened rather than softened them. If men ignore the revelation of God already provided for them in the Scriptures, how can they expect to respond to other means?

The story shows the sympathy of Jesus for the downtrodden. It also shows that His Kingdom is based on higher riches than material wealth. It shows moreover that He regarded the Law and prophets as a sufficient guide to repentance. It further shows that He could cast His teaching in traditional Jewish molds, although always with elements that mark its uniqueness. It would be a mistake to build a theology of the afterlife on the teaching of this parable. On the other hand, the force of the parable would be considerably weakened if the imagery bore no relation to the facts. Jesus implied that in the hereafter man will have self-consciousness and an awareness of others, and that destiny is tied up with attitudes and actions in this life. The servants of mammon cannot expect any place in the Kingdom of God.

Jesus' view of duty

Luke 17:5-10

Luke includes a parabolic saying that reflects Jesus' high view of service. He placed it after another saying of Jesus that seems to have been used on several occasions to illustrate faith. The power of faith was so great that a small amount of it, like a tiny seed, could accomplish such feats as casting a tree into the sea at a word of command. Such powerful faith involved responsibility. Some would be puffed up at the thought. The faith that Jesus was talking about was not the sort to create arrogant supermen, but rather, men with a deep devotion to their Master's service.

Jesus continued with an illustration from contemporary life. A farmer employed just one servant, who served as plowman, shepherd, cook, and butler. His terms of service were clear. No trade union restricted him to one trade. He could not, however, devote himself exclusively either to outside or to inside work. His responsibilities lay in both. Consequently, the master will not invite the servant to share his table when only half his job was done. The servant had no right to expect relaxation until everything was finished. When preparing the meal and serving at table, he was not doing the master a favor, but simply fulfilling his contract. He would not expect the master to give him any special thanks, for he had done nothing beyond his duty.

Jesus himself applied the moral to His disciples. They were to regard themselves as servants under contract. Their attitude must be one of humility. They must not overevaluate their own contribution. This teaching was highly demanding. It assumed that the disciples had no rights of their own, a view that shatters the plans of all self-seekers in the Kingdom. Members are expected to acknowledge, "We are unworthy servants; we have only done what was our duty." Duty is a sacred trust. This teaching as a pattern for modern industrial relations would be regarded as reactionary. Jesus, however, was not addressing Himself to industry, nor was He declaring a political manifesto. He was not laying down general principles of master-servant relationships. He was taking an illustration from contemporary life and using it to describe relationships in His Kingdom. The Messiah never intended men to glory in their own achievements. He wanted men who were more aware of their own unworthiness; men content to put duty before personal convenience.

An outsider's gratitude

Luke 17:11-19

At this point in his account, Luke introduces another geographical note — that Jesus was moving toward Jerusalem. The next incident occurred somewhere between Samaria and Galilee. Some have been puzzled by the fact that Luke mentions the areas in that order — as if Jesus was traveling away from instead of toward Jerusalem. Luke was less concerned about this than his critics are. He meant to show that Jesus was traveling eastward along the border. The proximity to Samaria explains why a Samaritan was among a group of nine Jewish lepers who met Jesus in the next village.

Jesus had encountered leprosy before. It was widespread, always with the same dread isolation, the same symptoms of loathesomeness and despair. Other men gave lepers a wide berth. Risk of contamination overrode whatever stirrings of compassion they might have felt. Nothing, however, could override the Messiah's compassion. He was prepared to face any human problem, however desperate. Moreover, the lepers themselves expected Him to do something. They shouted their request, "Jesus, Master, have mercy on us." By using the title "Master," were they professing to be disciples of Jesus, or were they driven by their desperate condition to own Him as Master? At least they possessed some faith, as the sequel shows.

How could ten men be brought to the same degree of faith at the same time? Some find this difficult, but weight must be given to their existence as a small, close-knit community. They shared a common misfortune, and it is not impossible that common despair drove them corporately to the same hope that Jesus could do something for them. When He told them to go and report to the priests, an act which required a considerable degree of faith, none of them hesitated. They well might have argued that there was no point in going since the evidence of their leprosy was still apparent, but they responded to Jesus' command. He might have healed them instantaneously with a word or a touch, as He did others on other occasions. But He evidently detected a real core of faith in them, which would be strengthened by the challenge to go.

Luke's interest in the story is not centered in the quality of their faith, but rather in its sequel. One of the ten men came back shouting praise to God. His action was symbolic of multitudes who would learn to praise God after being cleansed from the deeper leprosy of sin. The man fell at the feet of Jesus in sheer gratitude.

The thankfulness of this one man was heightened by the fact that he was a Samaritan. The nine who did not return were Jews. The contrast between the two racial groups in Luke's account is intentional. The Jews held contempt for the Samaritans' religion, and regarded their own as superior. These Jews, however, expressed no gratitude to Jesus. The incident vividly shows that the response to the challenge of Jesus transcends nationalism. A Samaritan praising God on account of a Jewish Messiah would not conform to Jewish expectations. The lone Samaritan acted individually. He was unafraid to go against the erroneous majority opinion.

The closing words of Jesus to the Samaritan sums up His approach to His mission. It is faith that heals. All ten lepers had exercised faith and were healed. Nine had experienced the healing impact of the Messiah, but they missed the best through lack of gratitude. Sometimes it takes those who are *persona non grata* to shame men into giving thanks. True faith and thankfulness are never far apart.

The Kingdom and the Coming

Luke 17:20-37

Luke mentions sayings of Jesus about the end of the age, some of which also find a place in Matthew's record of Jesus' discourse on this subject. In all probability, Jesus frequently mentioned the Kingdom and the Coming. In Luke's presentation there is an obvious connection between the two ideas, and Jesus clarified some misunderstandings about both.

We have already seen that the concept of a coming Kingdom was not altogether foreign to Jewish thought, although it was tied up with political aspirations. When the Pharisees wanted to know when it was coming, Jesus said that its coming would not be accompanied by remarkable signs. He had more than once been asked for a sign, but had declined. His temptation in the wilderness had showed that the Kingdom could not be inaugurated by spectacular means. Its most remarkable feature was that it could not be observed as a spectacle. No one would be able to say, "Look, it is here," or "Look, it is over there." It had no geographical boundaries. Rather, it was a way of life. The Kingdom was the reign of the King; it was a rule, not a realm. Such teaching cut across current notions. It did not appeal to matter-of-fact minds. It was too intangible. If it could not be seen, where was it? The answer which Jesus gave sums up an important aspect of His Kingdom teaching.

"Behold, the kingdom of God is in the midst of you." The future has become present. The new age has already dawned. Jesus was identifying the Kingdom with Himself. Here and now He was making royal claims and exercising kingly rule. The difficulties of recognizing such kingship must be admitted. Those conditioned to expect a powerful political Messiah would never have guessed that Jesus, with his unorthodox and strangely spiritual teaching, could be the coming one. The gospels clearly show that men needed spiritual illumination to understand Jesus. The saying could be understood to mean "within you" instead of "in the midst of you," and if this is correct, it would be even more evident why no one could ever say, "Lo, here" or "Lo, there." The strongholds of the Kingdom were people, not places.

This was not the whole picture. Jesus gave His own disciples further teaching about future days, which He called "the days of the Son of man." He again warned against expecting signs. Moreover, the Coming in the future would be no more obvious than the present Kingdom. Jesus used vivid illustrations to press home this point. The Coming would be like lightning, sudden and difficult to track. Prior to the Coming, men will reject the Kingdom, but this is not to be wondered at. In both Noah's time and Lot's time, men were unprepared when destruction came upon them. The Coming will be so unexpected that people on housetops will have no time to come down. The Coming will furthermore make great distinctions between people. Among those working side by side, some will be prepared but others will not.

The perplexity that followed such teaching can easily be imagined. The teaching was essentially spiritual, for the focus was on spiritual preparation. Even the minds of the disciples were not conditioned for it until after Calvary, Easter, and Pentecost. At this time they could think only in spatial terms. They asked, "Where, Lord?" — as if to tie down the Coming to some location. They missed the point. Their lack of insight is excusable, but those who live on this side of the resurrection should know better the present reality of the Kingdom and should be more concerned about the spiritual challenge of the Coming.

Jesus answered their naive question in proverbial form. Every Palestinian knew that when an animal died, vultures would gather and swoop on the corpse. The vultures symbolized judgment, and the corpse, the corruption that deserves judgment. Therefore, where judgment was needed, it would come. This is the sterner side to the Messiah's teaching. Those who stress His mercy and love must not forget that He also prophesied doom. Judgment can no more be averted than vultures can be kept from carrion.

Persistent petitioning

Luke 18:1-8

Probably Luke intended a link between the statements about the coming of the Messiah and the following parable about a judge and a widow, for the parable ends on a note concerning the Coming. The theme of the parable, however, is persistence in prayer. The characters in the story are exaggerated. The judge was a rogue, a disgrace to any judiciary. The widow represented the weakest possible claimant for justice. The judge, unrestrained in his actions by any thought that he was answerable to God, acted as if God did not exist. Many honest people do not fear God, but in the Jewish setting, justice was inseparable from a due regard for the law of God. Moreover, this man cared nothing for public opinion. He was virtually a law to himself. The pivot of the story is his persistent refusal to hear the widow's claim against her accuser, and the widow's even more persistent pestering.

Why the judge declined to take the woman's case is not stated. The story implies that his action was blamable. He was acting in character, and he was labeled by Jesus as "unrighteous." The widow, through persistence, won out in the end. The judge gave in because he did not wish to be bothered any more. He was concerned, not for the law, but for himself. He even contemplated that the woman might become violent (as the word "wear me out" could be understood). He did the right thing finally, but from the wrong motive, and was therefore still unrighteous.

Jesus asked three questions. The first was, "Will not God vindicate his elect, who cry to Him day and night?" The implication is that if such a rascally human judge can do the right thing, how much more will a just God. It is an argument from the lesser to the greater. The unscrupulous man does not serve as an example for a holy God, but rather is presented as a point of comparison. The parable must not be allegorized. If an unholy man vindicates, there can be no question that a holy God will do so. Another problem arises. Did Jesus suggest that divine vindication hinges on persistence in prayer? The idea is unthinkable. Vindication comes from the character of God, and the practice of prayer is based on the certainty of this.

A second question was asked, "Will He delay long over them?" The word for "delay" means "to be patient with," and the question therefore appeals to what is known about God. Patience and longsuffering are qualities of God. Who are the objects of His patience? They could be either the elect making the appeal, or the enemies. The former is better since it raises the very relevant question of whether God will withhold His action for any length of time. Delay in God is difficult to understand, but His timing is perfect. Jesus taught that justice would be given and the righteous would be quickly vindicated, although no specific time is given.

The third question followed: "When the Son of man comes, will He find faith on earth?" This was not a note of despair, for the Messiah faced His passion with resolute determination; it cannot be supposed that He feared the failure of His mission. Rather, His question is a reminder that faith cannot be taken for granted, nor is it a commodity that can be stored. It is a living relationship. The Son of Man had already come and found so little faith. What faith existed all but disappeared in the hour of His agony. Would the same happen at the coming? Jesus enjoined His disciples to a prayerful persistence that would match the widow's desperate appeals.

Two sample prayers

Luke 18:9-14

The challenge of the saying about the Son of Man finding faith on the earth would have left unmoved those who formed a high estimate of their own merit, having always included themselves among the elect and excluded everyone else. This constant self-estimation leads men to create their own targets of righteousness. They saw to it that the target was within their own reach, even if it was beyond the reach of many others. Jesus had His own way to deal with this type of person. His parable of the tax collector and the Pharisee shows a complete reversal of man-made values.

The setting is the Temple, the house of prayer, where two men entered to pray. They represented two very different types, although they both came ostensibly to pray. Jesus exaggerated the contrast between the characters, because the Pharisees despised tax collectors. They regarded themselves as religiously far superior. This antagonism forms the background to the whole story.

The Pharisee at prayer was broadly typical of Pharisees generally, although it cannot be supposed that all would have prayed in so self-centered a way as this man. He began with thanksgiving, but he was thankful for his own superiority. His reference to other men was derogatory, but he chose the worst types with which to compare himself, extortioners, the unjust, or adulterers. He then became more personal, by claiming superiority over the tax collector who had entered the Temple with him. He also included in his prayer a list of his own achievements — tithing and fasting. He assumed that good works would earn him favor with God. This was the fundamental weakness of the Pharisees. It engendered pride, and it was alien to the spirit of Jesus. The Pharisee in the story did not really pray at all. He had merely "prayed . . . with himself."

The other man, although a member of a socially despised class, is portrayed as a pious man; his posture suggests this, as does the downward look of his eyes and his beating of his breast. These were signs of repentance. The brief prayer, "God be merciful to me a sinner," was a vivid contrast to the Pharisee's prayer. It had no vestige of self-righteousness, nor any list of human achievements — only a confession of need and an implied trust in the mercy of God.

The parable not only teaches the true basis of prayer. It was also designed to show the true nature of humility. Only the tax collector went away justified. Luke does not say how the Pharisees reacted to the parable. They could not have accepted the possibility that a good-for-nothing tax collector would be more acceptable to God than a scrupulously upright man who was a model of religious devotion. This truth was profoundly disturbing.

Reactions in Jerusalem

John 7:10-31

For the Feast of Tabernacles, Jews from the outlying districts flocked into Jerusalem. It was a particularly festive occasion. It not only marked the harvest, but it served as an impressive testimony to their faith in God in a pagan world. The movement of pilgrims into Jerusalem was massive. The majority lived for the duration of the feast in booths hastily constructed from tree branches and set up by the thousands in open spaces, in the streets, and even on the roofs of houses. This all served to remind the Jews of the wilderness years of their forefathers. Jesus Himself probably lived in such an improvised shelter while attending this feast.

The highlight of the Feast of Tabernacles was the ritual of illuminations. The Temple blazed with light to symbolize that God alone was the true source of light in a pagan world. The vast concourse of people in and around Jerusalem looked up toward the magnificent Temple buildings, floodlit in the glow of the Temple lights, and were reminded that their forefathers were led by a pillar of fire by night. They felt afresh that God was in the midst of His people. These noble reminders of Israel's heritage should have enabled the multitudes to be well-disposed to recognize the Messiah when He came to His Temple. John's gospel shows that the very opposite happened.

The brothers of Jesus arrived at the feast for the opening celebrations, but Jesus waited until the eight-day festivities were half over. During the first part of the feast many expected Him to be present, and His absence prompted gossip. People began asking, "Where is He?" The answers came in conflicting estimates. To some He was a good man; to others He was a deceiver. The basis of judgment was mainly subjective. The gossip was hushed, however, because reports were circulating that the leaders were hostile to Jesus.

As soon as Jesus arrived, He began to teach in the Temple, probably in the spacious colonnade known as Solomon's porch. He soon gathered an audience from among the Temple pilgrims. Many were struck by the fact that Jesus was not one of the authorized rabbis. He was a Galilean untrained in the rabbinical schools. He was a layman in matters of theology. In His case, however, these standards did not apply, for He taught not on the authority of the Jewish schools, nor on His own authority, but He claimed to speak from God. Those with spiritual discernment could not fail to detect His note of authority, but those who

From the Temple area, the
view southwest through
the Gate of the Chain.

*". . . Jesus went up into the temple and taught.
The Jews marveled at it, saying, 'How is it that this
man has learning, when he has never studied?'"*
— JOHN 7:14, 15

thought only in terms of official certification missed His divine
authorization.

Jesus recalled the controversy over the Sabbath which had
blazed up following the healing of the lame man. He knew some
wanted to kill Him. These same people were prepared to waive
the Sabbath rule to circumcise a man, for rabbinic teaching held
that a positive command took precedence over a negative one.
Why were they not prepared to place the positive action of healing a man on the same level as circumcision? The opponents of
Jesus were inconsistent, and their method of assessment was
faulty. The remarks of Jesus, however, so perplexed the crowd
that they concluded that He was possessed by a demon — another example of the often illogical character of public opinion.

Some people were also perplexed at the dilatoriness of the
authorities. If they wanted to kill Jesus, why not arrest Him?
One suggestion, clearly rejected as incredible, was that the authorities had changed their minds and accepted Jesus as the
Messiah. They knew too much about the humble origins of Jesus
to do that, although He plainly told them that He was sent

from God. Some saw the point and believed. They could not imagine that the Messiah could do greater things than Jesus was doing. In spite of the generally hostile atmosphere in Jerusalem, faith was not totally absent. As the lights of the feast shone out over the city and beyond, some pilgrims became human beacons by committing themselves to the mission of Jesus.

17

Teaching From Events

An attempted arrest and its results

John 7:32-52

The evangelist John, looking at the development of events in the lifetime of Jesus, detected two opposing forces. On one hand were the human designs to arrest Jesus, to remove a potential threat to the hierarchy. On the other hand was the divine timetable for the Messiah's mission. John terms the latter His "hour," which was not yet due. Any attempt to arrest Him at this stage was doomed to failure.

The Pharisees, afraid that some were beginning to think that Jesus might be the Messiah, decided on immediate action. Police officers were sent to arrest Him, but their task remained unfulfilled because of the extraordinary effect of the teaching of Jesus upon them. They reported to their superiors that they could give no other reason for their failure to accomplish their mission than the incomparable teaching of Jesus. They had never heard anything to equal it. In John's gospel, the incident becomes all the more significant because of his great emphasis on the teaching ministry of Jesus.

First, they had heard Jesus say strange things about those who were seeking Him. He specifically said that they would not find Him, because He was going away. It is surprising that the officers did not at once seize Him for this before He escaped, but they did not. They heard the crowd murmuring, perplexed

231

about the saying and wondering whether Jesus was going to the "Dispersion among the Greeks."

The police officers present on the last day of the Feast of Tabernacles witnessed an astonishing incident. They were still looking for a suitable opportunity to arrest Jesus, when they saw Him stand up and invite thirsty people to come to Him. What did He mean? Was He referring to the water ceremonial that took place on the last day of the feast? Jesus clearly had no water to offer. They heard Him quote Scripture to describe how living water would flow out of those who believed. He must have been speaking of a different kind of water than that used in the Temple ritual. John, having afterward understood, informed his readers that Jesus was alluding to the coming of the Spirit, which would take place after Jesus was glorified. The contemporaries of Jesus would have understood water as symbolic of the Spirit, but they would not have known that the outpouring could only follow the death of Jesus. Neither the Temple worshipers nor the police officials would have had the key to the enigma. This saying of Jesus reveals His full awareness at this stage of His ministry that spiritual truth was to be communicated through those who were to believe in Him. As the water was poured over the altar by the Temple priests, so in greater measure would the Spirit overflow in refreshing streams from His followers to others.

The police officers, as they mingled with the crowds, heard further discussions about Jesus. Some were calling Him the prophet, the one specially expected by the Jews as foretold in the book of Deuteronomy. Others were nearer to the truth. They talked about the Messiah but were confused over His place of origin. Scripture pointed to Bethlehem, but Jesus came from Galilee. His birth in Bethlehem was not at this time known in Jerusalem. With two sections of the crowd taking a favorable view of Jesus, the police officials retreated from their mission to arrest Him. They may have come to the conclusion that their superiors were entirely mistaken about Jesus. John saw their reluctance as the divine overruling of the Pharisees' evil intent. Jesus' "hour" had not yet come.

Reactions were equally divided among the chief priests. Most of the Pharisees were convinced that the police officers had come under the spell of Jesus. They resorted to personal abuse because their authority had been flouted. They castigated the crowds who were attracted to Jesus as ignorant of the law and accursed. However, one of the "authorities" had come near to believing in Him. Nicodemus questioned the legality of condemning Jesus without a fair trial. This Pharisee might have been more forthright in showing his colors, but his challenge to the official approach nevertheless shows evidence of courage. Some of the Pharisees in their bigotry assumed that anyone who did not share their hostility was himself under suspicion. On geographical grounds they had concluded that Jesus could not be a prophet. The conclusion reflected the local snobbery of the Jerusalem authorities.

John's record gives the impression that Jesus rather than the Jewish leaders was the real master of this situation. He possessed a higher authority, which made a profound impact on those whose minds were not entangled by tradition. John knew as he wrote his story that the police officers were not the only ones who had been impressed with the uniqueness of the teaching of Jesus. The testimony came even more forcefully from the lips of those not officially well-disposed toward Him.

The adulterous woman

John 7:53-8:11

The opponents of Jesus were on the watch for fresh reasons to find a fault in Him or to test out His reactions to established procedures. His penetrating insight often brought out the worst in men. On one occasion a group of Pharisees and scribes resorted to action that was at the same time un-Jewish and unfeeling. They brought before Jesus, as a test case, a woman who had been seized in the act of adultery. They brought her to Jesus not because they respected Him as a judge but because they suspected that His judgment would differ from theirs, and in that event they would have evidence against Him.

The opponents of Jesus appealed to the law of Moses, which they claimed specified stoning for adultery.

It is highly improbable that the death sentence applied to

this offense in Jesus' day. The reference to it by Jesus' accusers was probably part of the temptation. An examination for such an offense would be carried out in private with witnesses present, and it must be assumed that this had already taken place. The focus of the story is the comparison between the woman and her accusers.

Jesus refused to be drawn into an action that was more political than moral. His opponents knew that the Romans reserved for themselves the right of executing the death sentence. They could hardly have expected Him to suggest an action that ran contrary to the Roman law. He said nothing, but instead wrote with His finger on the dusty ground. His silence goaded them to ask further questions. At length He gave His verdict. The man without sin was to cast the first stone. It was an indictment of the woman's accusers. They felt uneasy in the presence of Jesus and slowly drifted away, the oldest retreating first. They all left, for no man's conscience would allow him to stay, let alone take up a stone.

After all the accusers had withdrawn, Jesus turned to the woman. Probably then she first saw His face. Nothing is told of her thoughts while Jesus faced the challenge of her accusers. He asked her where her accusers were, and she reported that they all had left. He said that He would not condemn her. She never expected this. As the only one without sin, Jesus would have had the right to cast the first stone, but He had not come to condemn, but to save (John 3:17). Some have seen this pardon as a condoning of the woman's action. Jesus added, however, "Go, and do not sin again." The sinful nature of the act was not overlooked by Jesus, but He was more concerned for her future than for her past.

Although this story appears in John's gospel, it was probably not written by John. Some manuscripts place the incident in Luke's gospel. It is, however, undoubtedly of ancient origin, and there is no good ground for disputing the genuineness of the incident. Nothing in the approach of Jesus in this incident contradicts His thoughts and actions as presented elsewhere in the gospels.

Jesus, Light of the world

John 8:12-30

On the last day of the Feast of Tabernacles Jesus made an astonishing claim. The Temple illuminations sent shafts of light across the surrounding area. The light was symbolic to the more thoughtful among the multitude of tent dwellers. They were anticipating the messianic era in which the Jewish people would enjoy their superiority over the surrounding nations. Like the Temple candelabra, Israel would shine out when the Messiah came to His people. Few if any recognized that the Messiah was already in their midst. When He claimed to be the Light of the world, some Pharisees disputed His right to such a claim. They justified their skepticism on the ground that self-testimony is untrue. This, however, was fallacy. The determining factor was the character of the witness. The testimony of Jesus was unique. He knew why He had come, and He knew His destiny. He was the sent one, and the Father witnessed to this. The perplexity of His hearers at these sayings is understandable. It was one thing to

The southeast corner of the Old City including the Temple area is clearly visible from the Mount of Olives looking across the Kidron Valley.

"These words he spoke in the treasury . . . in the temple; but no one arrested him, because his hour had not yet come"

—JOHN 8:20

say that there were two witnesses, His own and the Father's, but where was the Father? Their question was superficial, but it may have arisen out of genuine perplexity. Jesus saw that the real problem was spiritual ignorance. The inability of these religious leaders to comprehend did not surprise Him. A knowledge of God could result only from a true understanding of Jesus and His mission. John simply records that no man laid hands on Him because His "hour had not yet come," although this was what the leaders most wanted to do with Jesus.

The subsequent discussion, which may have taken place in another part of the Temple area, exposed the spiritual darkness into which the Light shone. Jesus spoke again about going away, and some of His Jewish hearers thought that He was contemplating suicide. When He reminded them of their sinful state and the inevitability of death unless they believed in Him, they retorted, "Who are you?" Jesus reminded them of what He had already told them, speaking again of the Father who had sent Him. They were nonetheless wholly incapable of grasping His meaning. Some among His hearers, however, were more responsive. When they heard of the uplifted Son of Man they recognized in the claims of Jesus something they could not gainsay, and in some measure they came to believe on Him.

This occasion reveals much of Jesus' own perspective of these events. He was aware of the perfect harmony between His own actions and the will of His Father. He claimed to do nothing of Himself, which means that His own will was in tune with the mind of the Father. In this sense, He could claim to be always pleasing the Father. Such intimacy of fellowship is a pattern for His followers. All that obstructs that fellowship is spiritual darkness.

The problem of privilege

John 8:31-59

Those born and raised in rigid traditionalism cannot easily escape from it. Many who listened to Jesus were proud of their Abrahamic descent and were content to rely on it. Those who believed in Jesus had searching challenges to face.

Jesus talked about truth and freedom, ideals which have always appealed to the noblest minds. Most men, however, have

confused ideas about the nature of freedom, whereas truth itself
is too often equated with expediency. The importance of what
Jesus said about these themes cannot be exaggerated. He claimed
that His teaching was the gateway to truth, and that possession
of that truth brought freedom. In other words, the only way was
to follow Him and live by His standards. All lesser ideas of truth
must go. Liberty is not license, but a noble bondage to a new
ideal. Jesus expected and received reaction to this teaching. His
Jewish hearers appealed to privilege, for they were the children
of Abraham. The notion of bondage was totally foreign to them.

In response to their incredulity, Jesus spoke of a profound
bondage from which the Jewish people thought they were exempt. They would not admit that they were servants of sin. The
evidence nonetheless showed them to be men seeking to kill Him.
Their privileged position as Abraham's children did not prevent
them from yielding to the basest motives. Jesus had to tell them
that privileged descent counted for nothing in moral issues. Yet
they continued to argue about it. At length Jesus told them
bluntly that they were doing the devil's work instead of Abraham's. This was the basic reason why they had no desire for the
truth.

The Jews' angry retort to this rough handling is not surprising. They called Jesus a "Samaritan" and "one who had a devil"
— both terms of contempt. Ignoring their sneer, Jesus denied the
charge on the ground that He sought His Father's honor. Could
anything be further from demon possession? A demon could
never offer release from death. At this point, His opponents referred again to Abraham. Even the greatest of the patriarchs
had not been able to secure release from death for himself, let
alone offer it to others. There could be no mistaking that Jesus
was claiming to be superior to Abraham. His opponents made
no attempt to conceal their astonishment, "Who do you claim to
be?" It is a question men have been asking ever since.

They were challenging Jesus to compare Himself with Abraham, although their question had actually arisen from their confusion about what Jesus meant by "death." They thought He
meant physical death, but He was talking about spiritual realities. They did not really know God, although they thought they
did. All their misconceptions sprang from this. Since they had

appealed to Abraham, Jesus proceeded to make two astonishing statements about His relationship to the patriarch. The first was that Abraham had rejoiced to see His day. In what sense Abraham had seen it, Jesus did not explain. He may have been thinking of some glimpse of messianic glory when Abraham offered Isaac. Whatever the meaning, He was obviously claiming superiority to Abraham. The literal-minded Jews again failed to see the point. With an astonishing lack of imagination they compared the present span of Jesus' life with what it would be had He lived in Abraham's day. This was nothing less than ridiculing the profound statement of Jesus. Their minds were incapable of esteeming anyone greater than Abraham.

Far more violent was their reaction to the second claim of Jesus, "Before Abraham was, I am." This set Him far above Abraham. It was nothing short of a claim to preexistence. It was indeed more than that. The "I am" was a vivid reference to the divine revelation to Moses when he asked about the name of God and was told that it is "I am that I am." They could not avoid the conclusion that Jesus was making a concise claim to divine origin. Their anger aroused, His opponents recognized that further argument was futile. They rushed at Him with stones, but He escaped in the Temple crowds. Their action was symbolic. Many times since, men have reacted with violence to His claims. Had He only taken His place among Abraham's sons and been content with that, the Pharisees might more readily have accepted Him. But the Messiah could not conceal the truth, however unpalatable it proved to be to them.

Light for blind eyes

John 9

Many in Palestine had been blind before they met Jesus, but no one is more notable than the man in Jerusalem whose restored sight caused a controversy about Jesus among the religious leaders. John recognized a symbolic importance in this healing since he set it against the background of Jesus' claim to be the Light of the world. The blind man received more than physical sight, for John's account shows a gradual development of rare spiritual insight in a man whom the rabbinical schools contemptuously regarded as untaught.

When the disciples first saw the blind man they began a theological discussion about the origin of his plight. They debated whether it resulted from his own or his parents' sin. No other alternative came to their minds. Jesus, however, flatly rejected both alternatives and told the disciples to concentrate on the present rather than the past. He had not come to debate theological problems, but to work God's works. He saw the blind man as His subject. The process of healing was twofold; an anointing with spittle and a washing in the waters of Siloam. The brief interval between the two actions gave the man opportunity to exercise faith.

When sight had been restored, controversy began. The neighbors could not agree about his identity. Some said a remarkable thing had happened. Others, with a perversity not uncommon in human nature, decided that there must be two men looking alike, of whom one was sighted, the other not. It never occurred to them that their alternative proposition was more incredible. Moreover, the man's own testimony was decisive. On hearing how his eyes were opened, some took him to the Pharisees. This led to further controversy. The Pharisees' first reaction was to attack Jesus for healing on the Sabbath. They saw this as a technical breach of the Law.

His critics were also divided. The purists, knowledgeable of technical breaches, pronounced Jesus a sinner. Others, observing the restored man, could not understand how such healing could be performed by a sinner. Many since have had the same problem over Jesus. He may be faulted on man-made rules, but the uneasy feeling that the rules are wrong and Jesus is right remains. To dismiss the Light of the world in such a way is as ridiculous as refusing the light of the sun because it shines in the wrong place.

As the discussion between them progressed, the healed man grew increasingly confident, but the Pharisees became increasingly obdurate. First, they asked his opinion of his Healer. He called Him a prophet. Next, they denied that the man had ever been blind. When his parents confirmed the blindness, the Pharisees so intimidated them that they refused to say how their blind son's sight had been restored. Then they tried to silence the man's own testimony by declaring Jesus a sinner, but he showed impatience about the technical issue. For him, all that mattered was his new experience of sight. Then, they tried abuse. They had respect for Moses and the Law, but only contempt for Jesus and ignorance of His origin. At this point the man moved in to attack. He argued that they ought to know about someone who had such remarkable powers as to restore sight to eyes that had never been able to see. How could such a man be a sinner? Only one explanation occurred to his uncomplicated mind — this healing must be of God.

The Pharisees had no adequate answer to this. Their theology would not allow them to drop their charge that Jesus was a sinner. They had one recourse left — to cast out this troublesome, argumentative man. In doing so, they let slip their theory of the origin of the man's blindness. They said he was born in sin.

The story focuses not on the Pharisees nor on the healed man, but on Jesus. What effect did the healing have on the man's concept of Jesus? Jesus took the initiative to find him and ask him whether he believed in the Son of Man. The Messiah was personally challenging him for a decision. The occasion was momentous for the man, far more important than the moment his sight was restored. He gave an immediate response of faith. His spiritual as well as his physical eyes were opened. In contrast, the Pharisees, who were convinced they possessed spiritual sight, showed themselves groping in darkness when faced with the Messiah's works of mercy. Some of the Pharisees asked a leading question, "Are we also blind?" Jesus commented that those still blind see no need for spiritual sight. That some could be convinced of their sight and yet not possess it pictures man's pathetic unawareness of his own need. This miracle points to the true purpose of all the miracles of Jesus — to bring out sincere convictions in men about His own Person.

A pastoral allegory

John 10

Some of the stories of Jesus convey more detailed teaching

than others. Some are brief incidents with a single purpose; others are fuller stories with several aims. John records one of the fuller illustrations, drawn from rural life. So common was the sight of a shepherd leading his sheep that it supplied a pastoral picture of the relationship between the Messiah and His disciples. Most shepherds were good, but some were bad. The majority showed concern for the sheep, but some were interested only in their own welfare. These placed their own safety before the safety of the sheep. If wolves came they ran away.

Jesus presented His own situation in the requirements of a good shepherd. He had come to His sheepfold, the true Israel. There is only one entrance to this fold — Jesus Himself. Those who teach anything else are like robbers who shun the true entrance and climb over the wall with the intent to harm or steal the sheep. In claiming to be the Door, Jesus was asserting that He is the only way by which man can come to God. This vivid picture is taken from the shepherds' practice of lying across the access to prevent enemies from harming the sheep.

The imagery changes as Jesus described Himself as the Shepherd. He claimed to be the Good Shepherd, ready and willing to lay down His life for His people. This claim contains a hint of the meaning of the passion. He would be like a shepherd, sacrificing His life for His own sheep. He clearly indicated that this was His own responsibility. He was not to be sacrificed by others. This was His own choice. No one could touch Him without His permission. Had the Jewish people understood this, they would not have stumbled over the idea of a crucified Messiah. There is a further aspect of the shepherd imagery: the fold of Israel was not the only fold that would come under the Good Shepherd's care. Other sheep belong to the flock. Jesus had in mind the Gentiles who would equally share the privileges of the Shepherd's care and the Shepherd's self-sacrificial act. The Messiah saw wide horizons. His shepherd heart could not ignore the non-Jewish peoples of the world. His Church was to stretch far beyond the narrow confines of Judaism.

John remarks that some Jews considered, as others had done shortly before, that Jesus was demon-possessed. Not all thought so; some could not easily forget what had happened to the blind man. It was sound logic to them that devil-possessed people do not open blind eyes, for demons are the agents of darkness not light, of confusion rather than order.

The discussion over Jesus continued in the Temple court-yards. Crowds had gathered for the winter Feast of Dedication, which celebrated the cleansing of the Temple by Judas Macca-beus after its defilement by the hated Antiochus Epiphanes more than a century and a half before. It was celebrated in a manner similar to that of the Feast of Tabernacles. The colonnade, known as Solomon's porch, provided ample room for public dis-cussion, and a group gathered around Jesus. Some Jews chal-lenged Him to state specifically whether or not He was the Mes-siah. They expected a straight answer, but Jesus knew their in-tentions. Having already told them plainly, He reverted to the shepherd imagery. The sheep did not need to be told who the shepherd was, for they instinctively knew His voice. His ques-tioners, however, did not hear the voice of the Messiah. Had they done so they would have recognized why He could so authori-tatively pronounce on the destiny of His people. Indeed the Fa-ther and He were speaking with the same voice; the Father and the Son are one.

Whatever they understood by this extraordinary statement, the Jews decided to take action. They again attempted violence. For the second time they tried to stone Him in the Temple area. He calmly asked them for which of His good works they were stoning Him. They angrily retorted that they were stoning Him for blasphemy. The implications of the profound claims of Jesus had penetrated their minds. In this hostile situation, He was in-credibly calm. He reasoned that since in Scripture men are sometimes called "gods," why should it be thought blasphemous for Him to claim to be the Son of God? The works that He had done should have led them to discern the close relationship be-tween Himself and His Father. To them, nonetheless, He seemed to talk in enigmas. They tried to seize Him, but He escaped. The Messiah had come to His people as the Light, although most of them preferred darkness. Jesus then retreated across the Jordan. Many followed Him there. They recalled the testimony of John the Baptist and believed. The Good Shepherd's fold did not en-compass all Israel, but there were those who believed His works and believed in the one who did them.

News of a friend's death

John 11:1-16

During His brief ministry, in no home was Jesus more welcome than in the home of Martha, Mary, and Lazarus at Bethany. It was there that Mary had sat at His feet and listened while Martha bustled around doing the household tasks. It was there, too, that Mary later anointed the feet of Jesus. This family held a special place in His affections. It is instructive to note His reaction when adversity visited the home. Word came from the sisters that Lazarus was seriously ill. Jesus and His disciples were still outside of Judea when the news arrived.

Jesus' first reaction seems bewildering. In spite of His special love for Lazarus and his sisters, He made no attempt to hurry to the bedside. Instead, He did the opposite. He purposely delayed going to Bethany. Delay in such circumstances might suggest a lack of compassion, but Jesus' approach to His miraculous powers was dominated by the purpose of His mission. He explained His delay in an enigmatic way, which would not have been clear to the disciples who heard Him. He indicated that His major aim was the glory of God. Other issues were at stake as well as just physical illness. Jesus was more than a super Physician. His main concern was spiritual. The real question over Lazarus was not whether the illness was going to prove physically fatal, but whether it could be used to demonstrate the glory of God.

Two full days passed before Jesus made known His intent to return to Judea and go to Bethany. On hearing of His intention to make this journey the disciples objected. They remembered the attempts of some of the Jews to stone Him while He was in Jerusalem. To return to Judea would be foolhardy. Their reasoning was logical, but again they had completely failed to understand the true nature of the mission of Jesus. He was not a man groping in the dark, not knowing what to do next. He was no escapist, easily put off by hostile threats. Twelve hours of daylight enabled a man to see where he was going. The hours were not yet spent. His "hour" had not yet come. No evil designs of men could hasten it. Such was the supreme confidence of Jesus in the perfect planning of the Father. He knew that He would not be killed by stoning for His Father had other plans.

He told the disciples that Lazarus was asleep and that He intended to awaken him. They were mystified at this, for if Lazarus was only asleep they could see no point in Jesus making a hazardous journey to wake him. Moreover, the sleep itself would be beneficial. Although sleep was a widely used metaphor for death, they misunderstood this, probably because Jesus had already said that Lazarus' illness was not "unto death" (John 11:4). They missed Jesus' metaphorical intent, His use of the word sleep for death. He had to tell them bluntly that Lazarus was dead. He could have known of Lazarus' death only by supernatural knowledge. The Messiah was sensitive to the issues of life and death. Moreover, He saw in this death an opportunity to deepen the faith of His disciples. By the time Jesus and His disciples reached the tomb, Lazarus had already been dead four days. In the other instances of restoration from the dead there was no sufficient interval to exclude from the mind of the observers the possibility that the dead person might have been in a coma. In the case of Lazarus, death could not be doubted.

The disciples could not understand their Master. His plans completely baffled them. They were convinced that He was walking into a trap, and that He would die by being stoned. Thomas then announced the only course of action left to them. Since Jesus would not change His mind, they must stand by Him. They would all suffer together the consequences of what appeared to them to be an utterly foolish action. Thomas may have pictured in his mind that all the disciples would form a ring around Jesus so that if He were stoned they all would perish with Him. This was highly heroic, but it was a human arrangement and not according to God's plan.

18

Death, Divorce, and Generosity

A family bereavement

John 11:17-37

It is essential in the Middle East for funerals to follow soon after death. Four days had passed since the funeral of Lazarus. The sorrow of the sisters was intensified by the absence of Jesus. Others attempted to console them, but this could not compensate for Jesus' absence. When the news came that He was on the way and was nearing Bethany, Martha rushed to meet Him. Mary did not accompany her, but the reason is not stated. It may have been that she was more disturbed by Jesus' failure to come earlier. Many times during the last few days the sisters had said to each other, "If Jesus had been here, Lazarus would not have died." This expressed both their faith and their disappointment. They assumed that Jesus would have performed a miracle of healing simply because of His special regard for the family; but they were misjudging the Messiah. His mission was more important than personal connections. He had a profound message to communicate and a greater gift to give them through this event.

Martha confirmed her confidence in Jesus with a brave display of faith. "I know that whatever you ask from God, God will give you." When Jesus told her that her brother would rise again, her mind did not picture an immediate miracle. She thought of the last day, the final resurrection. Martha's reply was firm, concise, and specific, but she was looking beyond the mira-

cle of Jesus' own power and presence. Jesus therefore directed
her attention to Himself. Because He held the key to all spiritual
life He said to her, "I am the resurrection and the life." For those
who believed on Him, life and death would take on new meaning. Faith cannot bypass physical death, but it can secure spiritual life. Jesus challenged Martha to say whether she believed.
She confessed that He was the Messiah, the Son of God. This response of Martha was typical of the response that John expected
as a result of his book. What she confessed, John stated as his
purpose in writing (cf. John 20:31). There is, however, a difference between Martha's confession and John's intent for his readers. She knew nothing about the resurrection of Jesus, but John's
readers can read the record of it in his gospel. They are more
privileged than she.

Martha, her faith strengthened through contact with Jesus,
went and quietly told Mary that Jesus wanted to see her. She
needed no second bidding. She may have noted a renewed
gleam of hope in Martha's eyes. The mourning party at the
house thought Mary was going to the tomb, for she was weeping
as she went. Flinging herself at the feet of Jesus, she repeated
the same statement that Martha first made when she met Jesus.
At this point, Jesus was deeply moved and troubled. John describes this with a strong, almost vehement word, which is sometimes used of anger. The impact of the whole scene registered on
the mind of Jesus; He was faced with man's utter impotence in
the presence of death. Moreover, those present failed to recognize that the Messiah was conqueror of death. Jesus saw, too,
the pathos of human sorrow over personal loss. The deep stirring of His soul must be understood in the light of His own tears.
They were tears of sympathy and also of sadness. John shows a
Messiah who, so soon before the climax of His mission, could be
deeply touched with a feeling for man's weaknesses. The weeping Jews rightly interpreted His tears as expressive of deep love.

In the midst of this family sorrow, some of the Jews introduced a discordant note. They remembered the healing of the
man born blind and from this concluded that Jesus should have
prevented Lazarus from dying. They implied that what He had
not done He was incapable of doing. But very soon Jesus was to
show again His mighty power over death. John's portrait of the

Messiah shows not only Jesus' deep sympathy for men, but also His consciousness of the symbolic nature of His mission.

The defeat of death

John 11:38-57

Jesus, the sisters, the mourners, friends, and relatives arrived at Lazarus' tomb. The tomb was a cave, which probably belonged to the family. It was sealed by a large stone newly whitened to warn passersby of the risk of defilement. The whole company was shocked when Jesus requested the stone to be removed. Martha protested, pointing out that there would be an odor. Jesus was not unaware of the consequences in opening the tomb, but He knew what He was about to do. He calmly reassured Martha that she would see the glory of God.

Death had apparently conquered, but the Messiah, possessing the secret of all life, was preparing a shattering challenge. First, He stood in the entrance to the tomb and prayed. On other occasions, He prayed prior to some momentous event. On this occasion, the content of the prayer is recorded. It was brief, "Father, I thank thee that thou hast heard me. I knew that thou hearest me always, but I have said this on account of the people standing by, that they may believe that thou didst send me." This prayer breathed His complete confidence in the Father, with no pleading with God to act, no urgent request for additional power. The authority of Jesus was evident in the face of seemingly insurmountable difficulties. The prayer confirmed what was an abiding reality. Its deepest significance was its purpose. It was not for Himself but for the bystanders, that they might come to faith.

The account of the raising of Lazarus is brief. The loud command pealed forth from Jesus to Lazarus and the dead man immediately responded. He was still bound, each limb bound separately after the Egyptian manner. All that remained was for him to be untied. As the wrappings were being untied, the people must have experienced awe in the presence of the power that restored the ravages of death. Never before had death looked so powerless. It is not surprising that some of the witnesses be-

"Jesus said to her, 'Did I not tell you that if you would believe you would see the glory of God?' So they took away the stone"
— JOHN 11:40, 41

The Church of Lazarus, Mary, and Martha in Bethany, built over the site of their house. The village of Bethany lies on the eastern slope of the Mount of Olives.

lieved in Jesus. They saw in Him a Messiah of astonishing potential. They had witnessed the glory of God.

Stupendous miracles do not always soften the hearts of those hardened in unbelief. As is characteristic of human nature, some used this noble act for unworthy ends. They reported to the Pharisees, who saw it not as a thrilling triumph over death but as an ominous threat. A council of the leaders was summoned to consider the matter. Many feared that people would believe in Him and form a group that the Romans would regard as a political danger. The ruling parties were fully aware that they could not afford such a risk. Their own political future depended on the goodwill of the Romans, however much they hated them. Their greatest fear was the threat to their own institutions.

John somehow obtained a report of the proceedings within the council and recorded Caiaphas' summing up. He twice notes as significant that Caiaphas was high priest that year. In that capacity Caiaphas spoke supposedly on behalf of the whole people of Israel. He expounded the theory that it was better for one man to die for the nation than for the whole nation to perish. He regarded the actions of Jesus as a serious threat to national security. Was his theory justified? John does not discuss the matter, but he comments that Caiaphas' opinion was a truer prophecy than he knew. The words anticipate the meaning of the death of Jesus. He was to die in place of others. In dying for the nation He would also die for all the children of God scattered abroad. It is strange to find so prophetic a view of Jesus coming from a Jewish high priest. Only later did John and the early Christians learn the deeper meaning of it. There was first to be another empty tomb.

How evident is the paradox of men's reactions to the presence of the Messiah. The same event that saw the overcoming of death through the power of Jesus further prompted men to plot His death. Knowing of the plot, Jesus withdrew to the wild country northeast of Jerusalem, to a place called Ephraim. He left behind the intrigues and plots. Orders were given that anyone who knew where He was must report at once to the rulers.

Naturally, a miracle as striking as this has caused some to doubt its truth. It has been variously regarded as myth or fiction, as symbolic or as an acted parable. Most objections arise from the absence of the story from the synoptic gospels. If, however, the resurrection of Jesus is credible, then the raising of Lazarus cannot be regarded as impossible. It cannot be demonstrated. It must be accepted by faith, but there is no barrier to such acceptance if the nature of Jesus is what He claimed Himself to be.

More teaching on divorce

Matthew 19:1-12 (Mark 10:1-12)

Reference was made to the problem of divorce in the Sermon on the Mount, but Matthew records a further discussion about it between Jesus and the Pharisees. Jesus was entering Judea on His last journey to Jerusalem. Large. crowds followed Him. The Pharisees attempted to set another trap for Jesus through the issue of divorce. They were divided among themselves over this subject. The school of Hillel permitted divorce on almost any pretext, whereas the school of Shammai allowed it only according to the strict terms of the Mosaic law — that is, for adultery. They posed the question whether on any account it was lawful for a man to put away his wife. The crux of the dispute among Pharisees was not whether divorce should be allowed, but the grounds on which it was permissible. In practice, both Pharisaical schools were lax.

The teaching already given by Jesus on this subject had shown the Pharisees that His approach was more rigorous (cf. Luke 16:18). They therefore may have had some political motive since Jesus was at this time in Herod's country, and Herodias had good reason to be sensitive about the matter of divorce. The tetrarch and his queen would stand condemned by the teaching of Jesus.

When confronted by His tempters, Jesus employed a masterly technique. He did not directly answer their question. He used a counter question. He challenged them on their knowledge of the scriptural teaching on the ordinance of marriage. It is a divine arrangement, which should not be dissolved by man. The Pharisees at once saw that this conflicted with the Mosaic provision for a bill of divorce, and wanted to know what explanation Jesus would give of the supposed contradiction. In His answer He pointed out the permissive aspect of the Mosaic provision. The Pharisees should have recognized that it was made because of the hardness of people's hearts. They were wrong in supposing that Moses had commanded the provision of divorce rather than having reluctantly permitted it. The teaching of Jesus went back to the creation ordinance because it was ideally suited for family life. The one exception He allowed was divorce on the grounds of adultery, which destroys the original unity of marriage.

The Pharisees faded from the scene; they found the appeal to the creation ordinance unanswerable. The rebuff, however, did nothing to lessen their opposition to Jesus. The disciples, on the other hand, pursued the matter privately. Their reaction to what Jesus had said reflected popular opinion. The demands of His teaching appeared so rigorous to them that they concluded that the safest course was to remain single. Their comment shows that they had completely missed Jesus' point. God did not institute marriage to make a man and a woman a burden to each other. Rather, it was in man's highest interest that divorce should not be allowed for any cause. Moreover Jesus taught a higher status for women than was current in contemporary society. The prevalence of divorce was all too closely linked with the inferior status of women generally maintained among the Jews.

Jesus conceded, however, that some might be drawn to a celibate life. Some were celibate by choice, some had celibacy imposed upon them; whereas others chose celibacy as a definite policy in the interests of the Kingdom of God. The apostle Paul is a notable example of the latter. It is important to recognize that Jesus issued no command about this, but admitted that each must decide the matter for himself. There is no room in His teaching for an order of celibacy in the interests of the Kingdom imposed by the authority of men.

The Messiah and the children

Mark 10:13-16 (Matthew 19:13-15; Luke 18:15-17)

It must be noted that in the ancient world the Jews had a higher regard than most nations for the young. There was no practice among them, as among the Romans, of leaving unwanted children to die of exposure. Therefore it is remarkable that the attitude of Jesus toward children was resisted by the disciples. Apparently, they regarded the dignity of the Messiah to be too great for Him to allow children to hinder His work.

Jesus had already used a child as an object lesson to illustrate the necessary qualities for those entering the Kingdom. His striking visual aid had apparently been forgotten by the disciples. When people brought their children to Jesus for Him to place His hands on them and to pray over them, the disciples rebuked them. A word of strong censure is used, which suggests a particular officiousness on the part of the disciples. The parents and guardians of the children must have been taken aback. They had heard of the receptive attitude of Jesus toward the young. Yet, as far as the disciples were concerned, it was a matter of priority. They saw no reason why their Master should be preoccupied with so unimportant a sector of the community when crowds were waiting to hear Him. To Jesus, however, the child was as important as the adult.

The indignation of Jesus, recorded only by Mark, is strongly expressed and cannot be glossed over. The Messiah could be publicly annoyed at His disciples. He never sanctioned intolerance, even when it was ostensibly in the interests of the Kingdom. His response to the action of the disciples was both firm and tender. "Let the children come to me, do not hinder them; for to such belongs the kingdom of heaven." These words have been the charter for all who see the importance of teaching children the things of God. If the Messiah welcomed them, what right has any disciple to prohibit them?

They were reminded by Jesus of the terms of entry into the Kingdom. They, too, must become like children in their approach to life. Jesus demonstrated His point by holding children in His arms and blessing them. Those with spiritual discernment saw in His action the tenderness of God.

Wealth and spiritual inheritance

Mark 10:17-31 (Matthew 19:16-30; Luke 18:18-30)

Still traveling southward through Perea, Jesus was accosted by a young man seeking advice about eternal life. Such eagerness to hear of spiritual matters was unusual. The man ran up to Jesus, intensely earnest in his inquiry. Luke mentions that he was one of the rulers, and the sequel shows that he was very rich. It was uncommon for one of the ruling classes to seek out Jesus, for most of His hearers were poor. This man's attire would show that he belonged to the social aristocracy, and the disciples probably regarded him as a highly desirable candidate for their ranks. With deep interest they would listen to his conversation with Jesus.

When the young man addressed Him as "Good Teacher," Jesus asked why he called Him "good." God alone should be called good. Why did Jesus reply in this way? Was He implying that He Himself was not good? This is inconceivable. He must have meant that in calling Him good, the young man was in fact implying His divine nature. He went on to exhort the man to keep the commandments, naming several of them and ending with the injunction to honor his father and mother. As a Jew, the young man not only knew the commandments well, but recognized the importance of keeping them. According to Matthew, Jesus told him that if he kept the commandments he would enter into life. This seems to imply a doctrine of salvation by works. Such was the doctrine believed by every devout Pharisee. Jesus' remark must be understood in its context, however. When He added the positive command to love one's neighbor as oneself, the challenge became much greater. The Jewish lawyer to whom Jesus told the story of the Good Samaritan knew of the link between love to God and love to one's neighbor, but he quibbled about the interpretation of who his neighbor was. The young ruler did not question this. He confidently affirmed that he had kept all the commandments all his life.

Were it not for the evident earnestness of this man, it might be concluded that he was another example of Jewish self-righteousness. However, he did not make his claims in a boastful spirit, and Jesus did not challenge him on this score. He had made every effort to fulfill the Law as far as he understood it. So sincere was he that Jesus loved him. Matthew includes his further question, "What do I still lack?" Though he was not conscious of having disobeyed the commandments, he was nevertheless aware that more was needed. No wonder the Messiah was drawn to him. He was a genuine searcher after truth. Perhaps throughout the ministry of Jesus no one had shown greater promise. He was nevertheless immature. To be perfect he must sell his possessions and give to the poor. This suggestion by Jesus took him wholly by surprise. No rabbinical teaching required him to do that. His features reflected sorrow, for he could not face parting with his possessions. The offer of treasure in heaven in exchange did not outweigh what he thought he would lose. It must not be supposed that Jesus taught that no one with earthly possessions could also possess heavenly treasure. This was an individual case. The man thought too highly of his earthly treasure.

As Jesus traveled on with His disciples, He commented on the difficulty of rich men entering the Kingdom of heaven. He did not say it was impossible. He used the illustration of a needle's eye and a camel trying to struggle through it. This was a touch of humor. A rich man could no more hope to enter the Kingdom than a camel had a chance of getting through the needle's eye. This means that riches will never help a man through. Entrance to the Kingdom cannot be bought. Mark reports the disciples' great astonishment. They wondered, "Then who can be saved?" They evidently concluded that anyone who had possessions had no hope. Rather, Jesus was simply explaining that what seems impossible to man is possible to God. He meant that apart from the power of God no one could be saved. Salvation was not bought or earned, but received as a gift from God. It has always been most difficult for men to learn that the way of salvation is the way of utter dependence on God.

Peter realized that he and the other disciples were in a different position from the rich young man. They had left everything and followed Jesus. They had done what the ruler was not prepared to do. Peter asked, "What then shall we have?" Jesus assured His disciples that their rewards would be infinitely greater than anything they had surrendered for His sake. This truth applies to human relationships as well as to possessions. The spiritual gains will be 100 percent. For the apostles Jesus gave additional promise that they would occupy twelve thrones at the final Restoration. This is a difficult saying, but it seems to indicate that in the new age, high responsibility will be given to those who have followed Jesus faithfully.

The generosity of God

Matthew 20:1-16

Jesus had more to say about rewards. He did so through a parable. He compared the Kingdom with a vineyard owner. To ensure the proper care of his vineyard, work had to be done, and that necessitated the employment of casual laborers. The details are simple. The Jewish day was divided into twelve hours, and the owner went early to the marketplace to hire men for a full day's work. A set wage for a day's labor was agreed to by the workers. It was usual for unemployed men to wait in the marketplace until someone offered them a job. This employer went to the marketplace again at the third, sixth, and ninth hours and hired more men. There was still work to be done at five o'clock, and the owner found men still lingering in the marketplace. He invited them to do an hour's work in his vineyard. At the reckoning at the twelfth hour (six o'clock), all the men received the same pay, irrespective of the number of hours each had worked.

The climax of the story is the complaint of the workmen hired first and the response of the owner. The complaint seemed fully justified. Why should those who had labored so long, particularly through the hottest part of the day, receive no more than the men who had done only one hour's work? Modern industrial relations would not survive under such conditions. The parable, however, was not intended as a pattern for industry. Nevertheless, it is not without some value in showing the attitude of Jesus toward work. The first workmen could not deny that they had received a fair wage. It was the wage agreed upon before they began. The complaint was that others had received proportionately more, and therefore on a percentage basis the payment was unfair. Jesus does not enlarge on the advisability of the action. One might conjecture what would have happened had the owner tried to hire casual labor on the same terms the next day. He might have had difficulty in getting work started early a second time. The focus, however, falls on the owner and his rights, not on his methods.

The owner illustrates one aspect of the character of God — His generosity. He denied that he had wronged any of the workmen. He had faithfully honored the wage contracts. He could not be faulted in this respect by the most vigilant trade union. As an employer, moreover, he had rights — the rights of free choice to do responsibly what he wished with his own belongings. If he chose to go beyond the accepted rates of pay, he reserved the right to do so. "Do you begrudge my generosity?"

On this question the real crux of the parable lies. God is more generous than any man could ever be, and yet men have constantly questioned His generosity. The objection in the parable arose because men were judging from the wrong standards. It is equally difficult for men to learn that God works at higher levels than man works. If men begrudge the generosity of their fellows, it is no wonder that they cannot fathom the generosity of God.

The parable illuminates the thinking of Jesus. For Him, personal relationships were more important than material rewards. He emphasized less than the modern man the problem of equality. Communism, for example, is built on the concept of material equality. Whatever the merits or demerits of this concept, most would agree that it is more feasible in theory than in practice. The demands that Jesus makes on His followers are not without reward, but the nature of the reward is spiritual and therefore not quantitative. Of more importance is the idea of the grace of God. The Kingdom is not built on the principle that men will serve for what they can get out of it. Rewards should be left to the generosity of God.

Prediction and presumption

Matthew 20:17-28 (Mark 10:32-45; Luke 18:31-34; cf. Luke 22:24-30)

Jesus made several important announcements to His disciples on the way to Jerusalem. Twice before He had told them what was to happen to Him, but He knew that they had not yet grasped it. He told them a third time. The first three gospels all relate the saying, but Mark adds an interesting detail omitted by the others. He describes how Jesus went on ahead. The disciples, following behind, were amazed, but Mark does not say why. Perhaps there was something in the bearing of Jesus that filled them with premonition. His look may have revealed that His mind was on coming events. The disciples had been aware of dangers threatening Him, as when He returned to Judea following the death of Lazarus. Increasing fear took hold of them.

In this atmosphere of acute apprehension, Jesus again told them about His coming passion, now in more detail. Luke mentions the statement of Jesus that all that the prophets foretold concerning the Son of Man would be fulfilled, which shows the direction of His thinking at the time. The theme of fulfillment was of vital interest not only to the early Christians but also to Jesus Himself. As His "hour" drew near, these prophecies occupied His mind. He again referred to Himself as the Son of Man, who was to be betrayed, delivered to the rulers, mocked by Gentiles, scourged, spat on, and put to death (Matthew has "crucified"), but who would rise again. Only Luke relates the disciples' reactions to this statement. He says, "But they understood none of these things; this saying was hid from them, and they did not grasp what was said" (Luke 18:34). Some have supposed that Jesus could not have given such details about the trial and crucifixion at this stage, and they have therefore concluded that these must be the comments of the evangelists after the event. Moreover, it is reckoned to be incredible that the disciples would have been so ill-prepared for the events when they eventually happened if Jesus had foretold them in such detail. The objection, however, supposes that the disciples at this stage were able to apply the picture of the suffering Son of Man to Jesus Himself. Their minds were not conditioned to this kind of teaching. They would have found such ideas too painful and would have preferred to put them out of their minds. It was baffling to them as Jews to contemplate a crucified Messiah. As far as they were concerned, it was a contradiction in terms. Whatever the saying meant, they could not relate it fully to their Master. It is no surprise that they were caught unaware when the tragedy struck.

In the parable of the vineyard, Jesus had said that the first would be last and the last first. This puzzled the disciples. They had been the first to follow Jesus. They had stood by Him during His ministry. They may have begun to fear that they would lose their "seniority." This at least seems to have happened to James and John, who both belonged to the inner group. Their plan was to put a specific request to Jesus to ensure the perpetuity of their privileged position. They thought they were entitled to the highest places of honor — at His right and left hand. Matthew's version of what happened differs slightly from Mark's, in that in Matthew's account the question came from their mother, and in Mark's version, from the disciples themselves. It is natural for a mother to desire the best for her sons, but the blame for this extraordinary request cannot be laid only on her. Both Matthew and Mark record the subsequent indignation of the other ten disciples, which shows that they held John and James responsible.

That this request followed so shortly after the prediction of the passion shows the disciples' complete incapacity for understanding the mind of Jesus at this time. Most astonishing is the gracious way in which Jesus dealt with the request. He had a cup to drink — an appointed task to complete that involved the bitterest dregs of physical and spiritual experience. He anticipated a baptism of blood. Were they able to share this? The two men, with astonishing naïveté, pronounced their willingness with confidence. In both accounts James and John answered for themselves. Such a committal could not be made by proxy. They probably thought that the trials predicted were designed to prove their eligibility for the coveted positions. Jesus, however, reminded them that it was not His prerogative to allot the places of honor. It was the task of the Father.

One can only imagine the increasing sorrow that came to Jesus as the disciples' indignation rose against the two. Would they ever learn? He reminded them that their concept of the Kingdom was wrong. It was not like earthly kingdoms, whose kings arrogantly exercise authority over their subjects. Petty tyrants were in considerable number in Jesus' time. The Messiah was working on entirely different principles. In His view, the great are those who serve. He Himself had come to serve. He was wholly unlike what men expected the Messiah to be. Moreover, He had come to give all that He had as a ransom to save men. If the Master came for this, the servant could not expect to work on different principles.

19

Jericho, Bethany, and Jerusalem

Rejoicing in Jericho

Matthew 20:29-34 (Mark 10:46-52; Luke 18:35-43)

The synoptic gospels all narrate the healing of the blind on the outskirts of Jericho. Luke, who linked his report to the account of Zacchaeus, placed the event as Jesus entered Jericho, whereas Matthew and Mark placed it at the end of His visit there. Moreover, Matthew mentions two blind men; the others, only one. The precise location of the healing is of small importance, but some explanation of the differences in the narratives is necessary. A variety of suggestions have been made. Some have resorted to the unlikely theory that one man was healed as Jesus entered, and two men were healed as He left. The details of the story in both cases, however, are so closely parallel that the theory is highly improbable. Another suggestion is that the healing happened between the old and the new city. This theory makes it possible to account for the variant language of Matthew and Luke. Information is insufficient to lead to a final solution. It may be that Luke's source knew that the healing took place at the gates of Jericho but attached no importance to the timing of the event. That Matthew mentions two men and the other writers only one may indicate that there were in fact two men and that Mark concentrates on the one whose name was preserved — Bartimaeus. It has also been observed that Matthew has an affinity for twos that the other writers do not share. Another example of this is Matthew's mention of two animals in the narra-

tive of Jesus' entry into Jerusalem. Some think Matthew was arti-
ficially enhancing the narrative, but there is no good reason for
disputing that Matthew recorded authentic tradition.

Multitudes were thronging the streets of Jericho; some were
onlookers, some were pilgrims. Word of Jesus' approach may
have reached the town. The jostling along the roadway offered
little opportunity for the blind beggars by the wayside. They
could only inquire from whoever would listen to find out what
the commotion was about. They had probably already heard of
Jesus of Nazareth and knew of His power to heal. The opportunity was too good to miss. Their cries for mercy were at first
drowned by the noise of the crowd. Bystanders tried to silence
them. The cries interrupted their festive mood, but they mis-
judged the persistence of the men and the compassion of Jesus.
Efforts to silence the men led to louder shouts, for they would
not allow such an opportunity to slip. The Messiah might never
again come so near to them. They called Him the "Son of David."

Jesus stopped and asked what they wanted. All three accounts mention that He asked the question, "What do you want
me to do for you?" There was no hesitation. The desire of
any blind man is to receive sight, but in this case the statement
of that desire implied faith in Jesus' ability to give sight. Only
Matthew refers to the touch of Jesus on the blinded eyes, whereas
the other writers mention the expression of the faith of one of
the men. All were impressed by the immediate cure, and the
restored men (or man) followed Jesus. Luke's is the fullest account of the latter point, for he says that the man glorified God
as he followed, and that his words were accompanied with a
chorus of praise by all the people.

The spontaneous response of praise from the bystanders
ranks this event as one of the most notable among the healing
miracles. The people's praise must have heartened Jesus as He
continued to draw nearer to Jerusalem.

A tax collector's salvation

Luke 19:1-10

The city of Jericho was an important center for the collection of internal revenue. The head of the civil service department held a position of great influence in the political structure of that time. The method of collecting taxes was open to wide abuse, which made the populace regard those in the profession with hatred and contempt. The Jews were among the most heavily taxed people of the ancient world, and it is not difficult to imagine their resentment toward anyone connected with the system. Some collectors were notorious for extortion. Among these was Zacchaeus, one of the chief tax officers in Jericho. He may have been the most unpopular man in the whole city.

Although unscrupulous, he had some uneasiness in his mind. More than mere curiosity made him want to see Jesus. He probably had heard through his professional associations that Jesus often mixed with tax collectors, a social act no other rabbi would do. He may have heard about Matthew leaving his tax profession to join the small group of Jesus' disciples. If so, he would have assumed that Jesus possessed great personal magnetism to draw a man such as Matthew away from his lucrative profession. He felt a strong urge to see Jesus when he knew that He was passing his way. He went to considerable trouble to accomplish his quest, which indicates the seriousness of his purpose. The dense crowd was a problem, for few would make way for him. Because he was a short man, he found a vantage point in the branches of a sycamore tree.

The Messiah and His disciples edged their way through the crowd. Jesus was intent on His mission, but He never was too occupied with His own destiny to ignore the problems of the people around Him. He noticed Zacchaeus in the tree, but He saw more than a despised tax collector. He saw a representative of those whom He had come to save. Luke describes the brief encounter between Zacchaeus and Jesus. This tax collector was astounded when Jesus commanded him to come down quickly and act as His host for a meal. He was given no choice. Jesus treated the whole procedure as a necessity. Possibly, Zacchaeus wanted this to happen but never dared to hope that it would. He was overjoyed to receive such a command.

The crowds' reaction on seeing Jesus and His disciples walking to the home of a chief tax officer was typical. They attributed guilt by association. They hated Zacchaeus because he symbol-

"He entered Jericho and was passing through. And there was a man named Zacchaeus; he was a chief tax collector, and rich"
—LUKE 19:1, 2

Jericho, situated in the Jordan Rift Valley, is a tropical city of palms. Archaeological excavations have shown this city to be one of the oldest inhabited sites in the world.

ized a system that they despised. They did not see him as Jesus did, as a man in need. Jesus was totally unaffected by the customary categories by which people judge others. The gospels show unmistakably that He did not regard it as a matter of shame to be the guest of a "sinner," for He had come to "save the lost."

No hint is given of the conversation between Jesus and Zacchaeus at the table or after. The result, however, is clearly stated. For a tax collector to give half his possessions to the poor and to give back four times as much as he had defrauded was astonishing. In that brief interview the light of the mind of Jesus illuminated the darkness of Zacchaeus' life, and gave him the desire for better things. He had no time to lose. In spite of the fact that Zacchaeus was hated by the "sons of Abraham" (the Jewish people), Jesus saw him as a true son of Abraham. He had been saved from his baseness on that very day. Would there have been the same amount of murmuring from the populace had they known what the outcome would be? As the tax refunds were later being doled out with 300 percent interest, some might have regretted their scornful attitude toward Jesus' mixing with tax collectors. Perhaps some saw that His power transcended human barriers, even to reach those classes most despised.

On leaving the house, Jesus gave Zacchaeus a summary of His whole mission. His words suggest that He regarded Zacchaeus as symbolic: "For the Son of man came to seek and to save the lost." Such a mission found no place in popular Jewish messianic expectations. In the Jewish view, the Messiah would save the righteous, those who had already done much toward their own salvation. For a man like Zacchaeus, there remained no hope under the Jewish system. So near to the experience of Calvary, Jesus vividly demonstrated His concern for those who knew themselves to be outcasts both in a religious and social sense.

Resources to use

Luke 19:11-27

Somewhere between Jericho and Jerusalem, the disciples were discussing the Kingdom of God. In some measure they linked their Master with the Kingdom and had some premonitions that His approach to Jerusalem was fraught with destiny. They began speculating on the immediate establishment of the Kingdom, but again they misconstrued the spiritual nature of the mission of Jesus. Their minds focused on privilege rather than service; on receiving rather than giving. Jesus corrected their misconceptions by a parable. Luke is specific about the purpose of the parable, and this furnishes the key to its interpretation. The meaning, however, is not confined to first-century disciples, for it conserves universal principles.

The parable, known as the Parable of the Pounds, has similarities with another parable — that of the Talents, recorded only by Matthew. Many scholars regard them as different accounts of the same parable. The differences, however, are so significant that it cannot be maintained with confidence that both writers used the same source or that one used and modified the other. It is more reasonable to hold that the parables are distinct.

The setting of this parable may have been drawn from the history of the family of Herod. Archelaus, son of Herod the Great, journeyed to Rome in 4 B.C. to obtain confirmation of his claim to his father's kingdom, but a deputation of Jews had opposed him with the result that he was never ratified as king. Jesus pictured a high-ranking nobleman leaving home for such a purpose and entrusting various servants with responsibility during his absence. These various responsibilities are represented as "pounds," each of ten servants receiving a pound apiece. They were expected to trade under adverse conditions because of the hostility of the citizens and the deputation rejecting the nobleman's claims to the kingdom. The parable portrayed different reactions to responsibility in difficult circumstances. It illustrated what was still in store for the disciples. The Kingdom was not imminent; there was yet work to be done.

The nobleman, unlike Archelaus, received his kingdom and returned to reckon with his servants. Jesus gave samples of those who could be commended and He cited one man who had not taken his responsibilities seriously. The trading tested the reliability for further responsibility. One gained ten pounds and was appointed ruler over ten cities. Another gained five pounds, which led to an appointment over five cities. The details of the story need not be pressed. The principle is clear. Faithfulness in small responsibilities qualifies for proportionately greater responsibilities.

The man in the parable who was blamed is described in greater detail. He did nothing but hide his pound. He excused himself on the grounds of his estimate of his master's character. He called him a severe man, implying that his master was out for gain without doing anything toward it. The master pointed out that a savings account at the bank would have gained more than hiding the money in a cloth. The servant was a poor judge both of people and of circumstances. At heart he was a revolutionary, determined to deny his master any vestige of gain. His estimate of his master may have been right, but he had shown himself to be irresponsible. His pound was given to the man whose diligence had been most successful. When objections were raised that this procedure was unfair, the principle was given that those who fail to use what they possess lose the right to possess. The Kingdom of the Messiah requires that those who serve Him put to use the abilities given to them.

The parable ends with the rebellious citizens. They were

condemned to death. Why was this feature introduced? Was it to show the sovereign power of the newly appointed king, or was it to show the real severity of his character? Whatever the reason, it reflected the contemporary oriental scene of despotism against which the early Christian Church had to contend. The Kingdom of God would make no progress with members intimidated by circumstances. They must put their energies to full use.

At Bethany

John 12:1-11 (Matthew 26:6-13; Mark 14:3-9; Luke 7:36-38)

Bethany, situated about two miles southeast of Jerusalem, was a special place for Jesus, since it was the home village of His friends Mary, Martha, and Lazarus. It was the recent scene of the raising of Lazarus from the grave, and it was because of this raising from death that the Jewish leaders plotted to put Jesus to death. Jesus reentered this danger area. In Jerusalem many pilgrims already had arrived for the Passover feast. Some were looking for Jesus, wondering whether He would come to the feast. They debated whether the Pharisees' threats would keep Him away. They were wrong to suppose that Jesus would be intimidated. His mission was nearing completion. It could not be frustrated by men.

The atmosphere in Bethany was friendly. Simon, at one time a leper, invited Jesus and many others to share a meal at his home. Besides Jesus, the most notable guest was Lazarus. Suddenly, everyone's attention was captured by Mary's anointing of Jesus. Matthew and Mark say that precious ointment was poured over His head, but John says, over His feet. The latter action would have been the more unusual part of the process, which evidently struck John most vividly. He also recorded that Mary wiped the feet of Jesus with her hair, and that the whole house was filled with the sweet aroma. All three writers note adverse comments by some who witnessed the act. Matthew mentions that all the disciples were indignant. Mark mentions that some were indignant; but John confined himself to Judas' indignation.

The angry complaints centered in the wastage they had witnessed. They estimated the cost of the ointment at about

300 denarii (300 times a laborer's daily pay). The anointing obviously was extravagant. The bystanders thought of all the help to the poor that such a sum would provide. Often, concern for the poor comes to the forefront when other people's money is involved. They did not consider that Mary had a right to use her possession as she wished. Jesus, without earthly possessions of His own, had a different perspective. John adds that Judas was not concerned about the poor but about the extra money he could embezzle from the accounts of the apostolic band, for he was the treasurer. Unequivocally, John calls him a thief. This sordid side of these objections must have pained the heart of the Messiah. He alone responded favorably to Mary's generous action.

Her action must have been premeditated. She had sat at the feet of Jesus; she had listened intently to His teaching. She sensed what no one else apparently did, that Jesus' end was near. She knew of the threats of His enemies, and she feared the worst. She demonstrated her devotion by an act of extravagance unsurpassed by anyone else. Loyalty and love know no meanness. She sensed that she might never have another opportunity to do what she most wanted to do. The Master understood and supported her action. In silencing her critics, He reminded them that the poor were no new problem. The opportunity to alleviate their needs would not pass, but His present need they had not recognized. It is better to anoint the living than the dead. They preferred impersonal charity rather than costly personal devotion to Jesus. The woman's loving act will be unforgotten as long as the Gospel is preached.

It is well to remember that the Messiah welcomed an act considered to have no practical value. Those most devoted to Him have shared liberally with the poor. By contrast, those most critical have often done the least. Jesus, on entering the time of His passion, filled as it was with predestined sorrow, would remember the strange contrast between the fragrant ointment of Mary and the carping criticisms of the disciples. The "aroma" of devoted giving filled not only the house but the whole Church of Jesus Christ through the record of the event.

A crowd gathered outside the house to see not only Jesus but also Lazarus. The religious leaders, however, stepped up their plots against Jesus by including Lazarus as well. How could men be so perverse as to think they could remove by death one who had just been miraculously resurrected? Did it not cross their minds that Jesus could perform the same miracle again? Were they so obdurate that they refused to believe that Lazarus had ever died? Whatever the explanation, their intrigues intensified. They could not tolerate in Jerusalem one who claimed to be the Messiah.

A royal entry into Jerusalem

John 12:12-19 (Matthew 21:1-9; Mark 11:1-11; Luke 19:28-38)

The caravan of pilgrims threaded its way from Bethany to Jerusalem. As they drew near to the village of Bethphage, on the slopes of the Mount of Olives, Jesus requested two of His disciples to fetch a colt, which they would find tied at the entrance to the nearby village. Matthew records that they were requested to bring the mother of the colt as well, a reference that some attribute to his tendency to duplicate. More likely, Mark and Luke preferred to concentrate on the animal that Jesus was to ride on. Matthew's addition is of no importance in the event. Mark and Luke mention that the colt had never been ridden before. They obviously attached significance to this, not to demonstrate His riding prowess, but to present the whole occasion as unique. The untried colt symbolized that uniqueness.

Why did Jesus want to complete the journey in this way? John mentions the disciples' lack of understanding at the time, although later they came to understand the significance of the event. Jesus' decision to ride on an ass was not impulsive. The prophet Zechariah foresaw centuries before the coming messianic King riding on an ass. Jesus had this in mind when He sent for the colt. He was King in His own right, and as the Messiah He should come to Jerusalem in the royal manner prescribed by the prophet.

As the pilgrims approached Jerusalem they recited antiphonally, as was customary, the Hallel psalms from which came the responses "Hosanna" and "Blessed is he who comes in the name of the Lord." Praise burst from the crowd as Jesus mounted the colt. Some threw down cut palm branches and others spread their garments on the road before the colt as a special tribute to

Jesus. A second shouting crowd, waving palm branches, streamed out of the Jerusalem gates to join the pilgrims already with Jesus. The exuberant acclamation of Jesus as King must have surprised the disciples.

In light of this, how could a crowd only a few days later clamorously demand His crucifixion? It should not be supposed that the same people were involved in both scenes. The citizens of Jerusalem were less well-disposed toward Jesus than were the Galilean pilgrims. According to John, the raising of Lazarus ex-

Scanning the Old City, looking southwest from the Mount of Olives across the Kidron Valley.

cited the curiosity of many. The event marked Jesus from other
men. It prompted support from many pilgrims, and they ac-
claimed Him when they heard of His approach to the city.

Did Jesus exercise supernatural insight in procuring the ass
and colt? This need not be supposed. He may have known the
owner, who offered the use of the colt whenever He needed it.
On the other hand, the owner's willingness to lend the colt may
have been prompted by the widely circulating reports that Jesus
was to enter Jerusalem for the feast. Nothing else is known

"As he was now drawing near, at the descent
of the Mount of Olives, the whole multitude of the
disciples began to rejoice . . ."
—LUKE 19:37

about him. If he later became a member of the Church, he would have come to realize more fully the importance of his gesture on the day when Jesus rode into Jerusalem to die.

The swollen crowds slowly moved down the slopes of the Mount of Olives toward the city, loudly proclaiming the praises of God. Among the bystanders, Pharisees listened with astonishment, their anger rising. The people were praising God because of the mighty works of Jesus. Many of them, pilgrims from Galilee, had seen those works with their own eyes. Their enthusiasm was fired by the entry of Jesus riding on an ass, the nearest to royal confirmation that they had seen. The situation looked threatening to the Pharisees. They feared an uprising, which would seriously jeopardize their position. The sheer numbers of His supporters unnerved them. In despairing groans they charged one another, "You see that you can do nothing; look, the world has gone after him" (John 12:19). Desperately they appealed directly to Jesus to rebuke His overenthusiastic supporters. They were not prepared for His reply. "If these were silent, the very stones would cry out." The time had come. His "hour" had arrived. It was no longer necessary to urge His followers to tell no one. The Messiah on the eve of His passion was in no mind to silence the crowds.

From the slopes of Olives, the whole city was visible, crowned by Herod's magnificent Temple. The shining exterior of the buildings, however, shielded political intrigue, explosive emotions, and a disregard for a nobler piety that alone could contribute toward the peace of the city. Jesus foresaw the approaching calamity and wept. He looked ahead to the day when Roman troops would overwhelm it, when the city dwellers and their children would be mercilessly treated, when the Temple itself would lie a mass of toppled stones. These stones would cry out to the whole world that the city had met its judgment. The people were ignorant of the time of God's visitation. Few, if any, listened to this prophecy of doom and believed it. Forty years later, the Roman general Titus demolished the city and its Temple. No one else shared the tears of the Messiah over Jerusalem. To many, the tears may have caused misgivings. Their concept of the Messiah held no room for tears.

The fig tree

Matthew 21:18-22 (Mark 11:12-14, 20-25)

Jesus stopped to investigate whether there was fruit on a fig tree along the road, since He was hungry. Mark says it was not the season for figs. Jesus was certainly aware of this, for it would be some six weeks before the appearance of the ripened fruit. Fig trees, however, produce small knobs before the appearance of leaves, and these knobs are evidence that the trees have power to produce ripe fruit. The brown knobs, which are not particularly palatable, were sometimes eaten by the poor.

Finding no knobs on the tree, Jesus cursed it: "May no fruit ever come from you again!" The statement has caused some discussion. Some see it as an unwarranted outburst of anger against an impersonal object, totally unlike what would be expected from Jesus. The unusual character of the action must be admitted. When it is viewed, however, as a parable in action, it ceases to be an outburst of personal anger. The Messiah knew that He would find no spiritual fruit among the Jewish people. The nation was about to reject Him in spite of the show of piety. They had produced no fruits of righteousness.

The timing of the withering presents a further problem. Matthew says that it happened immediately, much to the amazement of the disciples, but Mark records that they did not observe that the cursed tree had been withered until the next day. Apparently Matthew compressed the events together. It was Peter who first observed the withering, and he drew the attention of Jesus to it. He and the other disciples were perplexed because the tree had not withered from natural causes; there had not been time for that. They asked Jesus how it happened. His answer can be summed up in one word — faith. What He had done they could do. They could even move mountains and cast them into the sea.

The disciples might have thought these words too extravagant, but neither Matthew nor Mark tell what their reactions were. Something of Jesus' train of thought may be surmised. His mind was turned to the recalcitrant city and its inevitable doom. What was the future of His mission? It must lay along a path of faith. There were mountain-like obstacles to overcome, but faith could do it. If all hope lay in the motley group of disciples, with their weaknesses and unbelief, the outlook was poor indeed. Jesus, however, at that moment of destiny, said to them, "Have faith in God." Jesus was the one perfect example of that faith. He knew that He would suffer, but He knew also that He would triumph through it. It was this absolute certainty that supported Him in the face of His passion. The same faith was available to His disciples.

At this time, Jesus linked three important aspects of spiritual life. Some of the sayings had been spoken before, but at this stage in the mission, the disciples needed to hear them again. Faith was linked to prayer, which in turn was linked to forgiveness. It is the prayer of faith that is effective. Even this will fail if there are bitter feelings in the heart toward another. This teaching indicates the attitude of Jesus toward those who were already harboring in their minds hostility toward Him. This same forgiving attitude reached its climax on the cross when Jesus prayed for forgiveness for the very men who crucified Him. No wonder the fig tree withered at once; there was mighty power in the command of such a person.

First scenes in the Temple

Luke 19:45-20:8 (Matthew 21:10-17, 23-32; Mark 11:15-19, 27-33)

It was inevitable that the Temple in Jerusalem should play an important part in the closing days of the earthly life of Jesus. Conversation centered around Him in the streets of the city. Men asked who He was, and some were answering, "The prophet Jesus from Nazareth in Galilee." It seems that no one approached any nearer to the truth than that. No one detected in the manner of His entry the marks of Israel's Messiah. Those outside the Temple courtyard were amazed when animals and men in chaotic confusion emerged from the courtyard. Jesus had driven them out. Inside the courtyard, the money changers' tables were overturned, and coins were scattered across the pavement. This prophet of Nazareth must be a man of considerable authority. As He stood in the entrance, none dared take their merchandise inside. With great moral power He declared, "My house shall be a house of prayer, but you have made it a den of robbers." He was quoting Scripture and powerfully demonstrating its truth.

This action caused the religious leaders to discuss further ways of getting rid of Him. Then, when from the Temple precinct came the ringing of children's voices crying hosannas to the Son of David, the leaders were indignant because Jesus took no steps to silence them. "Do you hear what these are saying?" Jesus again quoted the Scriptures, reminding them that perfect praise comes from the mouth of babes and infants. He would not support the restricting of praise to the ecclesiastically authorized. The children displayed more wisdom than their leaders.

The inevitable question of authority was raised in the Temple on the following day. Officials whose responsibility was to see that everything was done in prescribed order naturally regarded the actions of Jesus with suspicion. No one among the Sanhedrin had authorized the Temple to be cleared of undesirable elements. As for Jesus' remarkable teaching ministry, who had authorized Him to do that? Multitudes were astonished at His teaching. The officials asked Jesus to produce His credentials. Presumably, they reckoned that His failure to do so would provide legitimate grounds for them to take action against Him. They hoped to discredit Him in the eyes of the people.

Officialdom is often too conscious of its authority. Those who wield authority are prone to set themselves up as judges of the authority of others. With a tone of officiousness the spokesman confronted Jesus, "By what authority are you doing these things?" The real problem was, *who* had the power to bestow authority. On this point Jesus and the religious officials strongly disagreed. The moral dignity of Jesus the Messiah shone through. He would not be intimidated by their demands. He posed a counterquestion, mentioning John the Baptist: "The baptism of John, whence was it? from heaven or from men?" Its origin would substantiate its authority.

The critics were unprepared to answer the problem. They discussed it among themselves. They all recognized that they were in a dilemma. Their immediate answer would have been "From men," but the common people held John in too high respect for them to say that. They were afraid of being stoned by those who regarded John as a prophet. Moreover, John the Baptist had maintained an even more rigorous view of personal ethics than did most of the Pharisees, but they dared not admit that John's baptism was from heaven. They retreated from the challenge of Jesus. They replied that they did not know. Jesus claimed the right to decline answering them as they had claimed the right to decline answering Him. Yet in a sense Jesus did answer their question, for if John were a prophet and had testified to Him, His own authority could not be less than John's. The scene closed but not without revealing the futility of those attempting to bolster their own authority by challenging the claims of Jesus. His moral stature towered above them as they plotted to trap Him with a technicality. They would eventually kill Him, but only in His own time and with His own permission.

The Pharisees' lack of response to the preaching of John led Jesus to tell a parable which criticized their attitude. A vineyard owner had two sons, one of whom promised to work in the vineyard but failed to do so; the other at first refused but later went. The former illustrated the Pharisees who professed allegiance to God but were failing to carry out the spirit of God's command, while the latter illustrated those whom the religious authorities regarded as sinners but who had responded to John's preaching of repentance. Jesus could not tolerate mere lip service to God but emphasized the value of true spiritual response.

20

Parables and Questionings

The quest of the Greeks

John 12:20-36

Among the pilgrims at the Passover feast were Gentiles who
had been attracted to Judaism. These were proselytes who had
come to worship. Later, many of them were drawn into the Christian Church because the Gospel fulfilled the many hopes that
had been aroused in them through Judaism. Several of these
Gentile worshipers requested an interview with Jesus. They
had probably witnessed the entry of Jesus into the city, or had,
at least, heard of it. They may have imagined that He was about
to set up His Kingdom. John alone records the incident, but he
gives no reason why they came. Diplomatically, they asked Philip
to introduce them to Jesus. Philip may have known the Greek
language for he came from Bethsaida in Galilee, a district with
strong Greek infiltrations. It is possible that they personally knew
him. For some reason Philip consulted Andrew instead of taking
them directly to Jesus. He may have been uncertain of Jesus' attitude toward Gentiles and wanted Andrew's moral support.

John recorded, rather abruptly, the statement of Jesus that
the hour for the Son of Man to be glorified had come. He left
his readers to imagine what picture this would have conjured up
in the minds of these Gentiles. To them "glorification" may have
suggested the establishment of the Kingdom, but Jesus meant
the "hour" of His suffering. This He made clear by an illustration. No wheat harvest could be expected without the death

275

and bursting forth into new life of innumerable grains of wheat. The secret of productivity was in the self-sacrifice of the original grain. The imagery revealed the mission of Jesus. He was the grain of wheat. His hearers, however, could not recognize such a truth at that time. Perhaps later, these same Gentiles would learn and believe that the death of Jesus was necessary for the growth of His Church. The words were directed to all the disciples. They had to learn that following the Messiah involved gaining new values, even a willingness to rate eternal realities of greater value than life itself. Moreover, anyone who became His servant became the servant of His Father.

John's account next focuses on the inner life of Jesus. The Messiah stood alone among His people. His "hour" was pressing upon Him. He made no attempt to hide the fact that His soul was troubled. Those standing by heard Him debating whether to pray, "Father, save me from this hour." Then they heard Him reject such a prayer. It would have defeated the very purpose of His "hour." He offered, instead, the prayer, "Father, glorify thy name." A voice from heaven immediately answered. This was the last of the three recorded occasions when a voice from heaven testified to Jesus. The message was brief and direct — "I have glorified it, and I will glorify it again." The divine partnership between the Father and the Son is here clearly revealed. The message, although addressed to the Son, was not exclusively for His benefit. Jesus pointed out that it was for the sake of the hearers. The crowd, however, was not tuned in. Some heard what seemed like a thunderclap; others thought they heard an angel speak. It was necessary for the Messiah Himself to interpret the message.

In His further remarks, however, Jesus made no reference to the heavenly voice. He declared the present hour to be an hour of destiny. The battle was on. This world's ruler was about to be cast out. It was to happen in a totally unexpected way — by means of the uplifting of the Son of Man. The action would magnetically draw men to the Son of Man. The dullness of the hearers is again apparent through the narrative. They understood neither the nature of the uplifting nor the identity of the Son of Man. John notes that the uplifting referred to the manner of Jesus' death, but he wrote after the event. At the time he was as confused as they. The Messiah alone knew the awful reality.

Jesus made a final appeal to the crowd. The Light would soon be no longer with them. "Walk while you have the Light, lest the darkness overtake you," He warned, in imagery He had used before. It is common sense to walk in light rather than in darkness. Those walking in light are the sons of light. A similar description is included in the Qumran literature, but for the members of the Qumran community the Light had not dawned. It was the Messiah who was the Light of the world. The Light was shining, but many were remaining in darkness.

A horticultural parable

Matthew 21:33-46 (Mark 12:1-12; Luke 20:9-18)

Some parables of Jesus strikingly reflected the immediate historical situation. Such was the parable of the vineyard. It illuminated the mission of Jesus on the brink of His passion. The literary framework is simple. A vineyard owner had trouble collecting the fruit that the tenants were expected to pay as rent. A succession of servants were sent to collect it, but they were subjected to brutality. Some were beaten; others were stoned; and at least one was killed. The owner decided to send his son, believing that the tenants would respect him, but they reasoned that by killing the heir they could seize the vineyard. Swift retribution followed as the owner seized and killed the tenants and hired out the vineyard to others.

This parable has a pronounced allegorical element, more than is usually found in the parables of Jesus. The meaning was sufficiently clear for the religious leaders to grasp. They saw that it was aimed at them. The vineyard imagery was well known to them, and recalled the words of Isaiah 5:1 ff. The vineyard planted and fenced in, the winepress constructed, and the tower erected were no mere scenic details. The descriptions directly echoed Isaiah. The prophet had labeled Israel as the vine, and the listeners would have assumed that Jesus intended the same. Therefore, the owner represented God, and the tenants stood for the Jewish leaders. The succession of servants was a reference to the prophets, and the heir — the beloved son of the owner — could be no other than the Messiah. The killing of the Messiah was to take place very soon. Even as He was speaking to them, the leaders' murderous intentions were stirred to greater intensity, but they were afraid of popular reaction.

The details of the parable should not be pressed. It has been suggested that the false reasoning by the tenants about the inheritance is improbable, but the point of the story does not depend on this. Even if actual tenants would not reason in this manner, the Jewish leaders were, nonetheless, acting illogically toward the Messiah. They desired the inheritance of God's Kingdom, but they were planning to do away with the heir. Their folly resulted in the complete destruction of their city and nation no more than forty years later. The owner of the vineyard had taken action. At present the Messiah was still with them, although He knew that the time of His rejection was near. He held no illusions about His destiny. Could He have spoken so openly about His death in the hearing of His enemies? Some find difficulty in this and conclude that this narrative is a later parabolic interpretation of His death rather than a prediction. Because He was so deeply conscious of the dawning of His "hour" and knew that death was part of the purpose of His mission, it is not surprising that He spoke openly. His enemies had still to feign some charge against Him, but He knew that they would stop at nothing to be rid of Him.

After telling the parable, the Messiah appealed to their knowledge of Scripture, to the well-known passage about the stone rejected by the builders. He reminded them that the rejected stone had been chosen as the cornerstone of the whole building, a choice that was recognized as the Lord's doing, marvelous in the eyes of the beholders. He was quoting from Psalm 118:22, 23. The early Christians remembered the Lord's use of this passage and used it themselves (Acts 4:11; 1 Pet. 2:7). Jesus was not only the rejected heir, but also the rejected stone. Nevertheless, He gave a clear assurance of ultimate victory. Although rejected by His own people, the Messiah would be the cornerstone of His Kingdom. The vineyard would not be restricted to Israel. It would be given to another nation that would produce fruit. The other nation would be the new organism that would embrace all humanity, a figure of the Christian Church. The discussion ended on a note of judgment. A stone can crush.

The Messiah could not forbear this solemn note. This was not His prime purpose, however. His mission was not to judge, but to save.

A parable about wedding guests

Matthew 22:1-14

Matthew relates the parable about a feast that has some similarities with a parable in Luke 14, placed earlier in Jesus' ministry. The differences, especially the addition of the incident of the wedding garment, suggest that Jesus told similar stories on at least two distinct occasions. In Matthew's account the feast was of great social importance, for it was a marriage feast for the king's son. Those invited, however, refused to come. Servants were sent to urge them to attend, since all preparations were made, but they did not treat the invitations seriously. Some preferred their normal occupations. Others resorted to violence, killing the king's messengers. In the East, the refusal to accept hospitality by subjects of a king was regarded as much more than a personal insult. It was defiance of the king's authority, aggravated still more by political murder. This accounts for the king's anger, and he immediately despatched troops to suppress the offenders. Some have considered that armed suppression does not properly fit into a story about a marriage feast and have suggested that two distinct stories were edited into one. The angry reaction of the king, nonetheless, is not out of keeping with oriental despotism.

Instead of the invited guests, any willing to come were given the chance to attend. They were not screened. Their one qualification was willingness. As a consequence, the wedding hall was filled. One man, however, stood out from the rest by his totally unsuitable attire. He probably arrived in his laboring clothes, without having taken the trouble to prepare himself for the feast. This was equally an insult. It amounted to an acted lie. He was only pretending to be loyal to the king, whereas his actions constituted a snub. The king again showed his tyranical nature, and ordered the man to be bound and thrust outside.

The parable presents another example of an undesirable character illustrating a holy God. Jesus clearly did not mean to enforce the descriptive details in His stories. The application to the immediate historical situation was the major point. Israel, at least in her official representatives, was rejecting the invitation of her King. The common people were more disposed to respond. Even among these, however, were some who were not genuine. What was the meaning of the wedding garment? Some have suggested that the king had provided the wedding garment, which the guest refused to wear. If this was so, the garment probably represents the gracious provision of God that some foolishly scorn. It cannot be substantiated, however, that it was normal practice for special wedding garments to be provided. Others have regarded the garment as representing works of morality, but there is no suggestion of this in the parable, and since there was no discrimination between the good and the bad, this cannot be the meaning.

Jesus summed up the teaching of the parable in the concluding statement, "Many are called, but few are chosen." The story therefore illustrates the distinction between the "called" and the "chosen." Not all who were invited attended. The official guests, in spite of being called, showed by their actions that they were not chosen. The man in unsuitable attire equally showed himself as excluded from among the chosen, for he was not allowed to sit at the feast. The garment therefore symbolized eligibility to the feast. It must, therefore, represent sincerity of faith, without which no one can share the King's fellowship.

The imagery of a wedding feast at the inauguration of the Kingdom was not unfamiliar to the Jewish hearers. They commonly believed that the messianic age would begin with a banquet. The Dead Sea Scrolls, among other witnesses, bear testimony to this. Jesus knew, however, that the messianic feast would not take place until after the Messiah had been killed. While using an illustration of festive joy, Jesus was sad at heart at the hardening of many against His mission.

A question about tribute
Luke 20:19-26 (Matthew 22:15-22; Mark 12:13-17)

After their setback from discussing with Jesus the question of authority, the Pharisees tried a different method to ensnare Him. The political situation was tense, and they planned to get

Jesus to make a statement that would implicate Him with the Roman authorities. The hatred the Jewish people had for their overlords did not prevent them from making political capital out of it. They reasoned that if Jesus could be shown to oppose the Roman State, He would certainly fall foul of the Roman authorities. A difficulty arose for the Pharisees themselves, as they were notoriously the prime instigators of opposition against the imperial authorities. To solve the difficulty they gained the support of the Herodians, whom most Jews disliked because of their allegiance to Rome. A joint controversy with Jesus over the payment of tribute money would appear better than if the Pharisees proceeded alone. For such antagonists as Pharisees and Herodians to be in league shows their extraordinary determination to plot against Jesus.

Their plan to trap Jesus by His words to have some grounds to deliver Him over to the power of the governor was ill-considered. They did not anticipate the wisdom of Jesus. His enemies flattered Him, but their words had a hollow ring. They called Him Master, but they had no intention of following Him. They told Him that they were convinced He was true and that He taught God's way in truth, but they desired to plot His downfall. They acknowledged that He was not influenced by men's opinions — in this alone they spoke sincerely, much to their own chagrin. This latter point they hoped would be His undoing. They were convinced that He would not hesitate to speak against the emperor. They directly challenged Him, "Is it lawful to pay taxes to Caesar, or not?" Jesus had read their minds and had seen their hollow motives. He knew their malice. That Pharisees would ask such a question was proof enough of their hypocrisy. They paid taxes under duress, but they never admitted the legality of the taxes. In their view, no emperor had any claim upon them. Their sole allegiance was to God.

He challenged them outright, "Why put me to the test, you hypocrites?" He asked for a coin, a denarius. He held it up, showing them the emperor's image, and asked whose image it was. He touched a sore point with the Jews, who deeply resented having to handle such currency. It was an affront to the Jewish concept of theocracy, but they could not deny the validity of the currency. They admitted that the image was Caesar's. Je-

"But he perceived their craftiness, and said . . . 'Show me a coin. Whose likeness and inscription has it?' They said, 'Caesar's'"
— LUKE 20:23, 24

Denarius of Caesar Augustus, the famous tribute money with the image of Caesar.

sus' reply was crushing, "Render therefore to Caesar the things that are Caesar's, and to God the things that are God's." Matthew, Mark, and Luke all note that the hearers marveled, and Luke adds, "They were not able in the presence of the people to catch him by what he said." He had reduced His opponents to silence.

Jesus' reply reveals His own attitude toward the secular government. He had not come to be embroiled in political issues. His messiahship was of another order. He was content to allow Caesar to administer government affairs, whereas He concentrated on the affairs of God. In this, He set a pattern for His followers. In some issues the right of Caesar is not as clear-cut as in the question of taxes. Not everything on which the State has impressed its image rightly belongs to its province. When government conflicts with God's will, God must be given precedence. Taxes, although oppressive for the Jews, were not in that class.

The incident well illustrates Jesus' use of common objects to teach truths of universal application. Long after this silencing of Pharisees and Herodians by His words, men still marvel at His wisdom. A Jewish pseudo-concern for Caesar came to the fore again at the trial of Jesus when they threatened the governor with being no friend of Caesar's if he did not convict his prisoner. Nevertheless, the power of Jesus in that hour outlasted the power of human authorities.

The silencing of Sadducees

Luke 20:27-40 (Matthew 22:23-33; Mark 12:18-27)

The passion week was marked not only by a variety of controversies, but also by a variety of opponents. After the unsuccessful attempt of the Pharisees and Herodians, the Sadducees took their turn. Being more materialistic and rationalistic than the Pharisees, they denied the resurrection. They were the prototypes in some measure of modern rationalists, except for one important difference — the Sadducees accepted the authority of the Pentateuch. They appealed to the testimony of Moses, but they did not accept the authority of the prophets. Evidently, some of the Sadducees considered it possible to reduce the prestige of Jesus in the eyes of the general public by trickery and ridicule.

Matthew specially notes that the Sadducees brought their problem on the same day that the Pharisees and Herodians had come to Jesus. They, too, addressed Him as Master, but they used no flattery as the others had done. They appealed to the Mosaic law. They knew enough about Jesus to know that they would be on common ground in such an appeal. They thought up a problem relating to the levirate law (about brothers-in-law) in Deuteronomy 25:5, 6, which allowed a man to take his deceased brother's widow to raise for him a son to carry on his name. The law was not enforced and was severely limited in application in the time of Jesus. The Sadducees, however, thought they had found a way to expose the teaching of Jesus.

The test case was fantastic, although possible. A succession of seven brothers died and each in turn had taken the same wife because none of them had left any offspring. At last the woman died. The Sadducees wanted to know whose wife she would be at the resurrection. It was not a serious question, but Jesus took the opportunity to correct publicly their misunderstandings. They were in error on two points. They had a wrong view of God and a wrong view of Scripture.

Had they recognized the true nature of God they would not have supposed that the afterlife was no more than a continuity of this life. They had forgotten, or had never learned, that God was spiritual. Marriage, on the other hand, was confined to earth where it was necessary for the continuation and well-being of the human race. This was not so, however, in heaven. As children of the resurrection, men would live on an entirely new level. The Sadducees could not think in spiritual terms. It was beyond their experience.

Jesus exposed their ignorance of the content of Scripture by a reference from the Pentateuch. They could not question the validity of the passage to which He appealed. He quoted from Exodus 3:6 the words spoken by God to Moses from the burning bush: "I am the God of Abraham, the God of Isaac, and the God of Jacob." Jesus added a comment on this. "He is not God of the dead, but of the living." These words affirmed that the patriarchs were still spiritually alive, although long since physically dead. Such reasoning was based on no mere verbal quibble; it was based on a true understanding of the spiritual nature of God.

The evangelists record two reactions to the saying. Matthew notes the astonishment of the multitude at the doctrine of Jesus. Luke, however, refers to certain scribes who commented that the Master had answered well. These latter were probably Pharisees who were secretly glad that Sadducees had been silenced by Jesus. It is a sad commentary on human nature that men could be so blind in the presence of the Messiah. During the passion week, attacks upon Him reached their climax. His enemies used any device, legitimate or otherwise, to discredit Him in the eyes of His followers. They would have little difficulty in degrading themselves still further by engineering the crucifixion.

A question about the great commandment

Mark 12:28-34 (Matthew 22:34-40; cf. Luke 10:25-28)

The Pharisees put another test question to Jesus, and Matthew says it was because they heard that the Sadducees had been silenced. They were obviously motivated by rivalry. The Pharisees felt they could demonstrate their superiority in testing Jesus. They may have had some respect for His logic and relished pitting their wits against His. They had confidence in their knowledge of the Law in contrast to the homespun wisdom of Jesus, who had never been formally taught in the scribal traditions. The lawyer who brought the question had no sincere desire to know Jesus' interpretation.

He asked, as Matthew records it, "Which is the great commandment in the law?" Mark states it differently, "Which commandment is the first of all?" The two forms mean the same thing. All commandments were important in Jewish eyes, but one especially summed up the rest. Jesus cited the statement "Hear, O Israel: The Lord our God, the Lord is one," from Deuteronomy 6:4. This was a statement frequently on Jewish lips. Jesus added, "You shall love the Lord your God with all your heart, and with all your soul, and with all your mind, and with all your strength." So well-known was this that it is not surprising that on another occasion a lawyer gave the same words in reply to Jesus' question about the terms for inheriting eternal life. The command to love is notoriously difficult. Apart from the paradox of loving by command, there is also the problem of total devotion to God. The Pharisees, well versed in the letter of this law, fell far short in practice.

The added commandment, "You shall love your neighbor as yourself," is as difficult to observe as the first. The scribe who posed the question was concerned about orthodoxy, not practicability. When Jesus noted that on these two commandments hang all the prophets, a Jew would at once have understood. Jesus had selected the same commandments as any Jewish teacher of the law would have done. The scribe condescendingly remarked, "You are right, Teacher," and he repeated the answer. He added one comment, however — that to love as the Law required "is much more than all whole burnt offerings and sacrifices." This comment commended the man to Jesus, for He would agree with him, although many Pharisees would not have agreed. The scribe's interview with Jesus may have effected some change in him. Jesus himself commented that he was not far from the Kingdom.

He was not the first man who had challenged Jesus and instead found himself challenged. Jesus dealt with His questioners with unsurpassed moral dignity. It is not surprising that, as Mark notes, no one dared ask Him any more questions. All the evangelists agree that a time came when the critics recognized that verbal quibbles were useless in combating the influence of

Jesus. His enemies were to resort to more violent methods. In spite of professing to love God, the Jewish leaders were plotting against the Messiah. It is always easier to talk about love than to practice love. The great commandment has never been surpassed, but the Messiah was to introduce a spiritual enabling unknown before.

Jesus questions His critics

Matthew 22:41-46 (Mark 12:35-37; Luke 20:41-44)

When His critics no longer dared to ask Jesus more questions, He Himself initiated questions, a welcome change after the controversial problems that had been posed to trap Him. Jesus had no ulterior motive. It was not His mission to win word battles. He took this occasion to draw attention to profound spiritual truths. His own question was not framed in a spirit of argument. It was aimed to enlighten the minds of those who seemed utterly incapable of recognizing His mission.

In Matthew's account, the double question is asked, "What do you think of the Christ? Whose son is He?" The Pharisees standing by had a ready answer: "The son of David." Mark combined the two ideas in his version: "How can the scribes say that the Christ is the son of David?" Luke's account is similar to Mark's. One of the most-discussed questions in Jewish theology was the problem of the Messiah's descent. Amid a variety of views, Davidic descent was widely held. Some preferred to expect a heavenly origin; others, an Aaronic descent. The Pharisees were fully in support of a restitution of the throne of David.

Jesus quoted Psalm 110, in which David called the Messiah, Lord, and then He asked how David could do this, since the Messiah was to be David's son. Although many scholars view Psalm 110 as neither Davidic nor messianic, undoubtedly the Jews in Jesus' time considered the psalm as messianic. This can be confidently assumed, otherwise there is no point in the question that Jesus put to the Pharisees. In appealing to the passage, moreover, Jesus claimed that David spoke under the inspiration of the Holy Spirit. If the psalm is not Davidic, Jesus either was ignorant of the fact or was accommodating Himself to the beliefs of His hearers merely to win a verbal argument. Both alternatives make the discussion unworthy of the character and insight of Jesus. He, however, had higher motives.

In this psalm, the Messiah is placed in the position of highest honor — at the right hand of Jahweh. Moreover, a time is predicted when He will subdue all enemies under His feet. Jesus was looking beyond His passion when He cited these words. He needed no assurance regarding His ultimate victory over opposing forces. The words of the psalm nevertheless undergirded His present mission and was an open testimony to His hearers. They had been warned from His own lips that they were fighting a losing battle.

The critics gave no answer. They could have pursued the matter if they had a real desire to know the explanation. As a result, Jesus did not give an answer to His own question. They were in no mind to receive it. Even His closest disciples were incapable of recognizing that He Himself was the explanation. Not until later did it dawn on them that the solution lay in the human and divine nature of Jesus. As human, He was David's son; as divine He was David's Lord. This profound truth has taxed the thinking of men ever since, but there is no other way to explain the enigma of Jesus the Messiah, either in His person or in His mission. This incident shows how men well-acquainted with Scripture may yet miss its true meaning. It further shows that the key for solving many problems is the person of Jesus Himself.

21

Judgments and Forebodings

A general assessment of the scribes and Pharisees

Matthew 23:1-12 (Luke 20:45-47; cf. Luke 11:42-44)

Matthew records in discourse form many of the sayings that Jesus spoke against the Pharisees. After He silenced the Pharisees, many people gathered to hear what further comments He would make. Luke placed one or two similar sayings earlier in his gospel. On this occasion Jesus exposed the weaknesses of their position. The discourse can be divided into two parts — a general assessment and a series of specific "woes."

The people may have well expected Jesus to be hostile. The Pharisees had so often opposed Him. Although He said hard things against them, He did not challenge their position as religious leaders. He agreed that they sat on Moses' seat, a Jewish way of saying that they were Moses' representatives (the place in synagogues where the scroll of the Law was placed was also known as Moses' seat). Jesus criticized the Pharisees for not practicing what they preached, and He amply illustrated His point.

To observe the written Law was difficult enough, but the Pharisees superimposed a mass of traditions that made it all considerably more burdensome. Tradition became as binding as the Pentateuch and sometimes more so. Once imposed, however hard they were to bear, these traditions could not be relaxed. Many Pharisees were themselves adept at getting around the traditions, but they did not lift a finger to lessen the obligation upon others. Many maintained a firm line for fear of losing

288

face. Some schools, like Hillel's, were more lax than others, like Shammai's.

When spiritual life wanes and religious observance becomes mere formality, there exists the tendency toward love of self-display. The Pharisees of Jesus' day prove the point. Almsgiving, which was highly rated, they performed publicly to attract attention. They achieved the same purpose by ostentatious phylacteries, which were hollow cubes worn on the forehead and on the left hand, and fastened by leather straps. The cube for the head was divided into four equal parts into which were placed small pieces of parchment inscribed with the following passages of the Law: Exod. 13:1-10, 11-16; Deut. 6:4-9; 11:13-21. They originally served as a reminder at the time of morning prayers. The practice of wearing them at other times, which was later condemned in the Talmud, was intended to impress others with the wearer's superior piety. A similar impression was created by larger than normal fringes on garments. These were originally intended for the wearer to be reminded of God's commands and were not designed to be seen by onlookers. This outward show often hid dishonest behavior. Self-seeking was another vice. The best seats in the synagogue were grabbed, irrespective of the claims of others. Not all Pharisees were guilty of these weaknesses, but the system was wide open to these abuses.

Characteristically, the rabbis insisted on proper respect from ordinary people. The right title must be used in the marketplace greetings. This was alien to the spirit of Jesus. Although the greatest Rabbi of them all, He never courted titles of respect, nor did He desire His followers to do so. They were to regard themselves as servants; within a few hours' time, the Master would set the example of humility by washing their feet. Such an approach was far removed from the Pharisaic spirit.

Woes against religious abuses

Matthew 23:13-39 (Mark 12:38-40; Luke 11:39-53)

Anyone can decry, but the woes of Jesus are unique. They were delivered with an authority that arose only from a perfect understanding of the weaknesses of men. They have a far greater significance than the immediate occasion, for the spirit of Pharisaism lives on, and the Messiah's condemnation of His own times is equally relevant wherever the spirit of legalism exists.

Matthew records seven woes, and Mark and Luke include one not mentioned by Matthew. The cumulative effect is devastating. Some have judged the criticisms as unfair to the Pharisees. It is possible to cull from Jewish literature evidence that many good Pharisees existed who would have endorsed much of the criticism of Jesus. There was, however, enough abuse to justify condemnation in the strongest terms.

Jesus had come to announce the Kingdom, but He found the Pharisees at the gates, unprepared to enter themselves and determined to prevent others from doing so. They deserved the label of hypocrites, men who were acting a part. Pretending to be doorkeepers of the Kingdom, they turned out to be pickets. Some entered later, after the true nature of the Messiah dawned upon them. The Pharisees spared no effort to make converts, in spite of the fact that the Jewish people were not noted for missionary zeal. Jesus did not criticize the proselytizing movement itself, but rather, the disturbing results. The converts gained were made twice as bad as those who gained them.

The Pharisees were self-styled moral guides, but Jesus regarded them as blind guides. He quoted Jewish casuistry about oaths. An arbitrary graduated scale prescribed which oaths men were allowed to swear. Jesus had already taught in the Sermon on the Mount that oaths should be avoided as a means of adding weight to statements. Also, the Pharisees took their tithing rules to great lengths. They tithed everything, from the smallest products of the soil such as anise. In spite of their dedication in this, they neglected the important aspects of the Law such as justice, mercy, and faith. With criticism made more cutting by humor, He pictured them straining their beverage to avoid swallowing a gnat but ending inadvertently with swallowing a camel. The criticism is still valid for those who love external detail and forget the priorities of true faith.

Jesus directed the next two woes against false ideas of purity. The Pharisees maintained detailed rules on the ritual cleansing of utensils, which originally were valuable for hygiene. When accompanied by moral evil, like extortion, however, these rules became not only valueless but hypocritical. Also, Jesus compared them to whitewashed tombs, for they disguised with external rules their inner corruption. They erected monuments to the prophets, but they did not follow the teaching of the prophets. Other prophets were to come whose testimony would lead to a repetition of persecution. Righteous men had always been subjected to it, since Abel's time to the last of the Old Testament prophets, Zechariah. Jesus further compared the religious leaders of His time to a brood of vipers ready to attack. He Himself was their main target.

The woe not mentioned by Matthew but included by Mark and Luke was directed against the harsh treatment of widows and against inordinately long prayers. It is important to note that although many of Jesus' criticisms were harsh He concluded (according to Matthew) with a lament over Jerusalem. He longed to protect its citizens, like a hen sheltering her chicks. He scanned the Temple area, remarking how spiritually desolate it was. The Messiah would not return to it until He would come in greater triumph. In the place where He should have been most revered, He had been rejected. Instead of pronouncing blessings on the religious leaders, He was compelled to pronounce woes.

The real value of giving

Luke 21:1-4 (Mark 12:41-44)

Jesus, still in the Temple area, sat watching the people moving along the Temple terraces. He could see on the terraces the thirteen trumpet-shaped boxes into which worshipers cast their gifts. Since almsgiving was highly rated, the temptation to make an outward show of the act of giving was always present. Some sought added prestige by giving more than their neighbors. Abuse of this tendency led to a law restricting the proportion of a man's possessions that he might give away.

The Temple treasury was a valuable social asset. From its resources many of the poor were assisted. In days when social welfare was generally neglected, this Jewish concern was commendable. Jesus certainly was not critical of the principle that the rich should help the poor, but He saw deeper into the motives of the men who were giving. When concern for the poor is linked with ostentatious giving, alms become a snare instead of a blessing. The rich men who were casting their gifts into the treasury that day were unaware that a great mind reader was analyzing their motives. They would have been shocked to know His estimate of them.

The Messiah was looking for a last sign of genuine piety in Israel. This He found in a poor widow. Her dress revealed her poverty. Almost ashamed to come at all, she could only bring the barest minimum allowed as a gift for the treasury. She had no cause for ostentation. She hoped that no one would notice her as she slipped her meager offering into the box. What she put in was not worth much — a small fraction of a working man's daily pay. It would not significantly increase the treasury balance. She did not, however, consider that her gift was not worth giving. She could have been excused for doing so, for the gift comprised her total available resources.

Jesus called His disciples over and pointed out the relative values of the gifts that had just been given. The widow was still in sight, and the disciples must have been amazed at what Jesus said to them. How did He know? He must have observed more than they had. The idea that the widow's gift was worth most was difficult for men to grasp who were accustomed to judge by material measures. The Messiah was introducing a new scale of values. The new age would place a higher premium on spiritual worth than on material possessions. The disciples should have been partially prepared for this teaching, having listened earlier to Jesus. In the Sermon on the Mount, He had expressed the blessing on the poor in spirit, that they would possess the Kingdom. Here, visually illustrated, was the same truth.

Both Mark and Luke, in relating this story of the widow's gift, connect it with the woe against ostentatious scribes who "devoured" widow's houses. The widow's poverty may have been hastened by such extortion. Whether this be so or not, the contrast was no doubt intentional. Those who grow rich through the misfortunes of others cannot successfully salve their consciences by giving large sums to charity. The standard of assessment used by Jesus excludes such practices.

Ruins to come

Mark 13:1-4 (Matthew 24:1-3; Luke 21:5-7)

Although the Jews hated the Herods, they were proud of the Temple that Herod the Great had built for them. It still was not completed, but it was nevertheless a magnificent sight. As the disciples were leaving the Temple precincts its magnificence fired their imagination. It may have been the sunlight reflected on white marble. They drew Jesus' attention to the beauty of the stones. Their massive proportions gave an impressive appearance to the whole structure. The disciples marveled at the architecture. For Jesus it had deeper significance. He had called it His Father's house, and it was symbolic of the true worship of God. Its piety, however, fell short of its magnificence. Within its shining exterior were the seeds of its destruction.

Jesus predicted, to the disciples' amazement, that a time would come when not one stone would stand upon another, an incredible forecast, for the structure was so new and massive. How could its enormous stones ever be overthrown? It seemed to

The Dome of the Rock, viewing eastward. The ridge of the Mount of Olives forms the background.

"And as some spoke of the temple, how it was adorned with noble stones . . . he said, 'As for these things which you see . . . there shall not be left here one stone upon another . . .'"
—LUKE 21:5, 6

be the most stable part of the restless city of Jerusalem.

The disciples mused on the words of Jesus but said nothing until they had reached the Mount of Olives. Jesus first sat down apart from them, and so they had an opportunity to discuss what He had said. They then asked for an explanation.

They asked two questions: "When will this be?" and "What will be the sign?" — inevitable questions from men who look to the future. Matthew includes in these questions a reference both to the Coming of Jesus and to the end of the age. The disciples

The Temple was demolished in A.D. 70 by the Roman armies under Titus (left). The Arch of Titus (right) records the destruction of Jerusalem in a relief (below) depicting Roman soldiers carrying away treasures from the Temple, including the seven-branched lampstand.

"But when you see Jerusalem surrounded by armies, then know that its desolation has come near . . . and Jerusalem will be trodden down by the Gentiles . . ."
— LUKE 21:20, 24

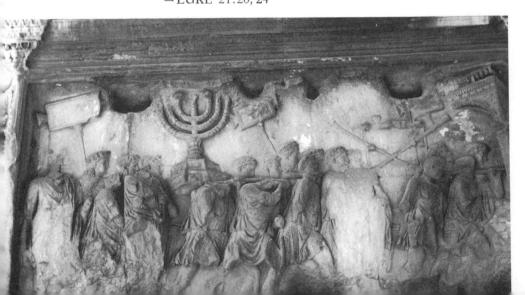

could not imagine a destruction of the Temple except as a calamity at the end of the age, and in His discourse Jesus related some sayings to one event and some to the other.

Jesus separated the Temple's destruction and the end of the age into two distinct events, which the disciples in their thinking had fused into one occurrence. Failure to realize this double strand in the whole discourse has led many to misinterpret the passage. Some who have denied that the discourse truly represents the teaching of Jesus think that the author wrongly attributed to Jesus a Jewish tract about the future. This theory has no foundation in fact, although it claims to absolve Jesus from the error of stating that the end of the world would occur when the Temple was destroyed. It is more reasonable to suppose that Jesus spoke of two distinct events. Another theory is that Jesus' predictions turned out to be wrong. This also conflicts with the facts, for many times Jesus predicted His own destiny. In interpreting the future, He saw two stages — one imminent, the other remote. Although not unconnected in thought, they are separated by a long interval of time not yet complete. The Temple was demolished in A.D. 70 by the Roman armies under Titus, but the end of the age is still future.

Most of Jesus' teaching about the future was given just before the passion. He was looking beyond the cross, to pull back the curtain of future events. The Messiah chose to speak of His Second Coming before the first had ended. The disciples found it difficult to separate the two.

Glimpses into the future

Matthew 24:4-44 (Mark 13:5-37; Luke 21:8-38)

Sitting with His disciples on the slopes of the Mount of Olives, Jesus talked about the distant future. Men are always curious about their destinies, but prophets of the future all too often mislead. Mere human foresight is inadequate for the task. Jesus is the best Guide, with His perfect insight into the pattern of human destiny. It must be noted, however, that what He revealed was not intended to gratify the curiosity of men. It was designed for an ethical purpose.

He first warned against deceivers who would come in His

name. Truth always has its counterfeits, and the mission of Jesus was not exempt from this tendency. The presence of deceivers would not in itself indicate the end. There were other means of telling — wars, earthquakes, and famines would occur, marking the beginning of the end time. The Christian Church has already lived through many such signs, but "the end is not yet."

The words of Jesus focused on the coming mission of the Church. His followers would bear testimony before governors and kings, but they were assured of the aid of the Holy Spirit. In spite of hostility, the Gospel was to be preached to all peoples. Those faithful to the Gospel would experience the hatred of men; even members of their family would become hostile to them.

Predictions of the more immediate future followed. The Messiah was looking ahead to the destruction of Jerusalem. In Matthew's and Mark's account, He spoke indirectly of "the desolating sacrilege," a term from the book of Daniel describing something utterly opposed to God. It would stand in the holy place, that is, the Temple. In Luke's account, the reference is more specifically to "Jerusalem surrounded by armies." Undoubtedly, both records refer to the siege of Jerusalem in A.D. 70, during which both city and Temple were laid waste. Jesus advised withdrawal from the city into the mountains. Great suffering was to fall upon the city and many of its inhabitants would become captives. The disciples knew of other captivities in Israel's history. As they listened to Jesus while surveying the city below crowned by its Temple, they found it difficult to grasp the predicted doom that awaited it. The Messiah knew that He was soon to be rejected in Jerusalem and He saw in this a symbol of the city's utter decline. Moreover, it was to be subjected to Gentile domination for a period called "the times of the Gentiles." The disciples had no clue as to how long that period was to be.

Throughout the whole period, false prophets and false Messiahs would arise. Jesus attached special importance to this, for He repeated the warning. The powers of deception by these prophets would be so subtle that even the elect would almost be led astray. There would also be signs in the heavens, as if the creation itself was keyed up to the coming crisis. The Jews were accustomed to such descriptions of catastrophic action. The darkening of the sun and moon would throw into brighter relief the glorious Coming of the Son of Man. Such optimism is all the more striking since Jesus spoke of it on the eve of His passion. Beyond the shadow of the cross He saw the glory to come. The swiftness of this coming in glory is, in Matthew's account, likened to the sudden swooping of eagles (or vultures) on carrion.

Although this far vista was mainly in Jesus' mind, a more imminent fulfillment was suggested by His parable about a fig tree. Its sprouting leaves and shoots signified that summer was near, a common enough observation. The Jewish nation, however, was the fig tree in the parable and its harvest of judgment was not far off. The Messiah read the signs, and He knew that within a generation it would happen. Just forty years later it took place.

Jesus brought the far-distant vista once more into view. The hour of the Coming of the Son of Man is unknown. The only fitting attitude for the members of the Kingdom is one of constant preparation. In another parable a doorkeeper commanded to watch for his master's return would be failing in his duty if he were not alert to open the door when the master came. Jesus had told His disciples about His future Coming so that they might learn to be watchful without being obsessed by events to come.

That Jesus talked about His Second Coming has seemed so alien to some that they excise it from the records of His teaching. The early Church, nonetheless, undoubtedly believed it, and its first leaders learned it from Jesus' own lips. It is to be the consummation of His mission. It is unthinkable that He left His people in the dark regarding future destinies. Neither the coming passion nor the subsequent resurrection would complete His task. Both Jesus and the early Christians were certain that He would come again.

Parables for the interim

Matthew 24:45—25:46

To help His followers have the right attitude while waiting for the Coming, Jesus told four stories, all recorded by Matthew. Their common theme is the importance of being prepared and the consequences of not being prepared. The first story is about household management. While the master was away he expected his manager to arrange the affairs of his household efficiently. He expected him to watch over the welfare of his subordinate. If the manager was a rogue who maltreated his servants, and took advantage of his master's absence, he would not escape punishment. The story was particularly apt for His followers as Jesus was preparing to go away from them. The Twelve would have greater responsibility than others. How would they react? Would they show wisdom or arrogance? By keeping their minds on the Master's Coming, they were to act at all times as if He were just at the door.

Jesus' next illustration told of a marriage feast. It was usual for a bridegroom to visit the bride's home for the marriage ceremony, after which he would escort her back to his own home. In the story, the bride had ten friends who had gathered at her house to escort the bridegroom into the house as soon as his approach was heralded. Evidently the bridegroom had to make a considerable journey and was uncertain of the time of his arrival. The maidens, aware of this, provided themselves with lamps in case they needed to go out after darkness had fallen. Five of them, however, failed to check their oil supply, and they discovered their lack only when the bridegroom's arrival was imminent. They begged to borrow oil from their companions, but these had no excess to share. While they were out to replenish their supply, the bridegroom came. They returned too late to escort him to the marriage feast. The details need not be pressed. The message is that of the first story—the need for watchfulness. The Messiah presented Himself as part of His own

Lamps of Palestine from New Testament
times. The larger hole at the top
was for the adding of oil.

"And the foolish said to the wise, 'Give us some of your oil, for our lamps are gone out'"
— MATTHEW 25:8

parable. He was the Bridegroom to come. He knew that many professing followers would not be prepared for Him, either in the present or in the future.

His third story was a parable from the commercial world. While the boss was away, his employees were responsible for the wise handling of his finances. Their responsibilities were not equal, since some had more skill than others. Three servants were made responsible respectively for five talents, two talents, and one talent. A talent was worth a considerable sum, and the boss expected the money to be put to good use. The first two servants gained 100 percent growth, but the third gained nothing. The master commended the two who had acted wisely and promised them both further responsibility. They would be partners of his pleasure. The other man, having formed a wrong estimate of his master, was scared that he might lose the talent and thus incur his master's wrath. Accordingly, he buried it in the ground. He at least saved the money, but the master was not impressed with his timidity. His business could never thrive on such methods. More serious was the servant's criticism of his character, over which he expressed his anger. He could at least have gained interest from the bankers. The master ordered the slothful servant to be cast out.

These three stories present contrasts between the wise and foolish, and the sense of contrast is extended in the fourth story. The imagery is of a shepherd with a mixed herd of sheep and goats. He separated them, placing the sheep on his right and the goats on his left. Jesus merged this rural scene into an assize. The shepherd became the enthroned King and the sheep became the inheritors of the Kingdom. Those on the left were rejected and punished. The grounds of acceptance or rejection were practical. Acts of kindness to the least of the King's subjects are counted as if done for the King himself. Where such kindness is absent, it amounts to an insult against the King.

A difficulty arises over this teaching. Is the inheritance dependent on works of mercy? If so, the mission of Jesus would be unnecessary. Instead of going to the cross, He should have organized a society for social relief. This was, however, the eve of His passion, and He knew the necessity of the cross. The interpretation of the parable must take account of this. It seems best to suppose that those who failed to be concerned about their brethren were those who never discovered the way and mission of Jesus. They were self-centered, but He by contrast was prepared to sacrifice Himself. He put others first.

Betrayed to IIis enemies

Luke 22:1-6 (Matthew 26:1-5, 14-16; Mark 14:1, 2, 10, 11)

Jesus had finished His public teaching. What He still needed to say was reserved for the disciples on the eve of His death. Ominous clouds were forming. He was fully aware of developments to come. Once again He reminded the disciples that He would be "delivered up to be crucified." He had mentioned crucifixion before, but now it was imminent. Matthew, who recorded it, gives no hint of the disciples' reactions. This is left to the readers' imagination. The stark reality did not strike the disciples until it happened.

The Jewish leaders were discussing a plot. They sought the best way of arresting Jesus without causing a riot, for they were still afraid of popular reaction. Their own opinion of the Messiah was already formed. They judged that He deserved death. There was no concern for granting Him a fair trial. They were not seeking justice.

Next in the grim drama occurred one of the saddest acts of history. The leaders' breakthrough to Jesus came from the inner circle of Jesus' friends. Luke and John state that Satan entered the heart of Judas. The result was the basest treachery. The leaders were delighted when one of the Twelve divulged the movements of Jesus so that He might be secretly arrested. Judas bargained for a reward for the information he gave; the amount agreed upon was thirty pieces of silver. Those who offered it were unaware that this amount had been predicted for the betrayal of the Messiah. They were fulfilling the prophecy of Zechariah (cf. Zech. 11:12). More significant was the fact that Judas was receiving the current price for selling a slave.

Those thirty pieces of silver in the hands of Judas Iscariot burned in his conscience until he could stand it no longer. He flung the coins down at the feet of those who had paid him. Why did he betray his Master? No one will ever know the actual motives in His dark Satan-filled soul. Perhaps it was a reaction to the announcement that Jesus was soon to die. Like the others, he had left all to follow Jesus. Judas knew, as treasurer, that the material resources of the little band were meager. Did he fear what would happen when Jesus had gone? Was he trying to salvage something from the wreckage of an unfulfilled Kingdom? Was he thinking he would be left destitute? Money would be useful, however obtained. His eagerness is best brought out by Matthew, who says that Judas took the initiative in extracting a fee. Wherever the gospels have circulated, his act of treachery has been condemned. He is representative of all who have betrayed Jesus after professing to be His friends. Material greed has too often turned men against the Messiah.

The leaders never knew the significance of their action. In paying the price of a slave for Jesus, they paid it from the same treasury from which the sacrifices used in the Temple worship were bought. They finally had Him in their grasp. Jesus, having already predicted His Passion, was not taken by surprise. His mission was bound up with their plot. Once He had been offered like the Temple lambs, no other offering would be necessary. Neither Judas nor the Jewish leaders got the point. They never knew that their victim was the Messiah. In contrast to their treachery, intrigue, and greed, the figure of Jesus stood in unimpeachable dignity.

22

The Upper Room

Preparing for the Passover

Luke 22:7-13 (Matthew 26:17-19; Mark 14:12-16)

During the last week of His life Jesus spent the days in Jerusalem, but He lodged each night outside the city. The day of unleavened bread marked the commencement of the Passover festival, one of the most notable festivals in the Jewish calendar. The Passover commemorated the ancient Exodus. The careful ritual, which every devout Jewish household observed, was highly symbolic. All trace of leaven, an emblem of evil, had to be obliterated. Every part of the house had to be systematically searched. All leaven would be collected and at a given time destroyed. Not until this had been done was the household prepared for the Passover feast.

Often, more than one household celebrated the feast together under the same roof, and those who owned property in Jerusalem placed their rooms at the disposal of others. The whole city was jammed with pilgrims, and the congestion caused difficulty in making arrangements for eating the feast. Jesus had special reason to keep this feast. It would be the last time He would do so. He knew, moreover, that His death would make all further Passover sacrifices irrelevant. Where was it to be held? Luke tells how Jesus told Peter and John to go and make ready. They naturally asked, "Where?" They probably thought it was out of the question to find a place. If so, they reckoned without their Master. Knowing His passion to be near, He left no details to chance.

303

He approached His destiny with calm deliberation. A meeting place for the feast was essential because of all that Jesus still planned to say and do in the presence of His disciples.

The two disciples were told that they would find a man carrying a pitcher of water. Water-carrying was generally done by women or slaves. The man concerned would certainly not be the owner of the room, but probably a servant. How were the disciples to know which man? They did not stop to question, for they had confidence in Jesus. (They no doubt remembered the colt tied by the wayside at Bethphage.) They found the man exactly as Jesus had said. Was it supernatural knowledge on His part, or was the provision of a room and the signal pre-arranged? Whichever it was, it shows the wisdom of Jesus. Only the two disciples would know beforehand the place. The betrayer would not be allowed to stop the sacred proceedings that night.

In Matthew's account of the disciples' instructions, they were to say, "The Teacher says, My time is at hand." This is significant, for it suggests that Jesus had had previous conversations with him. It suggests even that he was a follower of Jesus, for who else would understand the allusion to the Master's "time"? It may further imply that the Messiah's time for keeping the feast was different from the usual. Did He eat the Passover the night before most people were eating it? Many scholars think that He must have done so. He was investing the old feast with new meaning.

Another feature of interest is that whereas Jesus told His disciples to ask for the *kataluma* — the room that opened out on the courtyard, the owner allowed Him the use of the much better *anagaion* or *anōgeon* — the upper guest room. The upper room would be more secluded, and Jesus would more easily be able to impart His priceless farewell truths, which John has recorded. There may be significance in the fact that the only other use of the word *kataluma* in the New Testament is for the inn from which Mary and Joseph were turned away on the night when Jesus was born. Perhaps Luke saw some connection between the events as he related this part of his story.

The room was already prepared, furnished with seats for guests to recline at a table supplied with the necessities of the

The Old City of Jerusalem, looking west from the high tower of the centrally located Lutheran church.

"And he will show you a large upper room furnished and ready; there prepare for us"
—MARK 14:15

feast. Some think that the disciples would have had to prepare a lamb. If so, it would have been necessary for them to take a lamb and kill it at the appropriate time and place in the Temple. The owner of the house, however, may have provided the lamb. No Passover feast could be celebrated rightly without a lamb. But would Jesus have used a lamb when He knew that He Himself was to be the Lamb of God at that particular feast? When all was prepared and the disciples were seated in the room, Judas, the treasurer, perhaps wondered most how Jesus came to have the use of so splendid a room without his knowledge of it. He may also have wondered if the Master suspected his treachery.

An example of humility
John 13:1-20

The thoughts of Jesus in the upper room differed greatly from the thoughts of the disciples. He knew that His "hour" had come. He knew that this was His last meal with those who had accompanied Him for three years. They, however, had no understanding of the nearness of His end. They needed further teaching before leaving the room together. Much of what they were to hear was beyond them for the present, but when they remembered the words after the passion they understood.

The disciples had probably arranged the couches on which those sharing the meal would recline. It was usual to place them on three sides of the table with the fourth side left open to facilitate serving. The two main guests would sit at each side of the host. It is not clear in what order the disciples arranged their seating. It is unlikely that Jesus told them where to sit. His mind was deeply occupied with other things. The completion of His mission was of far greater consequence than matters of protocol. The order of precedence, however, meant much to the disciples, as is evident from the quarrels they had had as to which of them was the greatest. John apparently sat next to Jesus, since he leaned on Jesus' breast. Judas must have been somewhere near Jesus, and his nearness must have added to the Master's distress.

During supper, Jesus concentrated His thoughts on the Twelve. He saw before Him the nucleus of the coming Church. He knew, nonetheless, their lack of preparation and their need of a genuine spirit of service. They needed a lesson in humility. Without explanation, Jesus rose from His seat, took off His cloak, used a towel as an apron and poured water into a basin. The disciples watched Him. He was not acting like a normal host. He was doing a servant's chore. He began to wash their feet.

The action was strange and seemingly improper. It would have been more intelligible at the beginning of the feast as the guests had entered the room. It never dawned on the disciples that this was an object lesson for their benefit. As Peter watched, a growing sense of the incongruity of Jesus' performing so menial a task gripped him. He hastily decided that he would refuse to allow Jesus to wash his feet. His intentions were well-meant but misguided, for none of them needed this lesson more urgently than Peter. Jesus graciously assured him that he would later understand the reason for the action. Nevertheless, Peter became more insistent and declared that neither now nor at any time would he allow it. He had not yet learned that he had no right to dictate to Jesus. The mission of Jesus could not be managed in Peter's way. He would tragically discover this before many more hours had passed. Jesus gently reminded Peter that refusal to allow the washing meant rejection of his part in the mission of Jesus. This had not occurred to him. He compensated for his mistake by requesting a more complete washing, as if his loyalty was in proportion to how much of him was washed. Again he had misunderstood. The foot washing was symbolic. It was more than a physical washing — it was a cleansing of the heart and mind. The whole incident reflected Peter's immaturity as well as the warmth of his feelings. To Jesus it illustrated how little-prepared these disciples were for the continuance of His mission.

Most poignant of all was the Master's washing of the feet of Judas. Only Jesus knew of his evil designs. Had the others known, they would not have tolerated his presence. Jesus could read the mind of Judas. He told all the disciples that the foot washing had not made every one of them clean. The action did nothing to change the mind of Judas. He was too far gone. He probably despised the servility of the one he had determined to betray. If the Messiah could stoop to this kind of act, no hope remained for a real revolution. His Kingdom was not based on principles that appealed to the hardheaded Judas.

The lesson of humility was pressed home. He was the Master; they were the servants. He had given them an example. After Pentecost they learned the significance of that example. They achieved greatness, but not in the world's way. In the later history of the Church, symbolic foot washing was practiced, and it still is among some groups. The lesson of humility is nonetheless as valid now as it was on the eve of the passion of Jesus.

Focus on Judas

John 13:21-30 (Matthew 26:20-25; Mark 14:17-21; Luke 22:21-23)

It was a solemn moment when Jesus mentioned the betrayal. He spoke of having chosen the disciples, yet not all. He recalled Scripture that said that the one eating bread with Him was lifting up his heel against Him. He wanted to prevent the disciples from being too greatly shocked when it happened. He also wanted Judas to know that his plans were no secret. The disciples were mystified. They probably thought it was all a mistake, until they noted the emotional stress under which Jesus had spoken. He then told them bluntly that one of them was a traitor.

The atmosphere became tense. They wanted to know the betrayer's identity. The face of Judas revealed nothing. They were completely bewildered. Peter made signs to John to ask Jesus who it was. Whether all heard John's question "Who is it?" or whether it was merely whispered is not certain. Nor is it clear whether all heard the answer. They nonetheless all saw the action of Jesus in dipping the sop, probably consisting of meat, unleavened bread, and herbs, into the bowl. In the bowl was the *charoseth,* a mixture of wine and fruit. They also saw Jesus pass the sop first to Judas and then to the rest of them in turn. The others would not understand why Judas received the sop first. This was normally an honor reserved for the chief guest. Perhaps some of them resented Judas' receiving this honor. Only Jesus knew the true extent of his unworthiness. It was His last appeal to the man who had turned against Him. In receiving the sop, Judas' conscience must have been seared beyond feeling to accept it from the one he had come to hate.

The others were gripped with intense sorrow. They genuinely loved their Master and were horrified at the thought of His being betrayed. Their subsequent self-analysis is moving, as seen in the repeated question, "Lord, is it I?" Jesus answered each in the same way. The betrayer was one sharing the meal with Him. When Judas asked the same question, Jesus simply said, "You have said it." Apparently, the others did not hear.

Judas had eaten the sop. The others saw him suddenly move toward the door. They heard Jesus tell him to do quickly what he was about to do. They discovered only later what He meant.

At the time they were making two wrong assumptions. Some thought that Judas needed to hurry to buy something for the feast. Others thought that he was commissioned to give money to the poor. Neither was probable, but the disciples were too bewildered for rational thinking.

Writing later of those events, John states that Satan entered Judas at that time. There was no other explanation for his treachery. John mentioned that it was night as Judas left. He knew also that night had come to the life of Judas. So great was the moral failure of the man, that Jesus said to them all, even before Judas had left, that it would have been better had His betrayer never been born. The Messiah was alone with the eleven. John remembered and later wrote down some of the priceless things that Jesus said before they, too, went out into the night together.

Why Jesus chose a man like Judas will always be a mystery. He could not have been mistaken about his character. Jesus must have known that the time spent with him during the ministry would harden rather than soften the man. Judas seemed impervious to all the gracious acts of God through Jesus Christ. His presence in the apostolic band, however, may have been salutary for the training of the rest. The discovery that a traitor belonged to the group led to serious self-examination. Those who later became the spearhead of the Christian mission would not easily forget the grace that protected them from moral and spiritual decline like that of Judas. Moreover, they must have marveled at the patience Jesus had shown toward His betrayer on the eve of His passion.

A promise and a prediction

John 13:31-38

After Judas departed, the tension eased. The Messiah could now speak of what was nearest to His heart — over, He spoke of it in terms of glory. He wo ering clouds to impair His vision. Though H trayer was already putting his treachery in with calm confidence. There was no sugge sion would fail. The Son of Man was abou cause God had determined it. Man's most instruments of God in this process of glorification. Jesus saw the hour of His passion as the hour of His glory. His confident approach to the future went far to offset the disciples' shock at the news of betrayal.

Coupled with a certainty of the ultimate success of the mission, Jesus showed a special tenderness toward His disciples. He called them "little children." (Many years later John wrote to some of the followers of Jesus and used the same form of address. It had evidently deeply impressed him when Jesus used it that night.) The tenderness was timely, for the Messiah had to speak to them about His departure. It was a painful topic. He used the same words that He had earlier addressed to the crowd — "Where I am going you cannot come." That this saying was as mystifying to the disciples as to the other Jews shows how little they had learned from the previous predictions of Jesus. He would say more on this subject later in the conversation.

He gave His disciples a "new commandment." The commandment was "Love one another," so different from the usual demands of the law. Moreover, Jesus provided the standard by which the quality of a man's love could be assessed. The yardstick was no less than His own love for His disciples. There could be no higher standard. His mission was characterized by love. The badge of His followers was to be the badge of love. This, too, made a deep impression on John, for he wrote about love at length in his first epistle.

Peter, at this point, brought up again the subject of departure. He felt he must know more. "Lord, where are you going?" Receiving no answer, he was merely told that he could follow later but not now. This only increased his perplexity. The generous-hearted Peter wanted to know why, although he did not wait for an answer. He assured his Master that he was ready for the worst, even death for Jesus' sake. Peter's sincerity need not be questioned, but he did not grasp the truth that it was Jesus, rather, who needed to die for him. He had missed the real core of the mission of Jesus, which could never be achieved by heroics on Peter's part. It required the death of the Son of God.

The Messiah knew the weaknesses of Peter. He knew of his approaching fall. He predicted a threefold denial before cock-
. John left the incident there, but the synoptic writers filled

in additional details. Luke prefaced the prediction with a saying of Jesus that Satan had desired to sift Peter like wheat, but that Jesus had prayed for him. This throws a flood of light on the Messiah's own approach to the coming denial. He knew that He was wrestling with an evil power behind Peter's disloyalty. The mind of Peter was merely a battleground, as His own mind had been in the wilderness. He had gained a strength to share with others through that experience, and He urged Peter to do the same after he was restored. Peter must have been bewildered as he listened. He exclaimed that he would rather die than deny, as Matthew and Mark both note. Moreover, the other disciples proclaimed the same loyalty. Matthew also shows that Jesus' mind was musing on an Old Testament prophecy, from Zechariah 13:7, "I will strike the shepherd, and the sheep of the flock will be scattered." He knew that in a few hours His "sheep" would forsake Him and flee, in spite of their present vows of loyalty. The Messiah was treading a lonely path.

Themes from the upper room: the Paraclete

John 14.10, 17, 25, 26; John 15:26, 27; John 16:7-15

To prepare His disciples for His departure, Jesus made five statements about the Spirit's activity. The significance of Jesus' farewell sayings about the Holy Spirit was not fully appreciated until some six weeks later, when the disciples experienced the power of the Spirit at Pentecost.

The Spirit was named by Jesus as "another Counselor." He was to be to the disciples all that Jesus Himself had been. Moreover, He was to be the Father's gift in response to the prayer of Jesus. Such teaching would have been alien to those outside the circle of His disciples, but He expected His own followers to know about the Spirit, since He dwelt within them. This teaching became more real at Pentecost. The Spirit was given a special designation — "the Spirit of truth," a title which appears three times in this discourse. The name contrasts the utter reliability and veracity of the Spirit with all spirits of error.

The second saying makes clear that one of the Spirit's functions is to teach — a continuation of what Jesus had already been doing. The disciples still had much to learn after the departure of Jesus. They needed a competent teacher, and the Spirit was promised to fulfill that role. The basic curriculum would still be the teaching of the Messiah, which would be brought to their minds. Jesus knew the disciples had short memories, but the Spirit would prompt them. Through this, they would retain in their minds the priceless teaching of their Master. Whatever the methods or forms by which Christian traditions were to be preserved, their authenticity was assured by the Spirit. On the eve of His passion, Jesus looked confidently into the future. His teaching would not be lost, nor would its veracity depend on the fallible minds of men. He looked to the activity of the Spirit to ensure the trustworthy account of His sayings.

The third function of the Spirit's work is to witness to Jesus. The Spirit is His representative among His people. This function furnishes the norm by which any counterfeit spiritual agencies can at once be detected. All that conflicts with the teaching and claims of Jesus does not proceed from the Holy Spirit. Jesus knew how much His followers would need the witness of the Spirit. The success of His mission depended on the work of the Spirit. The book of Acts amply illustrates this fact.

The fourth saying describes the Spirit's work in the world. The Spirit would convict men of their sin, which they could never understand apart from the Spirit's help. The Spirit would show men their unbelief. The Spirit would also convince men of righteousness, because they would not see the point of seeking a righteousness beyond their own. They would otherwise fail to see the relevance of the mission of Jesus. The Spirit would also witness to judgment, making clear that in Christ the ruler of this world had been defeated.

The concluding statement reminded the disciples that the Spirit would be their Guide. Launched, as they were to be, into a hostile world to proclaim the truth, they needed an authority which only the Spirit could give. Not imparting His own authority, the Spirit's task was to glorify the Messiah and to speak of things that were to come. The mark of a Spirit-led disciple, as of a Spirit-led Church, is the extent to which Christ is glorified. It must be remembered that Jesus never spoke of His glory except in conjunction with His suffering.

All that Jesus had been to His followers would be continued

and expanded by the Spirit. This was the greatest gift that He could give to His Church after His own saving mission was accomplished.

Themes from the upper room: Jesus as the Way

John 14:1-30

Facing His disciples at the supper table, Jesus knew that many questions remained unanswered in their minds. Peter had asked, "Lord, where are you going?" and Jesus enlarged on this. In speaking of His Father's house He used a familiar illustration. It was a house of many guest rooms He said, and He was going there. This was a picturesque way of saying that He was going to the Father and assuring them that they would follow Him there. He mentioned His coming again, which some see as an indication that at His death He made a visit to that Home and afterward returned, but others see it as a more likely allusion to the Second Coming.

The disciples did not understand. Thomas asked, "How can we know the way?" It was an admission of confusion, but it gave the Master the opportunity to point to Himself as the Way. Before much longer it would dawn on the disciples that there was no other way to God except through Him. They would learn that this saying aptly summed up the purpose of the mission of Jesus, to provide a path to God.

Next, Philip requested, "Lord, show us the Father, and we shall be satisfied." This request reflects the disciples' bafflement, for Jesus had just said that those who knew Him would know the Father. Philip had not recognized in Jesus the perfect revelation of the Father. He deserved the gentle rebuke — "How can you say, 'Show us the Father'?" The disciples were earnest men but slow to understand. They were baffled at the moment, but Jesus proceeded to tell them that those who believed in Him would do greater things than He had done. It seemed incredible, but the key was to be found in the relationship between Jesus and the Father. The disciples were asked to believe. They should be prepared to do this for Jesus' own sake, on the basis of His own person. If not, they could at least believe as a result of seeing the works that He had performed.

The Messiah's own mind was filled with thoughts of the Father. It was the Father who would send the Holy Spirit. He would love those who loved Jesus. This, however, raised another question, put by Judas (not Judas Iscariot, who had left): "Lord, how is it that you will manifest yourself to us, and not to the world?" It was an important question. The disciples had to learn that God's choice is not arbitrary. Understanding would come to those who loved enough to obey the words of Jesus.

Understandably, the disciples were fearful at the thought of Jesus' leaving them, but He promised them His peace. It was a peace worth having since it could exist, as it did, in spite of the tensions of the coming passion. The Messiah made clear that what He was about to do was what the Father had commanded. The disciples would still have access to the Father through Him. He pointed out that the Father was greater than He was, in His present limitations. This could not fail to provide some encouragement to the disciples. In spite of the intense spiritual conflict within Himself, He knew the adversary had no authority over Him.

The way that Jesus spoke to His disciples is different from the way most people would have expected the Messiah to speak. He made no attempt to avoid the coming tragedy. He faced the future with a calm dignity born only of the certainty that the path of sorrow was the path to glory. The real Messiah could not be other than a suffering Messiah. However impossible men found the idea, Jesus Himself knew that it would lead to salvation for many.

Themes from the upper room: secrets of spiritual growth

John 15; John 16

Possibly Jesus at this point left the upper room. He may have passed a vine on the way to the garden of Gethsemane, which provided an apt illustration of a lesson His disciples needed to learn. He described Himself in the figure of a vine. He was the strong stem; the disciples were the branches for producing the fruit. It required little imagination to conclude what would happen when the branches were not attached to the stem. They could not even survive, let alone produce fruit. What better illustration could there be of the coming dependence of the disciples on Jesus! He spoke of their relationship to Him as an abiding in Him, which involved a particularly close connection. The life of the branches was to be the same as that of the stem. When the disciples spoke they were to speak the words of Jesus. That is why He could assure them that the Father would answer their prayers, for they would ask those things that agreed with the mind of Jesus. He Himself furnished the perfect example. He was "abiding" in the Father. What He was about to do, however tragic it appeared to men, was the will of the Father. He was producing fruit by bringing glory to the Father. In the same way the disciples were to produce fruit. The whole process would result in joy, the same kind of joy that Jesus was then experiencing. This was echoed later by the writer of a New Testament epistle when he spoke of Jesus enduring the cross because of the joy set before Him (Heb. 12:2).

Jesus next spoke of the greatest human love, as of a man laying down his life for his friends. This was His thinking on the passion. His suffering and death were to prove His love for them, and He wanted them to develop the same love for each other. He put it strongly, in the nature of a command. He was about to demonstrate His love by giving His life for them. It was not too much to ask them to show love to each other. They were people chosen by God to be fruitful, and the first and most important fruit is love, as Paul later noted (Gal. 5:22; 1 Cor. 13).

Spiritual growth is never easy. Jesus knew that the disciples would be in an atmosphere no less hostile than His own. The world (understood as all that is dominated by unspiritual principles) hated Him. It would also hate them. They could not expect the men of the world to treat the servant any better than they had treated the Master. Jesus was a realist. He never expected His mission to be popular. It was bound to run into persecution. Men who had no time for God would have no time for the mission of Jesus. They would ignore what He had done, but their hatred would be without excuse. It would lead to further persecution for the people of God. Jewish Christians, like the apostles, would be excommunicated. Moreover, the enemies of the Gospel would be convinced that they were doing God a service. The bewildered disciples would later remember that

Jesus had said these things the night before He died. They would recall how He forgot His own trials to reassure them. Later, when they felt the lash of persecution, the memory of His example brought a similar serenity.

The disciples remained mystified in spite of further assurances about the coming and work of the Holy Spirit. The suggestion that Jesus was going away still puzzled them. There was no need for them to ask further questions, for Jesus had read their thoughts. He gave them a paradoxical answer to their unexpressed questions. He told them they would weep when the world rejoiced. It would seem to them that they were on the losing side, but Jesus knew that just as surely as His own sorrow would be turned to joy — so would theirs. He mentioned the familiar human example of childbirth, when a mother forgets the anguish because her mind is on the joy of the newborn child. The disciples' sorrow when the stark reality of the cross confronted them would be transformed to joy on Easter morning.

When Jesus again spoke of the Father and His relationship to Him, the disciples thought they understood. They made a brave confession of faith in Jesus as having come from God. He knew, however, that in a few hours they would scatter in despair and fright. He could not say more. He could only reaffirm that He had overcome the world. This was the deepest assurance they could have.

23

The Passover and the Plot

The birth of a sacred institution

Matthew 26:26-30 (Mark 14:22-25; Luke 22:14-20)

Before leaving the upper room, Jesus inaugurated a new institution. In all probability, He was eating the Passover with His disciples the evening before the general observance of the feast. The apostle Paul gave expression to what Christians came to believe when he wrote, "Christ, our paschal lamb, has been sacrificed" (1 Cor. 5:7). This was no doubt in the mind of Jesus that night. The Jewish Passover was a memorial of the deliverance of the Israelites from slavery in Egypt, whereas the Christian "Passover" commemorates the greater deliverance of man from the slavery of sin.

During the Jewish feast, a son would ask his father, "What does this service mean?" This question would lead to a recital of the historical facts of Israel's redemption. These facts would be brought to mind in the symbolic ritual. In a similar way, Jesus instituted a pattern to commemorate His death. The simple actions, the plain bread and wine on the table, and the brief words comprise this impressive scene.

The Master took a piece of unleavened bread and raised it. Looking up, He prayed for a blessing on the bread. The head of every Jewish household would do the same as he presided over the Passover meal. Jesus may have used the same wording, but there were in His mind thoughts that never entered the mind of any other Jewish host. He knew that He Himself was to be the

317

Passover sacrifice. After giving thanks, He broke the bread into pieces, to symbolize the breaking of His body, which men were to witness within a few hours. He shared the pieces with His disciples, saying to them, "Take, eat; this is my body." Paul repeated the words in a fuller form, adding, "which is broken for you." This addition is valuable because it interprets. It highlights the vicarious nature of the suffering. Jesus was not sacrificed for His own sake, but for the sake of others. It was enough for them to know this at this juncture. Later, the apostles would come to know the meaning in more detail. Later still, Christian theologians would wrestle with its significance. The words of institution were kept to a minimum. Jesus wanted men to remember them. There was no time for more. Each time the disciples repeated the act, however, they would discover further meaning in the simple words.

The cup was also a familiar part of the Passover ritual, but new meaning was brought into this as well. As Jesus poured wine into the cup and held it, He offered another prayer of thanksgiving, His mind still on His coming sacrifice. It would involve the pouring out of His own blood just as He had poured the wine into the cup, a simple and effective reminder of what His death was all about. When the Old Covenant was ratified between God and Israel after the Exodus, it was ratified with blood (Exod. 24). Jesus inaugurated a New Covenant, which must also be ratified with blood — His own. He spoke of it as He handed the cup to the disciples — "Drink it, the blood of the new covenant shed for many." Luke's version is more personal — "shed for you," and Matthew's is more theological — "for the remission of sins." Both reveal the true intention of the Master. The benefits were to be shared by each of them personally, and the deepest meaning would never be grasped except in relation to sins. The Christian "Passover" was not instituted for righteous men, but for sinners.

According to Paul, both parts of the simple service had the same purpose — "in remembrance of me." Wherever observed, thereafter, Christians would remember that the passion of Jesus was a deliberate sacrifice on their behalf. Jesus spoke also of another feast, the messianic feast to come, which would inaugurate the future Kingdom. Jesus had told them earlier about that

Kingdom. They would know what He meant. The wine that was to be shared would be different — it would be new. Everything, in fact, would be new.

After that, they all sang a hymn, probably one of the Hallel psalms, and then went toward the Mount of Olives. The service, which was to play a dominant part in Christian worship, had ended, and Jesus — the central figure — moved on to fulfill the mission on which it was based.

The Messiah's parting prayer

John 17

This record of one of Jesus' prayers is more than a spiritual treasure. It is a guide and a pattern. To those with perception, it gives a deep insight into the character of Jesus. The prayer that He prayed in the hearing of the disciples before they reached Gethsemane has appropriately been called His "high-priestly prayer," since most of it consists of intercession for others.

Only the first part, which is the briefest portion, was offered on His own behalf. Although imminent events were much in His mind, He passed quickly over His own needs. He recognized that the "hour" had now dawned. It was the "hour" of destiny, not so much for Himself as for all mankind. In John's record, He had already rejected any selfish prayer to be saved from this hour. The other evangelists draw attention to a similar tension in Gethsemane, when the possibility of avoiding the "cup" was faced but strongly rejected. Here, Jesus desired one thing — that the Father might be glorified. This was no selfish prayer. It was an essentially outgoing prayer, for it requested that all who had been given to Jesus might have eternal life. As Jesus was talking to the Father about the glory that He had with the Father before the world was made, the disciples must have been overawed if they had realized that they had been living with one whose existence preceded the creation.

The second part of the prayer concerned the disciples. Their Master was praying for them. Some of His words were deeply challenging. They heard Him say that they had been given to

Him by the Father, as some precious legacy. They even heard Him say that they had kept the Father's word, that they knew that He was sent from God, and that they believed. He could still say such things in spite of their blunderings, constant quarrels, and failure to understand His simplest teachings. Nor was He unaware of their present need, for they heard Him pray, "Holy Father, keep them."

Jesus was thinking ahead. During the time that He had been with them, only one had been lost — Judas, the son of perdition. The rest were to remain in a hostile world. He might have prayed that they might be removed, but He did not. His very mission, though dependent on the coming Spirit, depended also on their presence in the world after Jesus' departure. Nonetheless, they desperately needed to be kept from the evil one. More than once, Jesus had warned them about the presence of this agency of evil, although He had assured them that Satan was already a defeated foe. To survive an adverse world, the disciples needed a special consecration, the same kind of consecration that Jesus had shown toward His own mission.

The third part of the prayer was a petition for the coming Church. The disciples were the firstfruits of a greater company. There was to be harmony and fellowship among the believers. He prayed for unity, the same kind of unity that existed between the Father and the Son, certainly more than organized unity. It is organic, springing from a common purpose to glorify the Messiah. Unity exists only to magnify Him. This kind of unity does not require organization to reflect it. Even the hostile world outside cannot fail to take stock of it.

The high regard that Jesus has for believers is seen from His petition that He might have them with Him to witness His glory. He knew some of them would witness His passion, but the suffering was transient. His glory was an essential characteristic. It did not become so by virtue of His passion. It had always been so — since before creation, as He had mentioned earlier in the prayer. He was fully conscious of His preexistence, and the passion must be viewed in the light of this. Jesus addressed His Father as "righteous," showing His awareness of the justness of God's redemptive plan. There was a cleavage between God and His world. The only way that the world could know God was not only through Christ, but also through His people. The Messiah had imparted both knowledge and love to His people, to be revealed through them to the world. On this triumphant note, Jesus ended His prayer. The close of that prayer marked the real beginning of the passion. Jesus had prefaced this event with prayer. It is in times of great crisis that a man's soul is laid bare, and this prayer of Jesus reveals something of His mind as He moved on to Calvary.

Gethsemane

Luke 22:31-46 (Matthew 26:31-46; Mark 14:26-42)

On the way to the Mount of Olives, Jesus surprised the disciples with the question, "When I sent you out with no purse or bag or sandals, did you lack anything?" Why did He suddenly ask this question? Was it to remind them that they were now on a very different mission from the former one? This was no mission of proclamation as the former was, but a spiritual conflict. The disciples answered, "Nothing"; they had found no lack. Jesus then gave them what appears to be conflicting advice. They were to have purse, bag, and sword. If no sword was available, they were to sell their cloak and buy one. The whole incident seems strangely militant. At first sight, it seems as if Jesus was advocating violence, but such an interpretation would be completely alien to His character. There is another explanation.

He quoted a passage of Scripture about Himself that He knew must be fulfilled, from one of the servant songs of Isaiah (Isa. 53:12) — a passage that speaks of the suffering Messiah. This theme was uppermost in the mind of Jesus on His way to the passion. He was conscious that this prophecy was about to be fulfilled in Himself, including the words, "He was reckoned with the transgressors." The disciples, on hearing these words, were still baffled, and they returned to the sword theme. They had discovered between them two swords, but Jesus merely said, "It is enough." If He had intended that His disciples arm themselves literally with swords, He would never have conceded that two were sufficient. He was speaking metaphorically. Not long afterward, when Peter used a sword to smite the ear of the

"And they went to . . . Gethsemane . . . And he took with him Peter and James and John, and began to be greatly distressed and troubled"
— MARK 14:32, 33

One of the ancient olive trees in the Garden of Gethsemane. The age of these trees easily reach back into early Roman times in Palestine.

high priest's servant, he received the rebuke that all who take the sword perish by it.

Jesus arrived at the garden, where His own spiritual conflict was to be intensified. Inside the garden, the Master and His disciples separated into groups. He left eight of them in one place. Then He withdrew a short distance with the other three disciples — Peter, James, and John. They soon noticed how distressed He had become. They remembered afterward His words to them, "My soul is very sorrowful, even to death; remain here, and watch with me." He urged them to pray that they might not be led into temptation. His words echoed the prayer that He had earlier taught all the disciples to pray. He knew how desperately they needed watchfulness and prayer. Moreover, He felt his own urgent need to pray.

He moved away from the chosen three to be entirely alone. This was the hour of His agony. They saw Him prostrate on the ground. They could hear Him praying. They never forgot it. The words became irradicably etched on their minds, "My Father, if it be possible, let this cup pass from me; nevertheless not as I will, but as thou wilt." Shortly after, excessive weariness drove the disciples to sleep. They were unable to plumb the depth of His anguish, nor has anyone ever been able to do this. He knew the cup could not pass, and yet He prayed that it might. His prayer reveals the perfect humanity of Jesus. It has heartened many of His followers who have passed through sorrows for His sake. In His mind it was the will of God that resolved all problems. This was no fatalistic approach, but an acceptance of the perfect planning of God. He had no desire to save Himself. The Father had sent Him to save others. The cup of suffering, however the flesh shrank from it, was His appointed lot.

With such sorrow upon Him, the disciples' failure to keep awake added further distress. It emphasized for Jesus, before His trial and crucifixion, the unutterable loneliness of His messianic mission. He could only urge them to watch and pray. He knew of their loyal intentions, but He was also aware of their weakness. Three times He prayed the same prayer, and each time when He came back the disciples were asleep. After the third time it was too late. The betrayer had arrived. The "hour" had begun to unfold and Jesus faced the time of His sacrifice. The disciples peered sleepily at the approaching rabble, unaware of what it all meant.

Luke adds one detail that the others do not record. He notes that while He was praying, Jesus perspired so heavily that it seemed as if great drops of blood were falling to the ground. As a medical man, Luke would know that the cause of this was intense strain. It demonstrates even more eloquently than words could do how massive was the spiritual conflict in which Jesus was engaged.

Betrayal and arrest

John 18:1-12 (Matthew 26:47-56; Mark 14:43-52; Luke 22:47-53)

Judas knew that Jesus had visited the garden of Gethsemane when He desired quietness. He knew that He would be there that night. He had informed the chief priests of this fact, and it had been arranged that a band of men were to carry out the arrest. To avoid mistaken identity, a sign had been prearranged. Judas was to kiss Jesus in greeting. He could hardly have conceived a sign more deceitful. In pretension of closest fellowship, the kiss was rooted in basest treachery. With the same lips that agreed to the infamous bargain of betrayal, Judas imparted the traitor's kiss.

All worked according to plan. Judas headed the rabble armed with swords and sticks. They shattered the stillness of the night and burst into the garden. Possibly, the other disciples did not at first recognize the features of the leader. They would not have guessed it was Judas. Their minds were still troubled about Jesus. No record is left of their reactions when, in the flickering lantern light, they recognized the betrayer. Three of the evangelists say that he was one of the Twelve, as if the disciples never got over the shock of it.

The rabble approached, but Jesus remained the real master of the situation. He showed no panic, only calm dignity. He asked whom they sought, although He knew the answer. Several shouted, "Jesus of Nazareth." He told them that He was the man. Those in the vanguard were overcome by the sheer dignity of Jesus. They fell back, seized by a sudden sense of awe. Why it struck them at this point when previously they had so often missed it, is difficult to say. Their sense of awe soon vanished. Jesus again asked them whom they sought and again received the same answer. He was not thinking of His own safety. He knew His "hour" had come, but He requested that His disciples be allowed to go. At the time of His own greatest need He was concerned for others. The crowd still made no move to arrest Him, as if uncertain whether He was really the one they wanted.

At last Judas nerved himself to give the required sign. Perhaps he regretted suggesting it, or, more likely, he thought it could be dispensed with since Jesus had twice admitted His identity. Mark telescopes the events as if Judas immediately kissed Him. John includes the earlier details but omits the kiss. Luke says that Jesus asked, "Judas, would you betray the Son of man with a kiss?," whereas Matthew alone mentions that Judas hailed Jesus as Master and that Jesus addressed His betrayer as "friend."

The moment was dramatic. The awkward pause ended. Some laid hands on Jesus. At once Peter impulsively struck out with a sword, a wild gesture of utter confusion. The tip of the sword sliced off the ear of the high priest's servant. Following the flash of the sword came the healing touch of the Master. He acted in mercy in a scene of violence. He had not come for violence. He commanded Peter to resheath the sword, for he would only perish if he did not do so. The Messiah had other methods. Peter's unthinking act of defense was a gesture of loyalty, but he wholly misunderstood the mission of Jesus. Jesus must drink the "cup" that the Father had given Him.

The multitude became sufficiently hushed, and Jesus spoke to them. He reminded them that His Father could send twelve legions of angels at His bidding, a company far greater than the multitude of His captors. The Father's plan, however, was the "cup," not the legions. The obedience of Jesus at His arrest involved a supreme act of powerful restraint. Nothing must hinder the Father's purpose. Even so, He challenged the mob at this critical moment, "Have you come out as against a robber, with swords and clubs to capture me? Day after day I sat in the temple teaching, and you did not seize me." Without waiting for an answer He acknowledged that the Scripture must be fulfilled, a point that must have been wholly lost on the crowd, but which was full of significance for Jesus. As He allowed hostile hands to grasp Him, He did so in the consciousness that He was wholly yielded to the Father's will.

Peter's burst of heroism rapidly turned to cowardice. Jesus found Himself alone, for all the disciples had fled.

Before two high priests

John 18:13, 14, 19-24 (Matthew 26:57-64; Mark 14:53-62)

Jesus was bound with ropes. The ropes eloquently testified to man's ineffective attempt to bring His messianic power to nothing. The spiritual and moral strength of the captive vividly exposed the real weakness of the captors. The Good Shepherd was voluntarily giving His life for the sheep.

He was led to the house of Annas, the former high priest, who also was father-in-law of the present high priest, Caiaphas. Annas was still regarded with great reverence by the people. The Romans had put him out of office, but not out of effective leadership. He faced Jesus with interest. He had been party to the plot to arrest Him, and he had had time to think up the questions that he would put to Him. He asked about His followers and His teaching, but he was not prepared for Jesus' reply. Jesus knew the reason for the questions. He knew that Annas was not seeking information, for he had no interest in the teaching of Jesus. His only concern was to support the plot against Him. The Messiah, however, had not come to waste words on those who had no intention of listening. He pointed out to Annas that there had been ample opportunity for him to find out for himself for Jesus had taught openly in synagogues and in the Temple. Jesus continued, "Why do you ask me? Ask those who have heard me, what I said to them; they know what I said."

Jesus' reply was both reasonable and right, but authority is sometimes insensitive to reason and justice. The high priest was more concerned with his own dignity, and his stooges, well-trained to guard that dignity, regarded Jesus' answer as an insult to their leader. At once one of them struck Jesus with his hand. Jesus challenged him to point out the wrong in His previous statement, if there was anything wrong. He knew that His accusers were not disposed to reason. The whole sequence of the passion events was one of the world's most potent witnesses to the irrationality of man. Neither the truculent officer nor the aged high priest took up the challenge of Jesus. Annas sent Him to his son-in-law.

Jesus was now confronted with the man who had previously said concerning Him that it was fitting for one man to die for

Descending from the House of Caiaphas on Mount Zion, these stone steps are part of the ancient road that crossed the Kidron Valley to Gethsemane.

"Then they led Jesus from the house of Caiaphas . . ."
—JOHN 18:28

the people. Caiaphas had been thinking of political expediency, but he had uttered a spiritual truth that lay at the heart of the mission of Jesus. He never grasped the meaning of his own words. Caiaphas and his advisers were ill-prepared for a serious examination of evidence. The arrest did not result from a well-thought-out charge. The high priest and his councilors were uneasy in the presence of the prisoner. They had no witnesses. They knew that truth would be fatal to their cause. Their hope lay in false testimony. Any plan based on false witness is precarious, for lies often contradict each other. Since the plot against Jesus had been in the minds of the hierarchy for some time, it is astonishing that no charge against Him had been planned. At this stage they seemed to be clutching at any straw. They needed witnesses who had seen Him do some indictable offense or had heard Him speaking seditious words. That they had difficulty in finding any who would give testimony, however false, suggests that they were not closely in touch with people who had had anything to do with Jesus. At last two were found who remembered hearing Him say, "Destroy this temple and in three days I will raise it up." It was unimportant that He had referred to His own body. The statement as they reported it had overtones of sedition. It was a simple matter to claim that Jesus had said He would destroy the Temple. This in itself might have served as a sufficient charge, but when the witnesses added that He would build another within three days, the charge itself began to look decidedly thin, for the existing building had already taken nearly fifty years to build and was not yet completed. They were desperate for evidence to proceed on a charge of this nature. Mark comments that the witnesses could not agree.

Meanwhile, Jesus was still standing bound before the high priest. So far, Caiaphas said nothing to Him. Neither had Jesus said anything in answer to the trumped-up charge. The high priest could tolerate the tenseness of the atmosphere no longer. Rising from his seat, he demanded that Jesus should answer the charge, but Jesus remained silent. Caiaphas challenged Him to declare under oath whether He was the Messiah, the Son of God. This had nothing to do with the charge, but had much to do with the intense animosity toward Him on the part of the hierarchy. When Jesus answered in the affirmative, the earlier charge was at once dropped. He had openly affirmed His position before the official representative of the Jewish people. Moreover, the Messiah wanted Caiaphas to know that the mission would be a powerful success whatever the opposition. He assured him that He would come again in power.

The Jewish council shows its true colors
Luke 22:63-71 (Matthew 26:65-68; Mark 14:63-65)

It was still the early hours of the morning, and Caiaphas had just extracted a confession of messiahship from Jesus. In dramatic response he rent his clothes, an accepted method of expressing the strongest disapproval. The real motives of the members of the hierarchy were now in the open. They had determined to reject Jesus as the Messiah. In fact, they had never seriously considered accepting Him as such. He was not their kind of Messiah. Moreover, His claim to be Son of God was in their eyes blasphemy.

The high priest declared that no further witnesses were needed. He was undoubtedly relieved, since no two people could agree on the former charge. He asked the council for their opinion over what action should be taken. They declared that He was worthy of death. Mark notes that this judgment was unanimous. It was the culmination of a nation's rejection of its Messiah.

The announcement of judgment was the signal for vicious mockery of Jesus. Some spat on Him and struck Him. Others blindfolded Him and then struck Him, calling on Him to prophesy who had done it. These rough soldiers were unable to appreciate His mission; it was no fit subject for this ribaldry. Jesus knew that these men as much as any others needed the redemptive act that they were unwittingly helping to accomplish. Their flinging abuse at Him could not humiliate Him. They were doing no more than debasing themselves. Their empty jibes rang hollow against the ultimate dignity of the Son of God.

None of the evangelists tells what happened to Jesus during the next few hours until daybreak. The judgment hastily arrived at during the night required ratification by the full council, which was called to meet at the earliest possible time. When the council was assembled, Jesus was brought in. His accusers went straight to the point. They again challenged Jesus to say whether He was the Christ. He pointed out to them their unwillingness to believe even if He answered their request. Their most significant question had been asked from wrong motives.

Again Jesus affirmed His coming triumph. The Son of Man was to be seated on the right hand of the power of God, which was to say that He would be next to God. No wonder He had said that they would not believe Him. Not even His disciples were prepared to believe at this juncture. The only one certain of this was Jesus Himself. His confidence in His mission starkly contrasted with the incredulous company surrounding Him. They further asked, "Are you the Son of God?" It is not clear what was in their minds in asking this question. For them the title may have been associated with messianic claims. It seems from their reactions that it meant much more. When He answered affirmatively, the Sanhedrin regarded this as a sufficient charge. They judged Jesus to have condemned Himself by His own words.

The action moved to Pilate's court, where the more official part of the trial took place. Nevertheless, the proceedings before the Jewish council demonstrated the real cause of hostility against Jesus. There is no excuse for the Jewish hierarchy. Some have accused the evangelists of giving a biased account, but history is obstinate in maintaining the premise that there was no established legal charge against Jesus. The gospel writers clearly state that He was falsely accused. The just was to die for the unjust, as Peter later remarked in his epistle (1 Pet. 3:18).

Denied by His own

John 18:15-18, 25-27 (Matthew 26:69-75; Mark 14:66-72; Luke 22:54-62)

One of the Twelve had already denied his Master. The other eleven had deserted Him. The Messiah faced His judges alone, yet not quite alone. The impetuous Peter had gathered sufficient courage to watch the proceedings from a distance. He chose the role of observer rather than participant. John notes that another disciple was with Peter, possibly himself. It was someone who had access to the house of the high priest, for he secured entrance for Peter. Since Peter was enough of an individual to stand out in a group, he must have known that he was running a risk.

He noted a group of people warming themselves by the flickering embers of a fire kindled in the courtyard to ward off the chill of the night air. They were members of the household staff. He felt that he would be safe among them. One of the women servants, however, noticing his features in the light of the flames, stared at him and charged him with having been with Jesus of Nazareth. Losing his nerve, Peter strongly denied that he knew what she was talking about. She had probably seen him that week in Jerusalem in company with Jesus. Her charge against Peter showed no sympathy for the mission of Jesus. She seemed to be implying guilt by association. Surely the chief disciple should have been proud to be so immediately associated with His Master, especially since he previously offered to die for Him. More than a few who have sought to follow Jesus have seen themselves in the cowardice of Peter.

In spite of his denial, Peter thought it wisest to withdraw to the porch. His thoughts were probably too confused to notice the crowing of the cock in the background. Satan was sifting him as wheat and the process was painful and costly. He found himself a second time accosted by a woman, this time not directly. She addressed the bystanders and announced to them Peter's association with Jesus. Some of them then directly challenged Peter, who, in extreme panic, denied all knowledge of Jesus. Could he fall farther than this? How could he be so blatant after his intimate association with Jesus through three years? Not one of the evangelists makes any attempt to gloss over it. Perhaps they all recognized that they would have done the same had they been there.

About an hour elapsed. No one knows what passed through the mind of Peter during that time. He was still utterly scared, and unprepared to stand by his Master in this hour of His passion. For the third time he was accused to his face. His former denials left one problem unresolved. Not only did he look like one of the Twelve, but he spoke like one of them. They were Galileans, whose distinctive accent marked them out from the city dwellers of Jerusalem. Moreover one of the men present was a relative of the man whose ear had been severed by Peter's sword. He would be none too partial toward the attacker. He asked Peter to confirm that he had seen him in the garden with Jesus.

The hunt was becoming too hot. Peter used oaths and curses to convince his accusers. He again denied knowledge of Jesus. At the moment of this third emphatic denial, Peter's eye caught the glance of Jesus looking at him through the doorway. At the same moment the cock was crowing. Something in the look of Jesus prodded the mind of Peter to recall what Jesus had predicted. He no doubt remembered his own rash promise to die for

Him. His conscience was battered. He went out and wept the bitterest tears he had ever shed.

The soldier's ribaldry did not cut Jesus' spirit as deeply as did the injuries from His friends. Was the training of the Twelve so much a failure that the most zealous of His followers stooped to deny all knowledge of Him? Jesus was not surprised. He had foreseen it all. He knew that this present bitter experience of Peter's would help to fit him for future leadership, after he had been restored. He had no fear of the outcome. He had already prayed for Peter that his faith might not utterly fail.

24

The Trial and Judgment of Jesus

The betrayer's remorse

Matthew 27:3-10

In Matthew's record, the remorse of Judas follows almost immediately after the bitter weeping of Peter. The two events present a remarkable contrast: for Peter, remorse led to restoration; for Judas, to hopeless self-destruction. The difference lay in the relationship of the two men to Jesus. Peter's denial was in the context of his genuine devotion to Jesus, whereas Judas' heart never glowed with the warmth of loyalty. He was completely out of alignment with the mission of Jesus, and yet he is said to have repented. What was meant by this? Matthew states that when Judas saw that the Jewish council had condemned Jesus, he "repented" — suggesting some change of mind when the matter became a *fait accompli*. Many men set on some evil course have tasted the gall of remorse when the grim consequences of their designs became visible, however much the consequences had been foreseen and in some sense desired. The worst of men can at times experience twinges of conscience. For Judas, the influence of three years with the Master could not be erased. If any mitigation of the evil of his treacherous deed is possible, it is this fact — that his conscience prodded him into some sort of repentance.

The thirty pieces of silver — the price of a slave and the price of the *Master* — symbolized his betrayal. Judas' desire for it vanished. He knew that Jesus was innocent. Disgusted with

333

his own action, and perhaps also disillusioned with the maliciousness of the religious rulers, he rushed to the Temple and declared that he had betrayed innocent blood, as if he hoped that such confession would reverse the verdict. The men in authority were little concerned with innocence. They had grasped their prey. In an act of despair, Judas flung the money on the Temple courtyard and left it there. He rushed out then, and hanged himself. Luke, in writing the book of Acts, mentioned that Judas fell headlong in a field. The high priests decided to use the money to buy the field as a burial place for strangers. They called it Aceldama, Field of Blood, a grim memorial to one who had at one time been numbered among the friends of Jesus.

Matthew, in relating the end of Judas, mentions the fulfillment of an Old Testament prophecy, which referred to a potter's field bought for thirty pieces of silver (cf. Zech. 11:12, 13). The parallel is remarkable. It appealed strongly to a writer whose mind was set on showing the fulfillment of prophecy by the life of Jesus. Not only events in the life of Jesus, but also incidental details of others implicated in the story, are subjects of ancient prediction.

How could a man so close in association with Jesus have so tragic an end? The tragedy of Judas had its roots in a wrong view of Jesus. Although he was acquainted with His mission and teaching, Judas never believed in Him. Jesus had earlier remarked that it would have been better if Judas had not been born. His unhappy end stands as a timely reminder for all would-be followers of Jesus. They should examine themselves to determine whether or not they belong to the real mission of Jesus.

Before the Roman governor

Mark 15:1-5 (Matthew 27:1, 2, 11-14; Luke 23:1-5; John 18:28-38)

The Jewish council decided its course of action. Jesus must be sent for judgment to Pilate, the governor. They escorted Him bound from the house of Caiaphas to the palace where the governor lived while in Jerusalem. It was no great distance away.

The Roman governor confronted Jesus, the messianic King. There is no question which of them was most kingly. By any

This coin and others issued by Pilate bear pagan symbols and reveal the arrogance of the man who, by the evidence of both the New Testament and Josephus, deliberately provoked the Jews.

". . . and they bound Jesus and led him away and delivered him to Pilate"
—MARK 15:1

standards, the Roman Empire did not have its noblest representative in Pilate. He emerged from this encounter bereft of honor. He was hated by the Jews and he in turn despised them. He made no effort to understand their scruples. He was cruel to the point of sadism. His record of misrule and violence led not many years after the trial of Jesus to his recall from office. This was the man who faced the messianic prisoner.

Since this was the official trial it was necessary for the charge to be formulated. Pilate, after asking what the accusation was, received an evasive answer. The Jews apparently thought that the governor would accept their charge, without being more specific, that Jesus was an evildoer. This shows the measure of their confusion. When Pilate suggested that they should judge the prisoner themselves, they declined because they possessed no power to pass a capital sentence. Having made this statement, they were required to produce a charge that warranted the proposed sentence. They knew that an appeal to Jewish scruples was useless. To make any sense to Pilate, the charge must be political. They decided therefore on a threefold accusation; that He perverted the people, that He forbade them to pay tribute to Caesar, and that He declared Himself to be a king. Pilate would not be impressed with the first, for he regarded the people as already perverted. He knew too well the hatred of the Jews for the Roman tax system, and would hardly have been persuaded by an accusation ostensibly in support of that system. He therefore took up the third charge. He asked Jesus, "Are you the King of the Jews?"

The accusers stood outside the judgment hall because their Jewish scruples did not allow them to enter a Gentile dwelling on the first day of a feast, for then they would be ritually unclean. Their concern for ritual purity was oddly incongruous with their plotting an innocent man's death. The governor tolerated their scruples to the extent of moving between Jesus in the judgment hall and the accusers in the courtyard. Because Jesus had not heard the conversation between the governor and His accusers, He asked Pilate whether he had thought up the question himself or whether others had put it to him. The reply stung the Roman; would he have thought up such a question! It was a typical Jewish question. The Jewish leaders had handed Jesus over, but Pilate was still perplexed as to the real reason.

Jesus refused to answer the charge against Him, but John records a private conversation between Pilate and Jesus that left the governor more bewildered than ever. Jesus could not answer the charge without defining what He meant by kingship. It differed from the way most men thought of it. It bore no relationship to an authority bolstered by armies. He was no political revolutionary, yet He was a king. Pilate understood at least this point, and asked, "So you are a king?" Jesus' answer to that question also perplexed the governor. He said that He had come into the world to witness to the truth. The Romans were not as noted as the Greeks for their depth of thought, and Pilate's further question "What is truth?" was asked cynically rather than from any desire for information. The tough administrator would not waste his time on such abstractions. The question was most likely spoken in a tone of contempt. Pilate's political history bore testimony to his own disregard for truth. The governor was nonplused by his prisoner. He announced to the Jews that he could find no crime in Jesus.

Before the Jewish king

Luke 23:6-12

Out of frustration, Pilate clutched at a remark made by the accusers of Jesus. They had said that He had been stirring up the people in Judea, Galilee, and "this place" (Jerusalem). Pilate suddenly asked whether Jesus was a Galilean, for in that case it would be Herod's responsibility to deal with Him. On learning His Galilean origin, Pilate sent Him to Herod.

Luke alone records this incident, and it forms no more than an interlude in the course of the proceedings. The interview between Herod and Jesus is notable for the light it throws on the character of Herod. At first he was glad of the opportunity to see Jesus, as if He were some curiosity to be gazed upon. Herod had heard much about Him. The early popularity of Jesus had not escaped his notice. He once thought that Jesus was John the Baptist risen from the dead. It had been reported to him that Jesus worked miracles. He thought it would be highly entertaining to see signs performed, but he was grossly mistaken to think Jesus would perform signs for no higher motive than curiosity.

He tried questioning Jesus, but his prisoner remained silent. Luke does not report Herod's reactions to this treatment. He probably had never before confronted such silent strength. Jesus did not engage in conversation because He was convinced that no useful purpose would be served by it. His demeanor throughout was eloquent with dignity. He would not satisfy the idle chatter of a man whom, on another occasion, He had called "that fox."

The chief priests and scribes became increasingly vociferous in accusing Jesus. The longer He kept silent the more they spoke. Yet His silence spoke louder than their words. The prosecution's behavior furnished a cue for Herod's soldiers to pour contempt and mockery on the silent prisoner. The king himself joined in the mockery. He draped over Jesus a gorgeous robe, but Jesus made no protest. This may seem to indicate weakness. Whose approach, however, has history shown to be more powerful — Herod's, or the Messiah's? Herod had met his match. Doing nothing to resolve the case, he could only send Jesus back to the governor.

The enmity that formerly existed between Herod and Pilate suddenly abated, because they were faced with a common problem that baffled them both. The crafty Herod would not have paid such deference to the haughty Roman governor had he been man enough to decide himself what to do with Jesus. These sworn enemies found an uneasy basis of friendship through their common bewilderment over Jesus. Although the Jewish king showed no restraint in his contempt for Jesus, the Roman governor showed unexpected unwillingness to find Him guilty. The presence of Jesus apparently disturbed Pilate more than it did Herod.

Jesus or Barabbas

Matthew 27:15-23 (Mark 15:6-14; Luke 23:13-23; John 18:39, 40)

The trial before Pilate resumed. The governor had called together the Jewish leaders to inform them of his decision. He had made up his mind, having realized that the charges brought against Jesus could not be sustained. The quiet dignity of the prisoner had driven him into a cautiousness untypical of his character. His usual rash and capricious nature seemed momentarily suspended. For this, some have questioned the veracity of the gospel accounts because of the supposed discrepancy between the Pilate known to secular history and the Pilate portrayed here. These critics, however, do not take sufficient account of the uniqueness of the occasion. Never before had Pilate been faced with a prisoner like Jesus the Messiah.

Matthew relates a revealing incident. A messenger came to the judgment seat with a note from Pilate's wife. She had heard some reports of the doings and sayings of Jesus, and she had experienced a dream in which she saw her husband condemning an innocent man. It distressed her deeply. Since it is unlikely that she often dared to give her husband judicial advice, she must have felt strongly to have done so here. Matthew, however, gives no suggestion that Pilate took any notice. Yet the strange premonition of his wife must have contributed to his uneasiness, for after this he tried again to release Jesus.

At this point in the proceedings, events took a different turn. The Jews appealed to Pilate's custom of releasing a prisoner at the feast. John says that Pilate himself reminded them of it, no doubt with the hope that he could rely on the popularity of Jesus among the common people to ensure His release. A difficulty has been raised because there is no certain knowledge from secular sources of such a custom. Obviously the evangelists who mention it did not invent it, and this may have been one of the few occasions when Pilate chose a policy of appeasement. Feast times were particularly explosive, and thus some measure of appeasement would be especially judicious.

The governor offered the choice between Jesus and Barabbas. Matthew states that Barabbas was a notorious prisoner. Mark says that he was in captivity among insurrectionists who had committed murder. He may have been a political hero among a certain sector of the community. In those days of fierce tension, troublemakers knew what to expect from the ruthless Pilate; they would be executed by crucifixion as a public example.

None of the evangelists say why Pilate chose Barabbas as an alternative to Jesus. There was no reason why an alternative should be offered. He could have released both Barabbas by popular request and Jesus because he considered Him to be innocent. He was desperately seeking a way out of his predicament. If he was seeking popular support for Jesus to offset the hostility of the Jewish leaders, he was ignoring the strength of the latter's hatred and their shrewd understanding of mass psychology. It took little time for them to infiltrate into the crowd and win support for Barabbas. They knew that a few loud voices could soon sway a multitude. When the governor gave them the choice, their answer was ready. It was Barabbas.

The pathetic perplexity of Pilate was never more visible than in his retort, "What shall I do with Jesus the Messiah?" It was again a matter for the governor, not the people, to decide. The crowd clamored for His crucifixion — the Roman's own method of torture and death for rebellious Jews. The suggestion marks the lowest point of Jewish degradation. They had already rejected their long-expected Messiah; here they actually demanded for Him the kind of treatment that Romans were constantly meting out to their compatriots. It had become the symbol of the deepest hatred of the Roman occupation. It was as if they had suddenly joined their conquerors against the noblest Israelite who has ever lived.

Pilate asked what evil Jesus had done, but it was futile. Explosive crowds are immune to reason. Pilate had completely lost command. He attempted to maintain order. He could have released Jesus in defiance of the Jews, for he knew that this would have been the just thing to do — but he feared an uprising among them. He would then have been forced to set the troops on the crowds to restore order. It would not have been the first time he had done this. In this situation, he preferred to sacrifice an innocent man.

The sentence of death

John 19:1-16; Matthew 27:24-26 (Mark 15:15; Luke 23:24, 25)

Faced with the demand for the crucifixion of Jesus, Pilate was forced to make a decision. John records an incident that reveals something of Pilate's thoughts at the time, which helps to explain his political dilemma. Sensing the governor's intention to release Jesus, the Jews had pointed out that such an action would show that he was no friend of Caesar. This was another instance of Jewish intrigue, for they had no concern that their governor, whom they loathed, should be loyal to the emperor. They would have rejoiced to see the removal of Pilate and his legions. Their comment, however, possessed deep political overtones. On too many occasions Pilate had acted with the utmost cruelty and injustice. He had every justification for fearing that

"So Pilate, wishing to satisfy the crowd, released for them Barabbas; and having scourged Jesus, he delivered him to be crucified"
— MARK 15:15

The Lithostrotos, or the 'Pavement,' of Pilate's judgment hall in Jerusalem.

Jewish complaints might reach the emperor's ears. Had he been noted for justice he would not have feared such a possibility. His appalling past hung like a specter over him. The high priests and their advisers were not unmindful of the tremendous influence over the governor that any mention of Caesar would exert.

The moment of decision had come. Pilate seated himself on the official judgment seat, set up on the paved area known as Gabbatha. Jesus stood before the vacillating governor, who haughtily presented Him to the people as their king. The situation was doubly incongruous. The people had already rejected Him as king; He was not the kind of Messiah that they wanted. Moreover, Pilate's statement was made in contempt. He had already crucified a number of Jewish revolutionaries. He scorned all Jewish "kings." The climax was reached when the Jewish leaders affirmed that they had no king but Caesar. Neither their recent nor their subsequent history was consistent with this sudden avowal of political loyalty. Why this *volte face?* Was their hatred of Jesus greater than their hatred of their Roman conquerors? It could not be otherwise. In spite of the harshness of the Roman treatment, the Jewish leaders were allowed considerable liberty in the conduct of their affairs. The Romans did not challenge their religious authority, but Jesus had done so. He had exposed them as whited sepulchres, and their resentment ran deep. Political hatred can sometimes be neutralized by religious resentment. Jesus the Messiah had become a greater threat to the religious authority of the hierarchy than the Romans had ever been.

Pilate knew the situation was out of hand. The clamoring of the crowds increased. He handed Jesus over for execution. In doing so he took a bowl of water and publicly washed his hands as a symbolic gesture, although he must have known that he could not wash his hands of moral responsibility for the judgment he was giving. It was futile for him to declare Jesus innocent and yet hand Him over to His hostile enemies. At that moment, Pilate judged not Jesus but himself. He renounced the dictates of his own conscience.

The trial was over, but it was a travesty of justice. In the mystery of God's plan of redemption, it had to be so. The just was about to die for the unjust. It was imperative that His innocence should be verified by the judgment of the highest judiciary in Palestine. In a local sense, Jesus was the substitute for the revolutionary Barabbas, who thus became a type of all other unjust men in whose place the Messiah died, as Christians later came to recognize. He was delivered to the Roman soldiers who would carry out the sentence that Pilate had never wanted to give.

The people cried out, "His blood be on us and on our children." They were answerable for their own attitude, but in their present hostility they were willing to transmit their accountability to their descendants. This typically Hebrew view of solidarity nevertheless suggests that no man can live entirely to himself.

What were the thoughts of Barabbas upon his release? He must have heard about the choice the people had made. If he had known anything of Jesus he may have wondered why the crowd wanted Him crucified. As long as he lived he would never forget that Jesus died in his place. It may have caused him to think. He may have concluded wrongly that his violence had paid off better than Jesus' nonviolence. How could he know that Jesus, through His death, was to build a community destined to reach the ends of the earth, whereas the only significance of his own release was its connection with the crucifixion of Jesus?

The scourging and the mocking

Matthew 27:27-31 (Mark 15:16-20)

Before releasing Jesus for crucifixion, Pilate ordered Him to be scourged. This was the usual barbaric practice. The evangelists do not dwell on the details. The lashing of leather straps would inflict severe physical injuries, a glaring symbol of man's inhumanity to man. It is sufficient to note that no cruelty was spared when men rejected the Messiah.

The writers are also silent about the thoughts of Jesus toward His physical sufferings. They had earlier mentioned the mental tensions that had troubled Him. Later, Christians recognized that He was like an unprotesting lamb being led to the slaughter. The vital difference, however, was the Messiah's power to protest and even to prevent the action had He chosen to do so.

No scene more eloquently expresses the passive acceptance of His messianic role than the way He submitted to the utter indignities and physical torture of the scourgers' whips.

Nor was this all. As if the scourging had not satisfied their sadistic cravings, the soldiers made Him wear an excruciating crown of thorns and arrayed Him in a purple cloak. There was no evidence in them of the pity and compassion that characterized their prisoner. They had no idea that their ribaldry would live on for centuries in the records of those grim events. They do not stand as unique. Their kind is found in all ages wherever men use violence as an instrument of rule. Twentieth-century barbarities have even exceeded the cruel sadism of those first-century soldiers. It is not surprising that the Messiah caught the brunt of human cruelty that day.

No greater contrast exists than that between the kneeling soldiers pretending to do homage to the king of the Jews and the true homage that was to be offered to the Messiah as King of kings. They missed their opportunity and substituted hollow mockery. They needed deep spiritual discernment to see in the ill-treated figure of Jesus anyone other than a misguided visionary, fit only to be the sport of callous men. Their ideas of strength and weakness were destined for an astonishing reversal in the near future. Some of them perhaps would later form the guard for the tomb and find themselves totally helpless to prevent the most incredible display of power — the resurrection of Jesus from the dead.

When the spitting and the smiting and the ridicule were over, the purple robe was removed, and Jesus' own cloak was placed on Him. All was ready for the crucifixion. The soldiers on special duty were marshaled by their officer — all part of a day's work. None of them imagined that this crucifixion differed from the hundreds of others preceding it. The sight of crosses outside Jerusalem and in other parts of Palestine was not unusual in those days.

The way to Calvary

Luke 23:26-31 (Matthew 27:32; Mark 15:21)

Condemned men were normally required to carry their crosses, but since frequently the scourging left them too weak, a

"And when they had mocked him, they stripped him of the robe, and put his own clothes on him, and led him away to crucify him"
— MATTHEW 27:31

Street scene on the Via Dolorosa, in the Old City, showing the *Ecce Homo* arch.

bystander would be forced to perform the grim duty. The Roman soldiers soon compelled a man to carry the cross for Jesus. He was a man from Cyrene named Simon. He had just arrived in Jerusalem from an outlying country district. He may have come straight from working in the fields. Possibly he joined the crowds mainly out of curiosity. He certainly never expected to carry a cross that day.

Nothing is known of his subsequent history. Whether or not he became a believer in the Messiah whose cross he carried is not recorded. Mark, however, identifies the man as father of Alexander and Rufus, who must have been known to the author and presumably also to the readers. It may be conjectured that Simon recounted his experiences that day. It could have been his sons' first knowledge of Jesus. Laboring along the *Via Dolorosa* with the heavy beams, Simon may have resented the task. Perhaps as he gazed at the figure of Jesus ahead of him he began to follow in a deeper sense. If so, he would never forget his privilege of helping the Messiah in His hour of need.

The procession wended its way through ranks of bystanders, some of them sightseers with nothing better to do. The doomed figure of Jesus meant little to them. There were also the usual clusters of women who took on the task of mourning for condemned prisoners on the way to execution. They were practiced in wailing. It was their way of expressing sympathy for condemned men. The comment of Jesus took them by surprise. "Daughters of Jerusalem, do not weep for me, but weep for yourselves and for your children." It was the first recorded word that Jesus had spoken since leaving the judgment hall. The statement showed His concern for others. Was it possible that some of these women had joined with the crowd in calling the blood of Jesus on themselves and their children? If so, the Messiah told them to weep for those children. He did not despise tears, for He had wept over Jerusalem. The coming destruction of that great city was clearer to Him than to its own citizens.

Barren women in Hebrew society were generally despised, but Jesus considered such to be more blessed at this time when the whole generation was heading for disaster. The childless would at least have no children to lament. In the hour of His own agony and suffering, Jesus set His mind on the coming judgment of the city. He saw a time when men would rather be crushed by rocks than expose themselves to the horrors of existence. It was a gloomy outlook. Jesus quoted a parable to the women — "For if they do this when the wood is green, what will happen when it is dry?" Apparently the "green" time was the present. The Romans were not crucifying merely an innocent man — they were crucifying the Messiah. When the times became "dry," which implies a considerable interval of time, would they act any differently toward the holy city? These words of Jesus reveal something of His mental attitude as He approached the cross. His thoughts were essentially for others.

25

From Golgotha to the Empty Tomb

The place called Golgotha

Luke 23:32-38; John 19:17-22

Outside Jerusalem a place was reserved for public executions. It was known as Golgotha, which means "the place of the skull." It was the scene of the dying agonies of many whose misdemeanors or political aspirations had led to their doom. It was to be famous for a supreme reason — it was the place of the execution of one who had never sinned.

To this place Jesus was led. Simon had carried His cross. The soldiers prepared for the sickening task — to them, almost routine. Their one touch of compassion was the offering of bitter wine to deaden Jesus' pain. The Messiah refused it, however. He would retain possession of all His faculties in the final accomplishment of His mission. Others saw His death as disaster and disillusionment, but it could not be so to Him. This was the purpose for which He had come. This was the voluntary laying down of His life, a conscious triumph over death, and He wanted to be fully conscious while carrying His purpose through.

There was no bitterness in the mind of Jesus, no resentment that men should treat Him so. He felt deeply moved for them. He prayed that His Father would forgive them. Their nailing Him there was symbolic of the attitude of man in general. It showed the need of the very act of redemption that they were helping to effect. As they heard that prayer, they would wonder that any man could be so gracious under such suffering toward those who were inflicting it.

The same men who crucified Jesus also crucified the criminals who were hanging on either side of Him. They heard no comparable prayer from them. They heard only curses, at first. The contrast could not have escaped them. This strange company in which Jesus was found was not without symbolic meaning. An ancient prophecy had predicted that He was to be numbered among transgressors. His cross, however, was distinguished from the other two, for it bore an inscription announcing Jesus to be King of the Jews. The inscription had been placed there on orders from the governor himself. The Jews, however, had rejected their Messiah. Their intrigues had put Him upon a cross. Their leaders had repudiated any king but Caesar. They could not stand for such an inscription as this. They at once protested to the governor. They claimed that he should have written that Jesus had *said* He was King of the Jews, but the distinction that existed in their minds was invalid. What Pilate had written was true. In a deeper sense than either the governor or high priest knew, He was King of a spiritual Kingdom infinitely superior to and more lasting than any earthly kingdom. But the spiritual significance of the event entirely escaped the official religious leaders. The governor, however, was obdurate. "What I have written I have written," he said.

Significantly, the title over the cross was inscribed in Hebrew, Latin, and Greek. It was intended that every witness should understand it. Perhaps the evangelists in recording it saw further and recognized the universal importance of what was taking place.

Some who saw Him die

Matthew 27:33-44; Mark 15:22-32; Luke 23:39-43; John 19:23, 24

Some witnesses of the crucifixion were deeply impressed; others saw it without being moved. The reactions of the following four groups are described by the evangelists.

The soldiers, those who had crucified Jesus and the two criminals, sat down to pass the time away, and they began to argue about the sharing of the dying men's clothes. Where it was possible, these were divided evenly, but when they came to the seamless cloak that Jesus had worn, they decided to cast lots for it. All the writers note this fact, but John alone mentions its deeper meaning. He quotes Psalm 22:18, a psalm that Jesus Himself had much on His mind during the Passion. He was shortly to quote it in His cry of dereliction. This remarkable psalm in many of its details describes the Messiah's crucifixion. John saw the casting of the lots as a direct fulfillment of this Scripture. None of the evangelists record any of the soldiers' reactions, however. They were men who in the shadow of the cross were mainly concerned about their own share of the booty. No one can say whether the man who won the seamless cloak ever thought more of its former owner than he thought of his prize.

Some of the passersby were more vocal. As far as the evangelists are concerned, they were an anonymous, even nondescript procession. They did not stop long enough to contemplate the crucified Messiah. They merely wagged their heads and threw out jibes. They had heard of the charge against Him, that He had threatened to destroy the Temple and rebuild it within three days. The charge was a distortion, but it made ready fuel for scorn. Anyone who could do a marvel like that could surely save Himself, especially if He were the Son of God as He claimed to be. They challenged Him to descend from the cross miraculously. They were partially right, but wrong at the most crucial point. He was not unable to descend, but unwilling. This was the climax of His mission. These passersby never imagined that anyone would stay there by choice. Because they missed the meaning of the passion, they resorted to derision. Their attitude is typical of many who fail to grasp the divine purpose behind the cross.

Even the ecclesiastical leaders added their taunts, and so increased their guilt in engineering the death of Jesus. They, too, thought that anyone making such claims as Jesus had done should be able to escape from the cross. Their jibes centered on His claims about Himself. "King of Israel" and "Son of God" seemed strangely incongruous for one in such desperate circumstances. It seemed to them that His present condition conflicted with His claims to save others. What was preventing Him from using the same power to save Himself? A further contradiction was His claim to trust God. Surely God would not leave Him such ignominy! Again, human reasoning had come to the conclusions because it started from the wrong premise. Their idea of salvation was false. The religious leaders should have known better than the passersby, but they lamentably failed. They had not grasped the fact that salvation involves self-giving, not self-saving. Their offer to believe if Jesus came down from the cross displayed a wrong approach to faith. They should have said that He saved others because He did not save Himself. It took the resurrection and the enlightening activity of the Holy Spirit to lead men to a faith like that.

To ridicule and scorn, Jesus gave no answer. He did, however, enter into dialogue with one of the criminals hanging beside Him. Both criminals began by taunting Him. They were no doubt influenced by the other groups, for abusive language is infectious. One of them, however, noticed a dignity in Jesus that strikingly contrasted to the blasphemy of his companion. He rebuked the other man for doing the same thing that he himself had done. Why the sudden change? Apparently it dawned on him that Jesus was innocent. He began to fear God. If Jesus really was who He claimed to be, then an urgent petition to Him should replace the cursing. His concept of the Messiah was probably vague when he asked, "Lord, remember me when you come in your kingly power," but it was enough. It revealed a Spirit-given insight, for there was no visible evidence of the kingly power of Jesus. His glimmer of authentic faith was acknowledged. Jesus gave him a special promise: "Today you will be with me in paradise." He had used the same word "paradise" earlier to describe the dwelling place of the just, and this apparently is the meaning here. There is some thought of unity with Christ in the words "with me," which finds a parallel in Paul's frequent stress on being crucified and raised with Christ. The gracious concern of the Messiah for this penitent criminal stood out in vivid contrast to the prevailing brutality that surrounded

Words from the cross

Mark 15:33-37; Luke 23:44-46; John 19:25-30

sus from the cross have already been men- r forgiveness for His persecutors and the offer of fellowship in paradise to the repentant criminal. The other sayings are equally revealing. The first is mentioned by Mark and Matthew. It was heard during a three-hour period of strange darkness, which dropped an atmosphere of physical gloom upon the surroundings. Jesus loudly cried out of the darkness. It was evident that a spiritual conflict as well as a physical phenomenon was in progress. So memorable was the voice that both evangelists record the exact words in Aramaic that are translated, "My God, my God, why hast Thou forsaken me?" These are the opening words of Psalm 22, which sum up the mysterious depths to which Jesus went to complete His mission. Did this desolate cry show a disillusioned Messiah? Subsequent events prove the opposite. The only reasonable explanation is that at this moment He suffered the full burden of the sin He had come to bear. It is the mystery of what the apostle Paul describes as His being "made to be sin who knew no sin . . ." (2 Cor. 5:21).

The cry, however, was misunderstood. The Aramaic word for "My God" sounds very much like "Elijah," and some thought that He was calling for the ancient prophet who had typified the Messiah's herald, John the Baptist. Some even suggested that they would wait to see if Elijah responded. One of the bystanders thought the cry was an evidence of thirst, and they offered vinegar on a sponge. In John's account, Jesus said just before He died: "I thirst." This cry draws attention to the intensity of thirst in death by crucifixion. In saying it, the Messiah was showing His true humanity.

Of the three other sayings, one was of special tenderness. The strong concern of Jesus for others never diminished through the ordeal of the crucifixion, as is so poignantly evident in His word to His own mother whom He saw standing with the beloved disciple, presumably John. He said to her, "Behold your son!" and to John, "Behold your mother!" That was all — but it was enough. John took her away from the scene and assumed responsibility for her. The simplicity of this episode illustrates again the attitude of Jesus toward family responsibility. Even in the hour of His death, He was concerned for Mary's welfare.

The evangelist John includes another saying omitted by the others. It was brief — "It is finished." This was not a cry of despair, as some have supposed, for the word means "accomplished" and suggests victory, not defeat. It is impossible to be sure what was in the mind of Jesus, but that cry was connected with His mission. He had reached its supreme fulfillment. The Shepherd was laying down His life for His sheep. The Son of Man was giving His life as a ransom for many. The Lamb of God was bearing away the sin of the world. The grain of wheat was falling into the ground to die. The hour had arrived. Everything that the Father had sent Him to do was finished. On the basis of this finished work, the Church was to emerge.

The last saying is recorded by Luke. In His last breath Jesus committed His spirit to His Father. Those standing by heard Him. The words show the triumph that issued from the seeming tragedy. His noble spirit expressed to the end the priceless quality of serene trust. There is no greater example of the godly attitude in death. It was the Messiah's last word, fully in keeping with His own teaching. The peace He gave to others was a reality to Himself.

Accompanying events

John 19:31-37; Matthew 27:51-54 (Mark 15:38, 39; Luke 23:47-49)

After the death of Jesus, the scruples of the Jews again became the most important issue. Condemning an innocent man to an ignominious death did not disturb their consciences, but having killed the Messiah, as they thought, their scruples about His dead body disturbed them. Their ceremonial observances overshadowed the moral issue of the justice of their proceedings against Jesus. It was nearing the Sabbath, and dead bodies still hanging on the Sabbath would defile the day. It was not uncommon for life to linger for many hours in crucifixion, and the "religious" Jews wanted the criminals finished off quickly, so they could observe the Sabbath in ritual correctness. They determined to be ritually clean, although they had crucified the Messiah. Some of them approached Pilate with the request that the legs of the crucified men be broken to hasten their deaths so that the bodies could be removed before the Sabbath.

Jesus, however, was already dead. Instead of breaking His legs, someone thrust a spear into His side. John particularly notes what happened: blood and water flowed from the wound. So important did John consider this event that he added a note asserting the record to be an eyewitness account. Some have concluded that the blood and water gives evidence that Jesus died of a broken heart. John's main concern, however, was to show that Jesus died an actual death in a real body, to counteract the error that He only appeared to have had a human body. Moreover, he saw the fulfillment of two separate portions of Scripture in the substitution of the spear thrust for the customary breaking of bones. The Passover lamb had to be preserved without broken bones, a highly significant fact for the early Christians when they came to regard Jesus as their Passover Lamb. The same thought occurs in one of the psalms (34:20), the messianic importance of which was also recognized by the early Church (cf. 1 Peter 1:19). John also remembered the words of Zechariah 12:10: "They shall look on him whom they have pierced." They spoke to him of the effects of the death of Christ. Men pierced His side, but they came to look to Him for salvation. As they looked, men would find that the symbol of condemnation had become a symbol of grace.

Two strange events happened, both recorded by Matthew and one of them also by both Mark and Luke. At the precise moment that Jesus died, the great curtain separating the holy place from the most holy place in the Temple was suddenly torn in two, with the rending starting at the top. According to Jewish tradition, two curtains were used, one within the holy place and one parallel to it in the most holy place, with a cubit between them. Whether this is so or not, the curtain seen by the priests was split into two pieces. Some have suggested that the earthquake shook the earth and at the same time split the linten supporting the curtain, causing the whole to collapse. The gospel records, however, suggest a more decisive rending than could have been caused by this means alone. Its significance is more important, as if the hand of God tore aside the separating partition, which for so long had made Him remote from the people of Israel. The death of the Messiah was linked with the new way of access to God. After the resurrection of Jesus, the disciples discovered the meaning of this. To the priests who witnessed the rending of the curtain, it could have seemed to only a portent of impending judgment.

The other strange happening was the mysterious opening of some of the tombs in the city. The earthquake might have shifted the stones that sealed these tombs. The altogether unexpected appearance of resurrected bodies, however, is less easy to comprehend — especially as it appears from Matthew's account to have happened prior to the resurrection of Jesus. There is no rational explanation of this. It was an exceptional event that coincided with the death of Jesus. It was symbolic of the fact that Jesus had conquered death. Matthew gives no details of the people who were raised. He merely states that they appeared to many after the resurrection of Jesus. The incident adds an air of mystery to the period immediately after Jesus' death. The earthquake itself could not have been fortuitous. It happened at the precise moment of Jesus' death, and therefore was clearly arranged by the Father to mark the completion of the mission of the Son.

At the final cry of Jesus and the earth tremors that split rocks before their eyes, many were overawed. Three of the evangelists mention one man who was deeply affected. He was the man in charge of the crucifixion, a seasoned soldier well-conditioned to scenes of horror; but he had never seen a condemned man die like this. He was more like a Son of God than a criminal. There is no knowing whether the man's insight went further when he heard later that Jesus had risen from the dead. Others, overcome with awe, smote their breasts in lamentation, although it was not the end as they supposed.

The burial of Jesus

Matthew 27:?? (Mark 15:40-47; Luke 23:50-56; John 19:38-42)

ce of the burial of Jesus was at once recog-
Church. One of the first statements of revela-
ed down is found in 1 Corinthians 15:3 ff.
e same form in which it had come to the
that Jesus died for sins, that He was raised
also that He was buried. The burial was
etween His death and His resurrection. All

The Church of the Holy Sepulchre
traditionally marks the site of Golgotha
and the burial place of Jesus. The
present building was erected by the
Crusaders on foundations reaching back
to the time of Emperor Constantine.

*"And with him they crucified two robbers,
one on his right and one on his left"*
— MARK 15:27

the gospel writers devoted space to it. Moreover, Jesus Himself
had mentioned His burial in advance to the woman who anointed
Him.

Romans were not concerned about the burial of their vic-
tims, but the Jews had careful scruples about burials.

A certain member of the Jewish Sanhedrin was a secret disciple of Jesus. His position made him cautious, but it also gave
him an opportunity to carry out the burial of Jesus in a decent

manner. Being wealthy, he had already prepared his own tomb, hewn from the rock. It had never been used. He could not have realized before that the first occupant of his tomb was to be none other than Israel's rejected Messiah, in whom he himself had come to believe. He had probably heard Jesus preach about the Kingdom of God, and the future possibilities of it had fired his imagination. He had joined the ranks of those who were looking for the reign of God to commence. He had a colleague on the Council who shared his views. John, in his report, specially mentions this colleague because he had mentioned him before. He was Nicodemus who had visited Jesus one night. He appeared still rather secretive about his allegiance, but he became bolder after Jesus was dead. He lent moral support to Joseph of Arimathea.

The governor's permission had to be sought for removal of the bodies of executed men. Joseph may have hesitated to make the request, since he knew that a Jewish deputation had already been to Pilate about the breaking of the legs. The governor was not partial to Jewish requests at any time. Joseph, however, was constrained by a stronger motive than fear. He was impelled by his love for Jesus. What was dormant in him now blossomed. Pilate was amazed that Jesus was so soon dead, but when the centurion confirmed this he conceded to Joseph's request.

Joseph and Nicodemus took spices, which the latter had provided at his own expense, and proceeded to take down the body of Jesus. Wrapped in linen, the body was anointed with the spices. Joseph's tomb was in a nearby garden. Its nearness facilitated the completion of the burial before evening when the Sabbath began. The body was placed on a ledge in a niche inside the cave. In the area in the entrance to the tomb, the burial rites were observed. No others besides Joseph and Nicodemus are named, but others may have been present. None of the disciples and none of the women were there, although some of the women followed at a distance and noted the position of the tomb. The circular stone was pushed across the entrance. It was easier to close than to open since the stone was rolled shut on an incline. After the tomb was closed, the stone was sealed. Joseph and Nicodemus and any others who were with them left the tomb and went away.

The empty tomb

Matthew 27:62-66; 28:11-15; John 20:1-10

The day after the death of Jesus was the most depressing Sabbath that the disciples had ever known. They were utterly bewildered and disillusioned. Their hopes of a messianic Kingdom were dashed. Their King had been crucified in shame. Nothing seemed to be left. Against this background of deep discouragement, the momentous event of the resurrection of Jesus must be considered. The first hint of it came a short while before dawn, when a group of the followers of Jesus, all women, went to anoint His body. They were unaware that this had already been done. Theirs was the honor of being the first to witness the empty tomb. That the massive stone had been rolled away from the doorway on the upward incline astonished them. They had discussed whom they could ask to move the stone.

They wondered how it had happened. Matthew reports one explanation — an earthquake and an angel. The chief priests had asked Pilate to set a watch over the tomb. This was not normal procedure, for body-snatchers would not operate in the East where corruption set in so rapidly. Why then this abnormal request? They told Pilate that they were afraid that the disciples would steal the body of Jesus. Their fear arose because Jesus had predicted that He would rise from the dead. Their knowledge of human psychology must have been limited if they seriously thought that the disciples would steal the body to bolster their own belief in the predictions of Jesus, for the disciples knew only too well that they would be deceiving themselves. Pilate's patience with the Jewish authorities was nearly exhausted, for he abruptly told them to set a guard. This request of the rulers shows them as men concerned lest the claim of Jesus to rise from the dead should gain popular currency.

The presence of the guards is an important factor in the assessing of the evidence. Apparently none of those on duty saw the tomb opened, nor did any of them see the risen Christ. They did feel the earthquake, and they saw the angel. If the resurrection of Jesus was miraculous, some miraculous accompaniments would not be unexpected. Whether men choose to believe in the reality of the angels or not, no one can dispute the fact of the empty tomb.

There is no need to discuss the once-popular theories that explain away the empty tomb. The well-known swoon theory that maintained that Jesus did not really die but revived enough to emerge from the tomb, can be dismissed as incredible. How could anyone who had been scourged as well as crucified have had strength to escape from the tomb? Nor can serious consideration be given to the theory that the body was stolen by the enemies of Jesus, for in this case the body would surely have been produced to give the lie to the basic message of the early Christians.

Some of the eyewitnesses to the fact of the empty tomb are mentioned in the gospels. The three women — Mary Magdalene, Mary the mother of James, and Salome — were there first. Soon after, Peter and John noted the same fact. These two disciples saw at once the significance of the arrangement of the grave clothes. The head cloth, which was apart from the other wrappings, was still rolled up. It was as if they were still wrapped round the body but without the body being present. This defies explanation. How could the body have been extricated from the undisturbed clothes except by a miracle? It must be remembered that none of the eyewitnesses who reported the event ever expected the tomb to be empty or the body to be absent. They were not seeing what they expected to see. Nevertheless, this evidence is in itself negative. The appearances of Jesus to His own people supply the only reasonable clue to the meaning of the empty tomb.

News of the risen Lord

Matthew 28:1-10; Mark 16:1-8; Luke 24:1-12; John 20:11-18

At least two of the people who went to the tomb early saw something startling. The angel appeared as a brilliant flash of lightning, terrifying not only the women but also the guards, who, shielding their faces, lay motionless until the light had passed. Only the women caught the message. A voice told them to stop being afraid. The angelic messenger knew that they were looking for Jesus, since they were at the tomb where Jesus had been laid. Yet, when the women heard that He had risen from the dead and would see them in Galilee, they could hardly believe their senses. They hurried to tell the disciples, but what degree of real faith they had is not clear, for fear was mixed with their joy.

It is difficult to sort out the varied reports recounted by the evangelists. Both Mark and Matthew mention Mary Magdalene in company with other women, but John refers to her as being alone at the tomb. It has been suggested that she at first went with the others but hurried back to Peter and John as soon as she saw the empty tomb, leaving the others to look inside. The angelic announcement was therefore not heard by her. Her message was correspondingly less complete. Her only conclusion was that her Lord had been taken away. The other two women, according to Luke's account, were challenged by the angel as to why they were seeking the living among the dead. The form of challenge was totally unexpected, for they were not actually seeking the living. They were seeking the dead. The challenge emphasized their inferior concept of the Messiah. They could not grasp the truth that He had risen. The angelic challenger reminded them that Jesus had predicted not only His death but also His resurrection on the third day. Ironically, the only people who seem to have remembered this were the enemies of Jesus. His friends needed their memories prodded. Even when the women went to report the empty tomb to the eleven, their words did nothing to jog their memory. They dismissed the reports as mere chatter. Faith came hard. Because it was difficult, it was all the more assured when it arrived.

One of the most notable experiences on that Easter day came to Mary Magdalene. Although she missed the angel's message, she had a more notable honor, for she was the first to meet the risen Jesus. She stood weeping at the tomb, her tears reflecting her grief that Jesus was no longer with her. Then she too received a message from an angel, but it went no further than to inquire the reason for her tears. At this point she became distracted by the presence of someone behind her. Mary did not recognize Him as Jesus, for her eyes were blinded with tears and her mind totally unprepared for the resurrection. Even when He spoke, repeating the same question as the angel, she thought He was a gardener who might know where the body of Jesus had been taken. She was seeking a corpse when the living Lord was standing before her. The miracle of the resurrection had happened, but she did not perceive it. An understanding of it could come only as a result of personal rapport with Jesus. When Jesus called her by name, she realized the truth at once.

In addressing Him as "Rabboni" (Teacher), she had not progressed beyond the former relationship. Jesus forestalled any attempt on her part to treat Him in the same relationship by touching His body. She had to learn that she could not retain Him by physical means. She was immediately given a message to take to the other disciples. Jesus told her that He would be ascending to the Father (His Father and theirs). In a flash, the significance of the resurrection was before her. A new era had begun. Jesus the Messiah was different. He was a spiritual presence that had become intensely real. What happened to Mary Magdalene would happen to many others during the next forty days, until the realization that He was alive had fully penetrated their minds.

". . . two men . . . in dazzling apparel . . . said to them,
'Why do you seek the living among the dead?' "
— LUKE 24:4, 5

A tomb with a rolling stone for closing its entrance. This burial place was found on the back slopes of the Mount of Olives, near Bethphage.

26

The Risen Lord

A memorable conversation

Luke 24:13-35

The shattering weight of disillusionment that Calvary had brought gripped the minds of even the staunchest followers of Jesus. They possessed no hope that any good would come out of the death of their Master. When the disciples heard rumors that Jesus had risen they were not in the least disposed to believe. They could not be deceived. Only substantial, firsthand evidence could break their profound pessimism. This atmosphere of despair clouded the outlook of the two men who met with the risen Lord and conversed with Him without knowing who He was. Their sadness showed in their faces. When the stranger requested to know the subject of their conversation, they were amazed that He seemed uninformed of the events that had so recently happened in Jerusalem.

Jesus knew what had happened. Better than anyone else, He knew the suffering and shame, but He knew also the power of the resurrection. His question, "What things?" was not to obtain information but to enable the travelers to articulate their sorrow. They spoke of Jesus of Nazareth as a prophet mighty in deed, but they had progressed no farther than that. They acknowledged what He had said and done, but they missed the point of who He was. They mentioned the grim facts of His death and their own disillusioned hopes that He would redeem Israel, whatever they meant by that. They then referred to some reports of the empty tomb, which evidently had not impressed them.

Then the Lord spoke. He told them what the prophets had predicted about the Messiah. They had probably pondered the same Scriptures many times before, but it had never dawned on them that the Messiah was to suffer. As He expounded these predictions to them, the Cross became less of a tragedy. The deepest lesson they learned was the importance of the Old Testament in interpreting the death of Jesus. Later, the idea of fulfillment was to play a notable part in the early Christian teaching and preaching. It is probable that the principles of interpretation

"Did not our hearts burn within us while he talked to us on the road, while he opened to us the scriptures?"
— LUKE 24:32

This Roman built road at Emmaus could be the actual place where the risen Messiah walked with the two disciples.

were learned during the period of resurrection appearances. What is recorded of these two friends, Cleopas and his companion, must have happened to many others, since the Messiah would not leave to guesswork the Christian interpretation of the Old Testament Scriptures.

There is no verbatim report of the conversation on that road from Jerusalem to Emmaus. Luke's summary of it is very brief. The two travelers wanted more of the wisdom of their unrecognized companion. They urged Him to dine with them at their home. They evidently intended to accommodate Him for the night, although there proved to be no opportunity for this, for He was soon to vanish from their sight. Before doing so, He ate bread with them. That was enough. He was their risen Messiah. Immediately after this recognition, He was gone.

This conversation completely transformed their outlook. Their gloom vanished. They began to reflect on what Jesus had said. It became more meaningful, now that they knew who He was. They retained something of the warm glow they had had during the walk. The incident provides an example of the spiritual impact of the risen Lord on those whom He met during the forty days of appearances.

The sequel to that conversation was a report to the disciples who as a group had not as yet met the risen Lord. The two travelers were so thrilled with their own experience that they had to share it. They thought nothing of the return journey of seven miles in spite of the lateness of the hour. On reaching Jerusalem, they learned that Jesus had also appeared to Simon, which gave them an immediate opportunity to tell how Jesus had come to them. The evidence for the resurrection was mounting, and with it, the expectancy of great things to come.

An interview with Peter

John 21

Impulsively, Peter had decided to go fishing, and six other disciples went with him. John does not name all six in his account, for he intended to concentrate on Peter. The fishing attempt on the Sea of Galilee was a failure. They fished all night without success. In their frustration, someone called to them to cast their net on the other side of the boat. It did not occur to them whose voice it was, but they obeyed — no doubt as a last desperate recourse.

Not until they pulled the great catch of fish into the boat did they give any more thought to the voice. John suddenly recognized that the voice was that of Jesus, and he exclaimed, "It is the Lord!" When Peter heard this, he jumped into the water and swam toward shore. The others struggled to get the loaded boats to land. When they finally landed, Jesus had a charcoal fire burning and asked for some of the fish that they had caught. Then He served His disciples a breakfast of bread and fish. John remembered the details of this experience so well that he recalled both the distance of the boat from shore at the time he recognized Jesus and the exact number of fish caught in the net.

The purpose of this appearance was evident when Jesus addressed Peter. The Messiah faced the man who had denied Him, but His mission was a mission of mercy. He administered no word of reproof. He simply asked Simon three times whether he loved Him. In His first two questions He used the word for the

"Just as day was breaking, Jesus stood on the beach; yet the disciples did not know that it was Jesus"
— JOHN 21:4

A view of the north shoreline of the Sea of Galilee. During the calm of daybreak, Jesus the Messiah called out from the shore to His disciples who were fishing.

noblest kind of love in the Greek language, but on the third occasion He used the word for a lesser love. Twice Simon strongly affirmed his love, but became disturbed because of Jesus' third question. Peter then realized that Jesus was indirectly reminding him of his threefold denial. Nowhere does the graciousness of the Lord show more vividly than here. Instead of complaint, there was a threefold commission for Peter — to watch over and tend the flock of God, the lambs as well as the sheep. Peter would understand the imagery. There was no need for a treatise on pastoral theology to prepare him for this task. Jesus summed it up in a familiar metaphor. He had called himself the Good Shepherd and He wanted the disciples to follow His example. In view of His unqualified reinstatement of Peter, the risen Christ is clearly revealed to be a forgiving Christ.

Jesus not only dealt with Peter's service but also with his destiny. He spoke of others who would stretch out his hands and take him where he did not wish to go. Tradition indicates that Peter was crucified upside down. John not only mentions the prediction of Peter's death but also adds a note to show that Jesus was speaking of the manner of Peter's death.

Peter was not overawed into silence by the thought of his own destiny. Some men never are. They immediately transfer their thoughts to others, as Peter did. He wanted information about his close companion, John. Jesus had no intention of giving him a glimpse into the future of other men. He would not reveal such matters to satisfy idle curiosity. He simply said, "If it is my will that he remain until I come, what is that to you? Follow me." Some thought that this meant that John would not die. John may even have thought that himself at first, but as he wrote, he was clearly dispelling a rumor to this effect. Peter, on his part, must tend the flock, not pry into other men's destinies. The gracious way in which Jesus dealt with His impetuous disciple is a high example of restoration. This was the method to be used in the continuation of the mission.

Two appearances to the apostles

John 20:19-29; Luke 24:36-48

The gospels record other occasions when Jesus appeared to

a group of disciples. At the first incident, ten were present. Missing were Judas, who had hanged himself, and Thomas, who was probably too disillusioned and discouraged to join them. The ten met in secret. They feared that the Jews, who had shamefully treated their Master, would do the same to them. Their fear is understandable. There was as yet no reason not to fear, except perhaps the report of Simon Peter that he had seen the Lord. Then, suddenly, Jesus appeared among them. They had not seen Him come. The door had not opened, but He was inside the room. Terrified, they thought He was a ghost. He asked them why they were frightened, but He did not wait for an answer. He spoke words of peace to them and then showed them His wounds.

Luke mentions the hands and the feet, whereas John mentions the hands and the side. For John, the side was of special importance, for he had noted in his record the blood and the water. Luke says that Jesus asked for food, which He ate before them; this would show that He was not an apparition. After they had recognized Him they were glad. According to John, after speaking of His peace, Jesus told them that He would send them as the Father had sent Him — a clear directive to continue the mission. Their work was to be an extension of His. They must have remembered that before His passion He had talked to them about this, but, of course, without the resurrection there could have been no mission. John also reports that Jesus breathed on them and told them to receive the Holy Spirit, who would give them power to forgive or retain sins. This apparently was a foretaste of Pentecost and pointed ahead to the era of the Christian Church. Although sins would be forgiven only on the basis of the work of Christ, the apostles were the agents for making this known. Some would reject the Gospel, and in doing so, their sins would be retained.

A week passed before the next incident. The disciples were gathered again in the same place. Again, it was the first day of the week, and on this occasion Thomas was present. He had been told what had happened the week before, but he was in no mood to believe. He was convinced that the others had imagined seeing the wounds. He would not have trusted his own eyes. He insisted on putting his finger in the nail wound. Because of this attitude, he has since been called "doubting Thomas." When Jesus appeared again and gave Thomas the opportunity to do what he wanted, he did not so much as reach out his hand. He must have been thoroughly ashamed and immensely overjoyed. The voice was enough, he would know it anywhere. He cried out, "My Lord and my God" — a momentous cry of remarkable insight. Thomas acknowledged the Messiah in a spiritual way. The resurrection had made all the difference. His reaction was a symbol of what would happen to everyone who came to true faith. His profound summing up of his new relationship to Jesus was unpremeditated. There was no time to formulate a Christology. He had seen Jesus in a new light, but it was the same Jesus with whom he had walked and talked for three years. The response of Jesus to his confession has been a source of great inspiration to multitudes of others. He had believed because he had seen, but those who were to believe without seeing would be even more blessed.

A farewell message

Matthew 28:16-20

On another occasion Jesus appeared to a group of disciples. Matthew refers to the eleven, but it is possible that this may be the occasion when the "more than five hundred" were present to whom Paul refers in 1 Corinthians 15. The number is less important than the message, which was addressed mainly to the apostles. Some of the disciples were still hesitant, although they were constrained to worship Jesus. They found it strange that when He was with them He would vanish without warning. It was like a dream. They were afraid that this intermittent fellowship would not last, and they dared not face the future without Him. They were passing through a transitional stage. They remembered Him as he was, a historical person, but they also were coming to believe in Him as the messianic Redeemer of His people. They were still confused.

There was, however, continuity between the pre-resurrection Jesus and the post-resurrection Jesus. Some modern scholars have asserted that after the Easter event no one could think back to Jesus as He was, but this view cannot be maintained. The more they thought of the former days the better they understood. The Messiah of their faith was undoubtedly identified in their minds with the Jesus they had known in history.

The message of the risen Messiah was reassuring. "All power is given unto me in heaven and earth" (KJV). They needed the promise of power. The mission of Jesus could never proceed without it. The disciples were faltering in indecision, but the possibility of being endued with the same power as Jesus possessed was transforming. His presence spoke to them of power. He had conquered death, and no power could exceed that. Jesus did not give a vague promise of power, but He left specific instructions. They were to go, to make disciples, to baptize, and to teach. Each separate command deserves careful thought.

Jesus intended His mission to be worldwide. Although He confined His earthly ministry to the house of Israel, His vision was never narrowly nationalistic. The ever-widening outreach of the Christian mission is recorded in the book of Acts, which presents the progress of the Gospel from Jerusalem to Rome. This parting commission of Jesus is the basis for the missionary endeavor of the Church.

The aim of the commission was to make disciples. This involved the application of the Christian message to the whole man. They would know the terms of discipleship from the previous teaching of Jesus. They knew it to be a difficult path. It involved a step of faith in a crucified, but now risen Lord, and it involved submission to a yoke of service. They were to win men for Jesus Christ, and having won them, to baptize them to signify their membership in the Christian community. The disciples were to be united in a common bond to Christ. According to Matthew, baptism was to be applied in the name of the Father, the Son, and the Holy Spirit. Some have regarded this as a later addition, when the Church had come to believe in the Trinity, but there is no objective evidence for disputing that Matthew recorded the specific command of Jesus.

Jesus emphasized teaching and this emphasis shows that evangelism is linked with instruction. The content of the teaching was to consist of all that Jesus Himself had commanded — His parables, His discourses, His exhortations, and His advice on a wide variety of themes. He had previously promised the Spirit's assistance to enable them to recall what He had taught. The gospel records themselves are samples of the working out of that promise. The teaching of Jesus was basic to the mission and was to be the foundation of Christian theology. Men would remind each other of His sayings and would create a firm oral tradition of what Jesus had said.

Matthew ended his story with the astounding promise of Jesus that He would be with His disciples always, right to the end of the age — that is, through the whole period of Christian history. His presence would be sufficient to allay their fears. This was the richest legacy Christ could bequeath to His followers.

The Ascension

Luke 24:50-53; Acts 1:5-11

Three of the evangelists do not mention the Ascension. It is Luke who focuses attention upon it. It took place at Bethany, where Jesus, having blessed the disciples with uplifted hands, vanished from their sight. This is all that is recorded in his gospel, but in his second book (Acts) he gives more detail.

In the Acts account, the disciples, when they were together with the Lord, posed a question, which must have frequently occurred to them during the forty days of appearances. The question was, "Lord, will you at this time restore the kingdom to Israel?" The form of the question reveals their lack of understanding. In spite of the teaching of Jesus, not only during His earthly ministry, but also during His resurrection appearances, they were still thinking of the Kingdom in inadequate terms. They could not exclude from their minds the thought that the Kingdom belonged to Israel. They expected their risen Messiah to perform some act of political restoration. The notion of the Kingdom as a spiritual reality or as a universal idea was still alien to them. This shows the difficulty that even sympathetic men had in grasping the true nature of the teaching of Jesus.

His answer was concise and challenging. The disciples were not to concern themselves with chronological calculations. They must leave future events to God. Interestingly, Jesus said nothing to them about the Kingdom itself, but there was nothing new on this theme that He had not already taught them. He desired to deflect their minds to more profitable channels. He reiterated the promise of the Holy Spirit with its assurance of power and spoke to them about their roles as His witnesses.

Although the Messiah was about to leave, He intended His mission to continue. His disciples were an unpromising group. The Messiah's only witnesses available were those gathered around Him. Most of them would have preferred to avoid Jerusalem for a start, but Jesus assigned this city as their first area for witnessing. He had attached importance to the fact that He was to suffer in Jerusalem. That city was the city of the Messiah. It was fitting that the first testimony to Him after the resurrection should be given there. Nevertheless, in that city the greatest hostility against Jesus had occurred and there was no reason to suppose that the disciples would find a friendly welcome. After Jerusalem, they were to witness in Judea, then Samaria, and then to the ends of the earth. The parting commission in Luke's account is universal, as is that recorded by Matthew. The message of Jesus Christ was relevant to all classes of people.

The actual Ascension followed immediately afterward. He went up out of their sight into a cloud. The disciples would no more see Him as they had done during the last forty days. A visible Ascension was necessary to convince them that a new era had begun. Otherwise they might have expected further appearances.

Luke comments that as they were gazing into the sky two angels appeared and addressed them, saying, "Why do you stand looking up into heaven?" The question implied either their expectancy that He would immediately appear again, or else it revealed their sense of utter helplessness because they realized that they would not see Him again. The heavenly messengers assured them that Jesus would return in the same way as He had ascended. They gave no indication of the interval of time that would elapse before that event. The disciples knew nothing of the centuries to follow, during which others would continue to look for the return of Jesus.

The need for a pause

Luke 24:49; Acts 1:1-4

According to Luke, Jesus had urged His disciples to wait in Jerusalem until they received power. Luke says this not only at the end of his gospel, but also at the beginning of Acts. It was obviously a matter of some importance. The appearances of the risen Jesus, according to him, stretched over a period of forty days, during which the disciples were adequately instructed in the matters of the Kingdom. Some of them may have wondered why there was need for waiting. Waiting is sometimes harder than getting on with the work. Their own human potential was totally inadequate for the strange message that they were to proclaim. They must wait for the vital power to carry it through.

Among the last promises that Jesus made to the disciples was the promise that He would send the Holy Spirit. He had spoken to them about this prospect before His passion. He had pointed out that the Spirit was in effect to be His other self. It was, however, a considerable transition from having the presence of Jesus with them to experiencing His presence through the Holy Spirit. Some transition period was essential. It turned out to be ten days.

Nothing is known of their conversations during those days, but transformation in thinking was certainly taking place. The Jesus of history was becoming for them the Christ of faith. This could not be finally effected, however, until they were filled in a special way with the Holy Spirit. This happened at Pentecost. The coming of the Spirit set the seal on the life and teaching of Jesus. Without the witness of the Spirit, neither the passion nor the resurrection would become personally relevant to those who were to be reached in the continuing mission.

One important question must be asked. During that waiting period and after, did the disciples lose their sense of what the historical Jesus was really like? Since they had begun to think of Him in a more exalted, spiritual sense, did this color all their previous memories of Him? If it did, this survey of the life and teaching of Jesus would have little value as history. Nonetheless, the events related in the gospels do not read like Christian colorations of the facts. No doubt, during that ten-day pause, many recollections occurred to them and many teachings and events that had previously been enigmas became clear. The resurrection made all the difference.

The appearance of Jesus to Saul of Tarsus

Acts 9:1-9

No account of Jesus the Messiah is complete without some mention of His unexpected appearance to the man who later became the apostle to the Gentiles. The apostle Paul includes this

". . . if Christ has not been raised,
then our preaching is in vain and your
faith is in vain"
—I CORINTHIANS 15:14

appearance in the same list as the various other appearances, and he clearly regarded it with the same validity. The risen Lord was seen through the eyes of one of His most hostile opponents.

Jesus suddenly appeared to Saul in a blinding flash of light as he neared Damascus to persecute the followers of Jesus. Struck down by the light, he heard a voice addressing him, "Saul, Saul, why are you persecuting me?" The same graciousness of Jesus that He showed toward His enemies during His ministry is evident here. Saul, however, seemed to be in some confusion

The temple of Apollo in Corinth. In his letter to the church in Corinth, the apostle Paul listed eyewitnesses to Jesus' resurrection, including himself.

over the identity of the voice. Foremost in his mind was his mission of persecution against the Christians. It had never dawned on him that the persecution of Christians was in effect persecution of Jesus Himself and that Jesus was the eternal Son of God.

In answer to Saul's question, "Who are you, Lord?" the answer came, "I am Jesus." It is significant that the risen Lord used His essentially human name, which means "Savior." He gave no description of majesty. He did not reveal Himself as an overpowering Judge. He chose to make a singular revelation to Saul in personal terms. He wanted Saul to know that He was identified with His persecuted people.

Saul was unique as a man "born out of due time," to use his own phrase. He was deeply aware of the importance of being an eyewitness of the resurrection, since this was the main condition attached to the apostolic office. When a successor was appointed to fill the vacancy left by Judas, the qualification was that the nominees were to have been eyewitnesses. By this extraordinary experience, Saul felt that he also was qualified. It was the intention of the risen Messiah that he should be convinced of his apostleship by this vivid appearance of the Lord.

Another fact must be noted. In writing to the Corinthians, Paul mentioned an appearance to James that occurred before the Ascension. It is left to imagination to conceive what passed between the Lord and one of His own brothers. James, like the other brothers of Jesus, was a man who previously had not believed on Him. That appearance of Jesus to him must have convinced him, for soon after that he became a leading member of the church in Jerusalem.

This does not conclude the life and teaching of Jesus, for the story of His influence on others is continued in the history of the Christian Church. With the completion of the personal mission of Jesus began the long history of the announcement of that mission by a succession of people who had come to believe that everything He said was true.

Subject Index

Scripture Index

Subject Index

Scripture Index